Copyright @ 2020 by Kathleen Mobilia

All rights reserved. Printed in the United States of America. No part of this book may be reproduced, scanned, or distributed in any print or electronic form in any manner without written permission.

For information, contact the author

        HugsAfricanKisses@gmail.com

Design by Kathleen Mobilia
Text set in 11 point Times News Roman
        Amaranth

Hugs African Kisses

My Adventures in
Liberia, West Africa
1973-1976

KATHLEEN MOBILIA

Dedication

A special thanks to my parents, Jimmy and Margaret. They had instilled in me the desire to travel and interact with new people. They encouraged me to dream big, to believe in myself, and pursue my dreams. They never questioned why their 23 year old daughter was going to work in West Africa. They knew I had to fulfill my dream.

I thank you Mom and Dad.

A special thanks to Dr. Jessica Kohout, my friend and editor. Simply stated, *Hugs African Kisses* has happened because of her belief in me. I thank you for not giving up on me and prodding me to finish the "damn" book.

I thank you Jessica.

A special thanks to Audrey F. McLaughlin for editing my book and giving me excellent advice.

I thank you Audrey.

A special thanks to my Edinboro Writers' Group for encouraging me in all my writing endeavors over the many years.

I thank you Barbara Reese, Beverly Renn, Joanne Munzert, and Becky Widdecombe.

A special thanks to my former student and now my friend, Joseph Siaffa Phillips II. He encouraged me and listened to Jessica talking about editing my book.

I thank you Joseph.

I thank you all for reading my story.

All mistakes are mine. All credit goes to those above.

Introduction

In August 1973 I was interviewed by the Erie Times, my local hometown newspaper, about my move to the Firestone Plantation in Harbel, Liberia, West Africa. I was going to teach at the Firestone Staff School. I also stated that I planned on writing a book about my adventures when I returned to Erie. In preparation for the book, I kept journals and took photos to document this time. However, the thought of typing my book was daunting because I couldn't type!

During the three years I taught in Liberia, I traveled all over, and grew to love the people. I was fortunate as a single women to be able to do so freely, photographing the tribal people, and experiencing life in Liberia.

I returned to teach in Erie, PA and never forgot about my book. I mentally planned my chapters for years and years. I did learn to type with four fingers on a manual typewriter, yet I wasn't skilled enough to type my book.

Life happened. Students, classes, and years passed. No book, just the many ideas flowing in my head. I watched as technology advanced before my eyes. Computers went from the size of a building to small enough to sit on a desk top and individually owned. Never did I imagined that I would own one. And then I did. Wonders of wonders when I discovered WORD! I thought, now my book could at last materialize.

And more life happened. Some chapters were roughly written. I needed to become proficient in WORD and so I took classes and classes. Chapters started to be written however, I now needed an editor who knew about life in Liberia and the Firestone Plantation. Dr. Jessica Kohout offered and our working relationship was forged. She had a wealth of knowledge of Liberia as her father went to work for Firestone in the 1940s. After a leave, he returned with his bride, Nickie, and then two daughters were born at the Firestone Duside Hospital and raised on the Plantation. Jessica was a perfect match for the much needed support with my book.

With writing my memories, the desire to visit Liberia grew stronger. But again life happened for me and for Liberia. She suffered a 20+ year civil war that devastated her people with tens of thousands killed. The civil war ended and slowly Liberia was on the road to recovery. Once again I began to plan a visit in 2015. Unfortunately, life happened yet again for Liberia with one devastating word. Ebola. It aggressively swept through the country killing many of her people. My trip was placed on hold. At last, in April 2018, I returned to the place that stole my heart 45 years earlier. Jessica, her son, Rob, and I experienced the people and land of Liberia once again. I met former students and was charged by their enthusiasm upon my return. My book must be written!

Upon returning from our trip, I began writing with renewed passion and completed my book. I am satisfied with the results. I know a year from now, I will want to rewrite it but, hopefully, life will take care of this need and just happen.

Some names have been changed and my story is according to my notes taken at the time and my memory be it good or bad. I also took writer's privilege in relating my story.

Ah, sweet Liberia. Forever in my heart.

The photo of latex in a cup hanging from a rubber tree is behind the first word of each chapter.

Liberia, West Africa

Firestone Plantations Company
Harbel, Liberia

FPCo map created by
Nickie Kohout 11/3/1959

Liberian tapper.

Liberian tapper cutting a rubber tree. Latex slowly drips into the cup.

Later in the day, the tapper returns and collects the latex.

Contents

	Title page	iii
	Dedication	v
	Introduction	vi
	Maps	viii
	Contents	x
1	Flying My Dream	1
2	My Bungalow # 79	15
3	Monrovia and Moonlight	24
4	49 D	38
5	Exploring Divisions 1, 40, 42, 43, 44, and 45	49
6	Isobel Lokko	54
7	Faculty Meeting ala Jim Smith	59
8	Mr. and Mrs. God	67
9	The First Day of School	75
10	The Nazi Problem	80
11	Moving-In Day	86
12	Marshall Beach via SNAFU Bay	92
13	Bat Man, Stewards, Leopold, Ah Ha!	100
14	Upcountry	110
15	Big Palava	127

Contents

16	The Legendary John Francis	136
17	Great White Hunters?	142
18	Calling via Ham Radio, Banana Mama, Green Mamba Visit	150
19	Coo Coo Nest and The Big Club	159
20	Charlies, Mahjong, and Buchanan	168
21	Red Paisley Drapes, The Pass, and Tuna Turkey	178
22	Freeport, Christmas Day, and New Year Party	184
23	Come As You Are Caper	192
24	John the "Duke" Wayne and Timbuktu	197
25	Mohawks Charging, Jupiter Rising, and Bathtub Christening	205
26	One People, One Fish	212
27	Monkey Bridges, Lepers, Mrs. Nixon, Oh My!	222
28	Vaitown, Cat Palava, Robertsport	235
29	Peter Cottle and Liberian Adventures	243
30	Chinese Dragon Attack and the Christmas Visitor	251
31	New News, New Teacher, New Dogs	262
32	To Be Wedded or Not and Gone Leopold Gone	272
33	Surprise Wedding, the Playboy Bunny, and Going Home	279
	Photo Credits	288
	About the Author	291

My friends Angie and Marty, sister Therese, and me
Erie, PA 1973

Chapter 1

Flying My Dream

The wheels of the Pan Am jet touched down and I let out a huge sigh. I was here. The Dark Continent had at last come to be. I knew I would conquer it as I had done with everything else I set my mind upon. And now, my mind was set upon Africa.

Since leaving JFK in New York, I had been wedged in between two people the entire nine hour trip. The jet was a Pan Am 727 and there wasn't an empty seat on board. I was amazed that so many people were traveling to the land of my dreams. On my left, next to the aisle was an older black woman wearing traditional West African lappa of burgundy, green, and yellow designs. Another lappa of equal beauty was wrapped around her head. She was traveling back to her home in Abidjan, Ivory Coast. In the window seat on my right sat a recent college graduate. He was dressed in faded jeans and a tie dye T-shirt and was sporting a big bushy "fro". The Afro hairdo was the latest rage in the USA. The guy told me he felt this new do would help him blend in upon reaching his new destination. He was an American raised in Sierra Leone by missionary parents. He was now returning as a Peace Corps volunteer and seeking his adventure in Togo. I was seeking mine in Liberia, I told them. Not Libya. I had to keep explaining that to my friends and family back home. It is Liberia, West Africa that I travel to. The lady had been there and knew that many people confused the two countries. And so we travel mates chatted easily about our goals and hopes. I earnestly pumped the experienced Africans about the new place that I would be entering and what West Africa was like. They most graciously obliged.

I was young. Twenty-three to be exact and going to live my dream of working in Africa. Ever since I was old enough to talk, I had spoken of the day when I would be doing this and what I would do. I was an Air Force "brat" and grew up mostly in Europe. My parents had always encouraged me to reach my goals. Now, I was. As a result of this positive attitude, my family and friends weren't surprised when I said that I had accepted a teaching job in Liberia, West Africa. And today, Sunday, September 2, 1973 was the day. I had just landed on this mysterious continent. What adventures lay ahead for me? What people would I meet? I was eager to leap off the plane and discover it all!

I had sent out many job resumes and applications as I knew American companies abroad had schools for staff children and would need teachers. I interviewed for many jobs overseas, but none were for Africa until now. My quest had all started on July 12, 1973 when I received a phone call from Ed Swinehart of the Firestone Tire and Rubber Company asking me to come to Akron, Ohio for an interview. The job was teaching third grade at the company's Staff School in Liberia, West Africa. The school was on their huge natural rubber plantation. The staff children would be my students. Would I come? I would soon learn that simple phone call was to change my life forever and I would finally realize and fulfill my lifelong dream.

I met Mr. Swinehart, a wonderfully personable fellow. Salt and pepper hair, middle aged, thick dark rimmed glasses, and checking out my legs! Gosh, what's with men anyway I thought? Throughout the interview, I smiled and radiated confidence that Firestone needed ME for the job. I explained that I had grown up in Panama Canal Zone, Ireland, England, and France being the product of a father who made the US Air Force his career. I stated that I was a first generation American as my mother was Irish and my dad Sicilian. I spoke French and had three years of teaching experience under my belt. With this background I knew I could handle the challenges that Liberia would present to me. After negotiating a decent salary, a furnished rent free house, a car, and a round trip flight home once a year, I accepted the position to teach third grade at the Firestone Plantation Staff School in Liberia, West Africa!

I believe that Fate plays a hand in what one does. You just need to listen and be ready. Just five years previously when I was a senior at St. Benedict Academy, I played Miss Angie Brooks representing her country of Liberia in the mock United Nations program run by Gannon College in my hometown of Erie. I had researched Liberia and knew her history well. And now Fate had selected me for the job of working for Firestone in Liberia, West Africa! My dream! I was listening!

For the next six weeks, I madly dashed about doing a million things that needed to be completed before one departs upon such an adventure. First, a series of shots and several trips back and forth to Akron. Then, I had to pack up my apartment and have my belongings stored until the actual move. Next, I shopped for a year's worth of items that were on my list given to me by Firestone. These household items included things such as clothing, sneakers, (I bought a dozen pair), linens, curtains, and paper products. There were limited stores in Liberia and I just couldn't go out and buy whatever I needed. Gosh, could I live without shopping? How I loved dressing up and going downtown in Erie to spend the day shopping with my friends. I decided this new experience would be an exciting trade off. I put much thought into my purchases, as it would be a year before I would be able to shop again. I made arrangements to ship my newly acquired items and other things over to the Plantation via the Firestone Terminal in Baltimore, Maryland.

Once there, my possessions would be placed aboard the next available Firestone ship to Liberia to arrive at the Plantation in about two months. Oops, almost forgot, I also had to sell my car.

No tears flowed as I made my goodbyes to my parents, siblings, Grandma, family and friends. Unfortunately, asking my longtime boyfriend, Tim, to wait for one year, proved to be more difficult than I had planned. He always knew that I had this need to work in Africa and I think that he was miffed that I was leaving as he didn't come to the airport to say goodbye. All too quickly, I was boarding the plane in Erie and leaving with no time for any regrets.

As the jet taxied to a stop I sat thinking about the rash thing I did before going to the airport. I had my hair cut so short that I couldn't pick it up with my fingers and then had it bleached blonde. Even my parents and friends did not recognize me at the airport and of course no one would know me in Liberia and what I had looked like before. My huge crystal blue eyes, flecked with green and gold, danced with excitement and adventure! I wore a Kelly green white polka-dot dress and white heels. The green I had decided would be both for luck and hope. I was finally off on the dream of my lifetime.

I had found the flight to be educating but terribly long. It was like waiting for the Christmas morning light to come so as to tear open what Santa had delivered. Instead this plane was delivering me to the Dark Continent for unknown adventures. We had landed on a small sliver of land squeezed in between tall dense green grasses, palm trees, and other trees I had yet to learn. I stretched to look out of the small window. My eyes fell upon a scene that resembled the Everglades of Florida and remote parts of Hawaii. Finally, when it was my turn to deplane, I quickly gathered my things and rushed forward.

Standing in the doorway and readying myself to climb down the stairs, the smells that filled my nostrils were intoxicating! The air was perfumed with the wild smells of grasses and flowers just wetted by a tropical downpour. Instantly, I fell head over heels in love with Liberia! I deplaned quickly and walked across the steamy, hot asphalt to the long, one-level cement block arrival terminal. The morning air was damp and intense. What awaited me? Who? Where and how far away was the Plantation that would be my home for the next year?

So many questions were flying through my head all at once. I walked toward the building and into my future. I followed the noisy crowd and found myself standing in a long line for customs. It was then and only then that I realized for the first time that I didn't know if anyone was coming to meet me! It also hit me that I didn't know anyone on this entire continent! Sure, sure, I knew this before I embarked on this adventure and I was seeking this kind of thrill but now, here I was. In Liberia! The knowledge of being alone on this huge continent hit me smack in the face! Fear gripped my heart…would Firestone send someone? A sweat broke out on my brow. My stomach flopped. I swallowed hard and forced the tears back. I willed them not to flow and planted a weak smile on my face. I had just assumed Firestone would be here waiting for me and had never inquired who would be my greeter.

Gosh, no one was approaching me. Of course, silly, no one knows what you look like. I needed to look for…who? Firestone? I picked up my little green carry-on bag, adjusted my white purse, and moved to the end of the line. I stood waiting in the humid terminal with beads of perspiration collecting on my brow. The line slowly grew shorter and I just sweated more! My eyes searched wildly everywhere. Looking for…a savior. Who's that over there? A short stocky black man wearing dark green pants and shirt stood peering at the quickly growing shorter line. Holding a bit of paper in his fist, he stared at everyone and then walked up and down the line trying to match a name on his paper to a name on a bag. Could he be looking for my name? He continued to examine the luggage tags. Finally, he looked at my name tag and a look of panic crossed his face! He looked upward at me. He abruptly turned and left but not before I glimpsed the miraculous simple red F on the sleeve of his shirt. Ahh, I whispered with relief-Firestone! Where was my savior? Vanished and why? This land was indeed mysterious. I waited and sweated. What else was I to do?

The line had dwindled down to just me and an important looking man took my passport and Firestone papers. I was questioned in a strange, fast speaking tongue where I picked up bits and pieces of English words. Firestone? Now even this black man was asking in a surprised voice. He talked rapidly and flung his arms madly about. The few people at the desk gathered their papers and fistful of rubber stamps and left through a small door. I followed to discover this was where our luggage was brought. I searched for mine and found that they weren't there. I looked for support and there was no one who looked to be in charge. Where were my passport and luggage? What was going on I thought as I settled onto an orange chair to await my rescuers. Would anyone come? I waited what seemed like years. I located a restroom and freshened up. I was in such a hurry to explore my world and where was it? Was anyone coming? I sat and continued to wait stoically. By now, everyone had departed the small building and it had become ungodly quiet. I sat. I was surprisingly calm considering my situation. Okay, I thought, I had seen the red F and trusted that someone would come for me. What a pickle I was in. No luggage and no passport! I knew I was never to lose visual contact with my passport, but that man had quickly disappeared. I sat and studied the long narrow room. The walls were cement block and someone had hung travel posters that were mostly European scenes. No windows, I noticed, and thought how interesting to see the decorative cut cement blocks work where windows should be. Only a few orange chairs, which indicated this was not a place anyone was expected to wait for long. But that was not the case for me. I was tired and scared and terribly alone. I sat. No telephone. Even if there was one, who would I call?

     I realized that in my excitement of leaving home, I never got a contact name and phone number. The dread crept through my body and yet I continued a weak smile. Push those fears away, someone will surely come. Finally that someone did. He arrived with soap still clinging to his wet, light reddish brown hair and a huge, surprised smile upon his face. He thrust out his hand and said, "Welcome to Liberia and Firestone Plantations Company! I'm Jim Smith and the headmaster of the Firestone Staff School. I'm sorry that I wasn't here when the plane arrived, but I simply slept in," he said while pumping my hand.

I did later find out that sleeping in and being late were not unusual for Jim Smith. His warm radiant way soon had me relaxed and ready to press onward as he showed me to his car outside.

"No luggage?" Jim asked.

"It didn't come on the plane," I answered and told him about my missing passport too.

Jim assured me that he would check on my passport and luggage on Monday. The next Pan Am plane from New York would be on Wednesday and my luggage should be on it.

"Here," he said reaching into a cooler that was in the trunk of his new gold LTD, "would you prefer a Liberian beer called Club Beer or a Coca-Cola? We will be eating breakfast at Steve and Gailann Lawton's place in a little while." I selected a bottle of Coke-Cola while Jim was opening the car door for me. "You must remember to wipe the lip of the bottle before you drink. Many times the tops are rusted and of course also in case of germs."

"Oh," I replied doing just that.

"Don't worry about your luggage, I will cable the pilot and ask him to search for it in New York. I know him and he'll do this favor for me," Jim told me.

Meanwhile, what would I be wearing until it arrives? Oh well…I learned a huge lesson that day that all travelers know. Always pack a change of clothes and carry it onto the plane.

"So, who cares about clothes when there is Africa to discover? Certainly not I!" I told him.

"That's the spirit!" he said as he threw the car into reverse and peeled away from the airport. He steered with one arm propped lazily upon the wheel as he pointed out the various sites and buildings, giving me a chance to study this man, my principal, or headmaster as he had called himself. He presented a clean-cut figure. Tall, but not too tall, about 5'10". Lean and muscular and sucking in his stomach which was obviously to impress me. He was going bald on top and sported a mustache a darker red than his hair. He must be the nervous type as he had the habit of stroking it as he talked. The top four buttons on his white shirt weren't fastened displaying his curly body hair. Light red. Like a bird's nest I thought. A thick gold chain. Macho guy...I knew that he was floored when he saw me and was visually taken back. Yes, this dress did show off my slender, curvy body, and emphasized my breasts. Maybe I should not have worn this mini dress as he kept staring at my legs and making me feel uneasy.

Jim said as we were passing the huge sign along the right side of the road announcing the Firestone Rubber Plantation at Harbel, Liberia, "This is the beginning of about 90,000 or so acres of planted rubber trees with 45 divisions in all. Each division is a little city unto itself with a Division Manager. You will be teaching the Staff employees' children. Kathleen, notice that Firestone buildings are made of the red brick. The bricks are made right here on the Plantation. Here's our Central Office and Mailroom."

"I just know that will become a favorite haunt of mine," I said as Jim pulled up in front and parked.

"Mail only comes in three times a week from the States," he said.

"Three? Gosh how awful to have to wait for news," I said.

We sat looking at the two story Central Office which was made in the shape of a U. There was an open porch that went around on the inside of this U. Jim told me that this made it easier for everyone to move about during the rains. We next drove by the factory, chemistry lab, carpentry shop, and more places that I would discover later.

"We'll save a tour of those buildings for another day," Jim said brushing my knee as he retrieved his fallen sunglasses. Jeez. Was that a deliberate move or just me getting the wrong signal? Time will tell I'm sure.

"Jim, am I able to send a telegram to my family? They will want to know I have arrived safely."

"Funny, you should mention this now as here we are at Firestone's Radio building." Jim said as we pulled up in front of a single story brick building and parked. "This is where you can send out radiograms to your family."

Gail Ruff, the man who ran the radio station, gave me a quick tour of how the place operated. "I know you want to send a cable to your parents announcing your safe arrival at the Plantation," he said.

So, I sent out a cable consisting of numbers that followed a form list of messages. I carefully selected ones that said I safely arrived. I decided that I would later write about my missing luggage, passport, and the crazy beginning I had had so far.

I asked Gail if I would be able to directly contact my dad who was a ham with an advance radio license. Gail was a ham and told me my best bet would be to contact Augie Le Monze, a Frenchman, who had the radio equipment to make US contacts. I was really excited to have the possibility of making radio connections with my parents! I also knew my parents would call Firestone's CEO in Akron if they didn't hear from me. So, I sent out my cablegram via the Firestone Radio Tower.

> Dear Mom Dad Stop
> Arrived safely Stop
> Things look great Stop
> Call Grandma Stop
> And friends Stop
> Hugs African kisses Stop
> Kathleen

Jim and I said goodbye to Gail and continued my tour by driving by the Factory and the auto shop. We drove about a mile further on when Jim pointed to a long narrow dirt road through the rubber trees.

"This is a favorite place of everyone after work called Sammy's Store. I'll be bringing you by this week to introduce you to more people. Oh, yes, there is a huge BYOB party in three weeks where you will meet many other Firestone staff," said Jim.

"Uh, what is a BYOB party?"

"It is a Bring Your Own Bottle party," Jim laughed. "You are not what we were expecting. I guess we thought you would be older and not so naive," he laughed and stammered.

"Oh? Well, I can handle myself and don't you worry at all," I told him. But I knew that he would be someone I would have to contend with in the near future. But now I decided I would simply enjoy the Plantation with its beautiful green rubber trees. My home for the next year.

"Did you know the rubber trees all lean toward their 'God' in Akron, Ohio?" I heard Jim saying. Gosh, I thought this is an incredible place and with such fascinating stories. This is definitely my kind of place!

Jim drove his big LTD easily around while giving me lots of history about the Plantation. Every now and then I caught him staring and he would blush.

Liberians were walking all about alongside the road. They were dressed in traditional clothing. Brightly colored lappas decked the heads and lower parts of the women. Many women were bare on top with their breasts swaying as they walked. Most carried something on their heads and a baby wrapped around their waists on back. I did see some women wearing bras but with no shirt. Funny to see this and no one seemed to care. National Geographic in Technicolor and moving! Men wore pants and went with or without shirts. Most were barefooted with a few wearing floppy sandal-like shoes. How wonderful to be able to experience this. Everywhere I looked there seemed to be so much more for me to learn.

By now, I had guessed that Jim was stalling. Something was awry and I was soon to discover it. He slowly pointed out my home to be as we drove past.

"Why are the houses up on pillars?" I asked.

"That is to keep out critters and for air circulation," Jim told me. "No, you'll see your home later," he said as I begged to see where I would be living for the next year. We turned and drove into a large compound of homes. We passed a few homes when Jim pulled into a semi circular driveway planted with red flowering Hibiscus. Walls made of woven palm leaves were under the home that stood on brick legs. Some beautifully decorated tables were neatly arranged in this jungle-like environment. I had thought it was to be only Steve and Gailann Lawton at breakfast, however, waiting there was a group of about 16 people. Everyone greeted me as I stepped from the car into the bright sunlight. I just knew these smiling people would become my friends and my family.

Gailann and Steve had pulled together a brunch for me upon receiving a frantic phone call earlier from Jim. They quickly called some people to come over and meet me. Apparently I was not expected this Sunday morning but was to come in on the Wednesday flight. So, I shook hands and smiled but I was terribly hot and sticky from traveling in the same outfit for the past 24 hours. Gosh, 24 hours ago I had left the comfort of family and dear friends to now find myself surrounded by these charming people.

How sweet of Jim to drive me around stalling so as to give everyone a chance to gather for the brunch. Fresh pineapple, papaya, grapefruit, and oranges graced the beautifully decorated tables. Houseboys served us Bloody Marys and champagne. What a wonderful way to be welcomed after the unusual start I had had!

Everyone was chatting and telling me so much. Would I remember it all? Jim told them all that my luggage didn't make it and I needed clothes. "Clothes? Don't worry," Gailann said, "We'll fix you up."

Ye gads, what's this? One exotic looking lady grabbed my breasts with both hands, feeling them, and said in a thick accent, "I have a bra to fit her!"

What was going on here? What have I gotten myself into? Look at everyone! No one seemed to mind that this lady was holding my breasts and sizing me up! What was I to do? Jump back? Scream? These were parents of children I would be teaching. How I handled myself now would be terribly important. So, I just stood, doing nothing but listening and definitely looking and feeling like a fool with some stranger holding my breasts! Someone was saying she had dresses, underwear, a nightgown, and the like. I would be taken care of and was not to fret about clothes and such. I was embarrassed to have my personal clothing and body discussed so calmly by these people. This was a strange but a helpful lot…maybe??? Didn't my mother tell me there would be days like this?

The names swam in my head…must remember them as I will be teaching their children. Gillian, Lokko, Johnson, Witteveen, Phillips, Hugg, Hegarty, Cooper, and Field. My face was beginning to hurt from smiling so much and my breasts were throbbing, too. After eating, Jim pulled me away saying he wanted to continue my tour and this time it was to go to the school. I eagerly obliged and said hurried goodbyes.

After a few quick turns, we approached the Firestone Staff School that housed the eight grades. Grades 1st through 4th were on the right with grades 5th through 8th on the left. The office/library was in the center and was the only room that was air-conditioned and the restrooms were also in this area. All along the front of the building was a wide covered porch.

"We have recess in the porch area when it rains," said Jim holding the door for me.

At last, I entered my classroom. It was almost double the size of my room back at Diehl School in Erie! So this is where I will spend the greater part of my day. The blackboard was at the front and at the back were cupboards and a sink. Why, there was even a refrigerator back there, too!

"Why a refrigerator?" I questioned.

"The children bring a snack to eat at 10 o'clock and it's necessary to keep it refrigerated because of bugs. You're not afraid of snakes and such are you?"

"Oh no," I said. "It takes a lot to frighten me."

Along the side walls were low bookshelves about 2 feet high. Above them were crank-out windows that reached to the ceiling. Doors were in each corner on the driveway side and another door by the blackboard in the front going out to the large open field. Hanging high in the middle of the ceiling were two huge oscillating fans.

"It is nice and cool in the room now because this is the rainy season. Just wait until dry season when there isn't any electricity. Pretty awful as dry season begins about early November and ends with the rains returning in March. This area of Liberia averages about 200 to 250 inches of rain per wet season and is why Harvey Firestone built the Plantation here," Jim said.

"Oh," I said as I was busy counting the desks. "Wow! Twenty! After teaching 36 children last year this is wonderful news!"

"No," said Jim, "you will have ten to thirteen children. Not twenty!"

"Ten to thirteen???!!! Now, I know I am in heaven! And I'm being paid no less!" I smiled.

"Most teachers use all the desks by having a permanent reading group in the back of the room and using the other desks for the rest of the day's work. But do whatever you want. You're the boss lady!"

Thank goodness I am a morning person because Jim told me the school day begins at 7 am and ends at 12:45. He told me that we begin early to take advantage of the cooler temperatures.

"Teachers are to report by 6:45 and leave at 1:00."

"Okay…great. But Jim, the jet lag and the thrill of being here are taking a toll. I am exhausted and want to clean up and rest."

"Then it will be the Firestone Guest House for the next stop so you can do just that. You will be staying there for about three weeks to a month."

"Why weeks or a month? Why not my house?"

"Well, you will need to select paint colors for the rooms and it will take that long for the work to be done along with spraying the house for pests."

I wondered what pests he was talking about but chose not to ask. We drove about 2 or 3 miles and pulled up in front of the Guest House. Wow, was it fantastic! Set up very similar to the school with the rooms being off on both sides and the dining room, living room, and other areas in the center. Brick again. The time was now 5:00 p.m. and any bed looked inviting!

I thanked Jim for his help as I just wanted to shower and sleep.

"Don't sleep until 9 or it will mess up your inner clock," he told me.

"Nine??? I just want to crash!" I knew I was beginning to feel and act silly from lack of sleep but did so want to keep up a good impression.

So, I showered and changed into the borrowed clothes left for me by the various women. And yes, the bra fit. Meanwhile, Jim was back in the kitchen getting the staff to fix us a light supper.

We ate and Jim continued to talk to me keeping me on a tropical time schedule. One other person was staying at the Guest House. Charles Lorenz was up from Firestone's Cavalla Plantation for business. How wonderful it was to have men waiting on me and doing the cooking and cleaning up! When living in Europe and South America it was always the women who did this work. I'm going to like this place I smiled. But, I was struggling with sensory overload and I needed sleep. I found myself staring at the beautiful white wicker screen dividing the dining area from the sitting space. So much information. Will I ever learn it all? This Jim fellow was too overly nice. No principal in the States would ever behave this way. What was going on here? Why was he so overly kind? Would I ever find out?

Finally, Jim saw me to my room and said goodnight. I closed my door and with a plop, fell exhausted but smiling in sheer happiness, onto the bed.

I was home at last!
Africa!
Hugs and kisses to you, dear Africa!

My Bungalow # 79

Chapter 2

My Bungalow # 79

Lazily, I rolled over and stretched. Umm, what a wonderful dream I was having of finally being in Liberia and meeting so many interesting people. I then felt like someone was watching me and my eyes popped open to find a little black man gazing at me! Smiling and speaking quickly in a tongue I didn't know! I screamed and he jumped back still holding onto a robe for me to get into. Oh no, this can't be. I'm still dreaming, but no, as he continued to talk and stand and wait. Grabbing my sheet, I rose and gingerly slid into the robe. He was now pouring coffee while I looked slowly around the room. Was this a dream? Yet, this is not my bedroom at home and yes there was a black man pouring coffee in front of me. Then I realized that I was indeed in

Liberia and memories flooded into my mind. The plane, tour, people, brick buildings, passport, more people, and my breasts? It all came back! The room was cold from air conditioning and then I saw my green dress hanging on a hanger. Not where I had put it the night before. What? Did this man come in during the night and hang it? Gosh, it even looked cleaned and ironed too! He left the room talking the whole time and I sat smiling nervously and watched him go out the door.

  I showered and dressed remembering how I had arrived in Liberia without my luggage and all that had happened to me yesterday. No, I concluded that I wasn't dreaming. No one could dream in such detail. This had to be reality. Whoa! Even the reflection in the mirror that looked back at me was different! The haircut and the color job…oh yes, now I remembered what I had done to my hair before leaving Erie. If I was dreaming then I didn't want to wake up as this was cool! I decided to explore my surroundings to discover if this was a dream or reality.

  I slowly opened the door and stepped out onto a screened veranda to the delicious smells and sights of colorful tropical flowers. White wicker rockers and sofas created an inviting restful area for idle conversations. Gosh, I don't remember them from yesterday…everything was…such a blur. I heard voices and followed the sounds through the lounge or living room and then the dining room. Umm, some of this did look familiar.

  Quick smiles and laughter greeted me. I didn't understand a word but the gestures indicated for me to sit and eat. The food arrived and it was wonderful. I indeed was hungry! Sectioned grapefruit, freshly squeezed orange juice, warm bread, and eggs were laid before me. I tried to get the men to bring me tea but they served coffee instead. I laughed along with them, as the Liberian English language was so strange to my ears. Okay, this had to be reality I concluded!

  I had no idea what time it was since I had forgotten to set my watch to the new time zone yesterday. Judging from the sun's position, I knew it was late morning. I decided to do some exploring on my own around the Guest House. What incredible colors of plants and so many shades of green! I must get to know their names. The view was terrific, too. I could see other Firestone brick houses and perhaps a golf course? The houses were situated on top of rolling hills with winding driveways lined with trees. Intermittently there were colorful plants and lots of palm trees but wherever possible there were the rubber trees, all leaning to the west or their "god Akron", as Jim had told me.

Jim? Where was he? I was anxious to get out and see more of the Plantation and my bungalow. I returned to the veranda and was absorbed in the view when Jim pulled in.

"Good morning Kathleen! Have you eaten?" he said thrusting his chest out and walking toward me with his arms inward and swinging in a very distinctive way.

"Yes, and now I'm looking forward to seeing more of the Plantation and perhaps seeing my house, oh, I mean, bungalow. Uh, Jim, a strange thing occurred. Someone entered my locked guest room last night, tidied up, washed my clothes, and then this morning a black man woke me as he was returning my clothes! I am very concerned about my safety."

"That's what your houseboy will do for you and is nothing to be worried about. Okay? They will just do their job, well, providing you will hire a good one. Anyhow, I have planned our afternoon with a stop at your bungalow and then to get you your car at the motor pool. Are you ready?"

"Great!" I exclaimed as I got into his car.

Driving along the main road allowed Jim an opportunity to point out different people's homes until we drove into the bachelor compound. All the homes were a single bedroom. We climbed a small hill to my bungalow-to-be where I could see the layout of the area.

"The design of the compound is a figure 8 with four houses on a circular drive on each side of your bungalow that sits in the center of this figure 8. All your neighbors are single men and will keep their eyes on you…uh, that is, if you require any help," he quickly corrected himself blushing. "Are you aware that you are the only single white woman on the Plantation and probably even until you get into Monrovia, the capital?"

"No. Really?" Now it was my turn to blush and so I changed the subject thinking this is probably why he is so attentive to me. Just plain darn lonely. "Which bungalow is yours?" I asked.

"Oh," he quickly said, "I live at the Hydro Lake and you'll see it later this week when the school's staff come for a welcome luncheon meeting to start the school year off."

Jim drove into my horseshoe-shaped driveway that was lined in the middle with pretty red flowering bushes and growing in the very center of this circle was a tall 15+ foot purple flowering tree. The other side of the driveway leading to the bungalow was edged with spider lilies. "The red hedges are Hibiscus and in the center is a Bougainvillea," explained Jim. "However, you can plant and landscape the gardens as you wish by contacting the Botanical Research Division. They'll do whatever you desire."

"Oh, wow, I just love to garden but, I do need to learn about tropical plants."

"Just ask anyone and they'll help. Notice the tree by the steps of that bungalow across the street? It will be flowering red on top in the dry season and is a very common Christmas decoration back at home," Jim told me what it was upon seeing my confused look. "It's a Poinsettia tree!"

"You are kidding me? A Poinsettia?"

"Yep, this is a total surprise to everyone. The other trees are a variety of fruit. Let's see, there's papaya, lime, avocado, grapefruit, and banana. That's pineapple growing over there. Boy, I can see you have a good stock of fresh fruit. Someone previously planned and planted this garden well."

My bungalow was also on "brick pillars" and had closed-in spaces underneath.

"Firestone designed the older homes this way before there was air-conditioning. This allowed for greater airflow and also to keep unwanted critters and termites from entering the home. You will park your car underneath. There are two rooms for your houseboy and night watchman and also a bathroom for their use. Did any men come around asking for a job this morning?"

"No," I said.

"They will be around soon. Read their letters of reference and make sure you hire the oldest night watchman you can get. They will have a lot of family that will protect you. It is a Liberian way."

"Wow!" was all I could muster as we climbed the cement stairs to the screened in covered porch which was about 12x10. I knew I would enjoy many evenings sitting out here. We walked into a very large open living and dining room about 16 feet wide by 20 feet long that had double French door windows on the three exterior walls. A single swinging French door led into the kitchen. The white walls were 9 feet high. The room was furnished with a beautiful Cushman maple furniture dining table with six chairs, a sofa, and two armchairs. The sofa and wooden chairs had cushions on them-pretty old and worn looking, too! A coffee table and two end tables with lamps completed the ensemble. A beautiful African tie-dye tablecloth was on the table along with table settings and candles. Also hanging on the windows were odd-looking green and white curtains.

"I wanted the place to be inviting for you and so I took the liberty of doing a little decorating early this morning. I'm loaning you these items until your shipment arrives from Baltimore which should be in about two months."

My first thought was again, why was my principal being so nice to me? Am I safe with him or will he jump my bones in the bedroom?

"Uh, where is the kitchen?" I asked quickly.

"Through the swinging French door but, don't you want to see the bedroom and bath first?"

"Gee, Jim you know women really want to see their kitchen and…and I just like to see the place where I will be cooking my meals."

"Oh, you won't be cooking! Your houseboy will be doing that along with the cleaning, washing, and ironing. You have surely landed in the good life!" He said as I pushed open the French door and swept into the kitchen via a long passageway that connected the kitchen to the house.

"Oh," I said looking at the bleak but functional room.

"This hallway has a concrete floor that will protect the house in the event of a fire," Jim added.

The kitchen didn't have any cupboards, instead, there were three shelves, one counter by the sink, and a small table with two chairs. Everything was painted white. Again, some dishes, pots and pans, glasses, and other stuff courtesy of Jim.

"Boy, I didn't realize how bleak this room was until just now but, we can requisition the carpentry shop to build you anything you want and just charge it to the school," Jim said when he saw my disappointed face.

"I can design my workspace, cupboards, and all?"

"Yep. We'll go by the carpentry shop later to place the order."

"Gee, what's this closet for?" I said as I opened the door.

"It's called the chop cupboard and all your food is stored there. You must keep the heater on at all times to keep the moisture from ruining the food. You have another closet on the other side in the bedroom," he said, touching my shoulder prodding in a suggestive way leading me to the bedroom.

I did follow, maintaining a safe distance. The bedroom was opposite the living/dining room and was the same size with a huge bed covered in a white bedspread. A lamp was on the bedside table. Again the walls, windows, and paint color mirrored the other rooms. The bathroom was large also about 16 by 20. The bathroom was like the kitchen with a toilet, hanging wall sink, and a tiled shower but, no bathtub. Back in the bedroom's interior wall was the walk-in-closet with a tall chest of drawers in the center. Whoever lived here before liked the color white. I was already thinking of my room colors-soft yellow for the bathroom and bedroom, kitchen a pale blue, and the living/dining room a soft green or beige, probably the latter.

"You will need to keep both closets locked or else your things will begin to disappear. By the way, these are twin beds that I put together to make a king bed. Most single people like this huge bed."

"Really?" I remarked.

Jim said, "Decide on what color you want the rooms painted in and we'll go next to place the work order. Your bungalow should be ready in about three to four weeks."

Okay, paint colors, great. King bed… hum no way I want to keep the beds this way as it could just be encouraging him or any other guy for that matter. Then who knows what I could be getting myself into.

I can see it now back home…

> Dear family friends Stop
> Lonely men lined Stop
> Up to see king bed Stop
> With queen Stop
> In it Stop
> Hugs African kisses Stop
> Kathleen

Oh yes, everyone would have interesting chats over tea, eh?

"Gosh, it will take three to four weeks to paint the place? Guess the Guest House will be home until then," I answered.

"That's right. And tomorrow, Kathleen, we will be going to Monrovia to select the fabric for your sofa and chair cushions. The upholstering takes about the same length of time as painting. All this is on Firestone's tab as we want to make and keep you happy."

"Wow," I said but thinking about the unreal treatment and how this would never happen in the States. And… who really wants me happy I thought…Firestone or Jim Smith?

While locking the bungalow up, the sky released a downpour soaking us as we scampered to the car. The drops were the largest I'd ever seen! But, when I looked down the little hill, it wasn't raining.

"What's going on here?" I questioned.

"Oh, this is a typical Liberian rain shower. It will be over in a few minutes. That's how it rains here; off and on for short durations. Though, sometimes it will rain for a couple of hours or maybe even days. But that is unusual. Always warm rain and seldom a cold one," Jim said as we drove down the road with the wipers trying to keep up with the rain. And then the rain stopped.

My mind was racing about trying to plan and think about all the decisions that go into the nesting routine. Ten minutes later, we drove past the factory buildings and stopped at the carpentry shop. After a couple of hours, we had ordered the cupboards for both the kitchen and bathroom and the wall colors that I wanted for my new home. I was amazed by how the shop had blueprints of every building on the plantation! It was so easy to plan my kitchen and bathroom.

"I am so excited to be doing this as this is my very first time! I can't wait to see the completed job," I told Jim.

"Just want to keep you happy and I aim to please. A happy and contented teacher will stay and give the Company their very best! Anyhow, I'm starving and I bet you are too."

Hum, I thought, stay? Have there been problems with teachers leaving before? If he keeps coming on so strong…I'll just be leaving too. Okay, Kathleen just keep a cool level head and watchful eye…I told myself. "Truthfully, I'm both hungry and tired. I would like to rest after we eat."

"Didn't realize how late it is. The motor pool is closed so we'll get your car tomorrow. Sorry about that. We simply had a late start today."

"That's all right," I said, "I'm really tired from all the excitement of today." How many times do I need to say I am tired? I just wanted to be alone and quiet. I needed time to reflect.

Back at the Guest House, I freshened up and then we ate. A repeat of last night occurred with Jim entertaining me until 9 pm.

I stretched and yawned sleepily after dinner wanting to avoid sitting in the living room as he had suggested. "Jim, I am super tired and need to rest for the big day tomorrow. Couldn't I please go to sleep earlier tonight?"

"Why yes, I guess so…but there is so much to tell you."

"I will be here for a year or more and couldn't it possibly wait until another time?"

He agreed and insisted on walking me to my room where he lingered like he was going to maybe kiss me??? This is crazy! He is my boss! I've been here for only two days and don't know if I am interested in him or not! No tingles...

"You know Kathleen, I think you are a terrific person and really happy that you are here to teach at the Firestone School. I am positive you will add much to the school environment and people's lives," he said trying to corner me into his arms.

I managed to dance around his awkward attempt at an embrace, said goodnight, and got into my room alone. Again I fell into bed feeling somewhat settled but questioning why he was so overly nice to me and hovering around like he owned me or something? Maybe I am sending out the wrong signals. I just am not tingling with him. Yes, he did say I was the only single white girl around for many miles. I certainly hope he's not the only single white man! He's so old...I bet 10 to 15 years older than I am. And he doesn't impress me in the least! But it does look like I'll be contending with him sooner than I had thought.

What an interesting cable home this would make...

>Dear Angie girls Stop
>Place is neat Stop
>Boss comes on Stop
>Strong await my Stop
>Letter love Stop
>Hug African kisses
>Kathleen

I slowly drifted off to sleep pondering my second day on the Plantation. Ahh. Africa...dark mysterious continent.

View of Monrovia from the Dukor Palace Intercontinental Hotel 1973

Chapter 3

Monrovia and Moonlight

I awoke to the steady sound of rain pelting on the tin roof. How comforting it is to listen to its rhythmic beat. I am liking this place more and more! This Africa! A glance at my watch showed it to be 6:00. I am on my US body-clock-time schedule I thought. But again someone has been in my room when I was sleeping turning the air-conditioner on. I don't like the thought of a man coming into my room while I sleep. Liberian way or not. Gives me the creeps and I'm angry with myself for sleeping so soundly. But sleep comes so easily here, which was definitely not like at home. Thanks Jim, for telling the Liberian to let me be. Still wearing the thin, borrowed, pale blue negligee; I stepped outside to welcome the dawn. Wisps of fog greeted me as I stood on the veranda and watched the now gentle rain spray the lush green tropical vegetation.

Ahh, I sighed; I truly have found a paradise!

I wonder what today will bring. School begins on Monday and I haven't been able to work in my classroom yet since Jim has kept me so busy. Maybe when I get my car...I won't have to be as dependent upon him as last night was terribly awkward. I am anxious to meet my children and get into the school year. Hopefully things will be different with Jim once the school starts and we are on our own schedules. I surely hope so! I just want to maintain a friendly non-dating atmosphere between us. I am reading the signals that he wants us to be more. Must be that his biological clock was ticking. After learning that I am the only single white woman around...well, he's probably thinking I could be his last chance at having a relationship. Not the way I want to have a man and besides, I'm not "tingling" with him. I'll know when I meet the man of my dreams, as the tingling will start.

I step back into my room to shower and dress. I decided to wear my "coming to Liberia" dress and not the borrowed ones since we were going into Monrovia. Hopefully, my own clothes and luggage will arrive on the Pan Am flight on Wednesday. I can't wait to have my things here and get into my own routine.

Jim arrived in top spirits while I was eating my tropical breakfast. He acted like last night never happened. He cheerfully announced, "Good morning Kathleen, your car is ready! First today, you are going to take your driving test so as to be able to drive your car back here before we go to Monrovia."

"But I already carry an international driving license," I said, "why do I need to take this test?" Okay, I can act like last night didn't happen either.

"It's the Liberian law and now here is something to remember to do before sitting in the car," he said as I slid into the passenger seat of his car and he closed my door. "The officer, a PPD or Plantation Protection Department person, will not tell you this as he expects you to know it already. You must walk around the car and kick all four tires."

"What? Kick the tires? Why on earth?" I said in total astonishment.

"Because of snakes," he smiled, stroking his mustache, "and then stoop down and look under the car."

"Okay, I give. Why this?"

"Chickens or goats could be underneath! You never want to kill a chicken, a goat, or a sheep. The Liberian government could deport you after a lengthy trial," laughed Jim. "Then get in the car and drive where he tells you. Yes, I'll be in the back to translate for you. Remember this is very serious and don't laugh."

"How come I haven't noticed you or anyone else doing this particular inspection ritual around cars?"

"Because you only perform this when an officer is in sight. Otherwise he will fine you,"

"Nothing like this at home. When can I get back to my classroom as I want to start preparing for the children and school?"

"Plenty of time to do that. Don't worry," he said as we pulled into the PPD parking lot.

I was introduced to a Liberian who just stood there gaping at me. So, in my white heels, I kicked all four tires and looked underneath whilst noticing how the men were also taking a lookie at me stooping. We all got in and I drove Jim's big LTD around. I smiled, as this was the strangest test I had ever taken. There was Jim telling me what the Liberian was saying and me trying to drive and not make any errors. Will I ever understand this strange English?

"Great!" I said because there would be no written test. What a strange way this PPD officer shook my hand with a snap of the fingers at the end of the shake congratulating me on passing the exam.

"Liberian handshake," Jim informed me as I saw him shaking the officer's hand with a green bill being placed in it. Okay, a little bribery must also be the Liberian way. Little did I know that I would soon find out about their way of "dashing".

Jim said, "How about us getting your car now? I know you are anxious to be driving around on your own. When that errand is done, we'll be able to go to Monrovia."

"Super!" I responded, eager to get my own car to explore the

Plantation on my own as I hadn't seen much of it yet. And then, of course, I wouldn't be obligated to my boss to take me around.

Over at the Motor Pool, Jim introduced me to Jerry Elam, an American, who ran the garage for cars and trucks. I also met Hans Lutz who headed the department for the heavy-duty equipment for the company. Jerry had a slender build and blondish brown hair and a big welcoming smile. He was wearing green pants but had on a white T-shirt with a pack of cigarettes in his rolled sleeve. Hans, a stocky Swiss, pumped my hand for what seemed like hours welcoming me to Liberia.

"My children go to the Staff School and are anxious to meet you as we are to have them go back to school. They are driving my wife, Mitzi, crazy," he said with a thick German accent. Must be from the German side of Switzerland I thought.

"You are assigned that Ford Zephyr over there for one year," Jerry said. "It is number 49 D. Next year you'll move up to the C class of car. Jim drives an A class as he is in charge of a department." Looks like a reward system I thought, the better the job, the better the car.

"Wow!" I said upon reaching the car. Well, if one could call it that. The hood and driver's side door were white, trunk beige, and the passenger's side door light blue, the right rear fender was dark green, and what was remaining on the car was black. The whole car looked like it had just experienced an accident or was going to go out looking for one. My feet barely reached the petals and thank goodness it was an automatic as I adjusted the seat in closer.

I laughed, "Looks like I won't be carrying any passengers since there isn't any floor on that side!"

"Floor? Do you want one?" Hans asked like it was usual not to have one.

"Well…I'll let you know if I have need of one. I don't want to be any trouble." I just thought this was a pretty interesting car. Plus it gave me liberty from relying upon Jim.

"I like it! It is distinctive and unique!" I said seeing how disappointed Jim was that I was going to be driving this piece of trash. I, however, saw it as my African vehicle of freedom that would help me explore this marvelous land! Well, as far as 800 miles per month on the company's gas allowance. That's what Jerry said I was assigned.

"Plenty of miles and you will probably only use about 200 a month."

I shook both men's hands again and said bye knowing that 800 miles would not be enough for me. They didn't know me yet and I would see how I could finagle more miles.

Whoa! Jim sped off wanting me to follow him back to the Guest House but, I couldn't get this car to go very fast. Gee, I could walk faster...well, it looks like my top speed is 50 miles an hour and that's traveling downhill! I still liked the crazy car and planned to travel as far as I could get it to go.

The Guest House steward had packed us bag lunches and we went back down to the Motor Pool to get gas for Jim's car. While gassing up, I saw Jim talking to a very large, muscular, good looking Liberian wearing the Firestone clothes of green shirt and pants with the red F on the sleeves. Boy, I really like Firestone's outfit as it reminded me of my savior from Sunday. I was introduced to him using the Liberian handshake. His name was David Sharwillie.

"Welcome Missy," he beamed as he held opened the back door for me to climb in. Jim entered from the opposite side. David got behind the steering wheel. Hum, now what is up I thought?

"I usually take a driver to Monrovia and the company recommends that all staff do the same. Sign up for a driver a day in advance. David is the best and most difficult to get. He's the General Manager, Jack Carmichael's driver. Right, my man?" Jim asked David. They laughed some shared secret laugh.

Now all kinds of crazy thoughts flashed through my mind. I knew that Monrovia was about an hour or so away from the Plantation, but a driver? What was Jim really up too? I moved closer to the door and carefully watched how I positioned my legs. Got to keep a conscious eye on what I do so I don't give him the wrong impression. After all he was my boss and I wanted to keep ours a working relationship. How would I explain this to my boyfriend back home? I decided, when I saw an opportunity, I would drop this bit of information.

On the way to Monrovia, Jim gave me a brief history of Liberia. "Liberia was founded by the American Freed Negro Society back in 1822. This US organization help fund the return of freed Negroes back to Africa. Many ships brought the freed families along with weapons, seeds, tools, and such things needed to start a new settlement on the west coast of Africa. The families selected the bay by Monrovia establishing their fort and settlement. They named it after President James Monroe the fifth president of the United States."

I let Jim go on, not interrupting as he really did enjoy telling me. So, I smiled and let him talk and tried to absorb as much country and sights as I could. Let him do his bit I thought remembering how I had represented Angie Brooks in my local home town's mock United Nations. Miss Brooks was the first African woman delegate to the United Nations and she later became the United Nations General Assembly's first African president in 1969.

Once we left the Plantation and passed Robertsfield Airport, we also left the tall thick bush, trees, and rolling hills. The scenery became very flat with low grasses and occasional palm trees swaying in the breeze. The sky was an intense blue with many massive cumulus clouds floating lazily. The road was paved but in really bad shape by Plantation standards. David swerved all over to avoid the potholes.

"The road is in great shape," remarked Jim noticing my discomfort. "It was paved last year when Mrs. Richard Nixon came in January 1972 as a good will ambassador from the US. Mrs. Nixon visited the JFK Hospital and President Tolbert."

"Gee, this is good?" I said being bounced all over and trying to keep some sense of modesty. "What are the country roads like?"

"Bad-o!" piped up David. "Only drive them between seasons. If you want to go upcountry, I drive you. I got plenty of friends."

"Can't I go by myself?"

"No-o, you can't do that thing! It wild there!" David laughed.

I noticed how I could understand David's English much better than other Liberians. Jim told me that David speaks slowly because he drives so many Firestone people when they visit from Akron.

We sped through a large brush fire that was burning on both sides and even across the road. "Why are those people burning the ground and brush like that?" I asked.

"The people get their farms ready for planting rice," said David.

"It's the slash and burn technique," filled in Jim, "you will see this all over the country. The people are pretty superstitious also planting soap stone carvings of large penis gods of fertility. The Charlies will be around and could get you one. They are great conversation piece to have especially if the penis is huge!"

Gosh, talking about penises so causally with my boss is weird and it is just what every single teacher needs in her house too! I could maybe…well…my mind just wandered…

"We'll do some bargaining when we are in Monrovia so you'll get the hang of it. The Ivory Charlies and Liberians really like a good chatter while selling and might even give you a low price if you play the game with them…and they often will even gift you as a thank you. Good entertainment if you have the time."

"Boy that sounds intriguing as I do like to chat and get bargains!"

Every now and then we'd pass a few grass huts but, otherwise the view was pretty simple and nothing stood out. We slowed down from 55 miles an hour to about 35 when we came into the outskirts of town. So far it had taken us a little over an hour to travel the 50 or so miles. I'll be sore tomorrow I thought as I rubbed my lower back.

Monrovia! Ahh, Monrovia! My eyes flew back and forth from left to right trying to see it all. Wow! So many cars and so many people! No traffic lights and stop signs…horns tooting and arms flailing, such commotion! I loved the bustle of the place. Small shops thrown together with tin roofs and weak walls. People selling goods spread out on the ground. I leaned out the window to snap pictures.

"That's the car wash. It's just a small creek where you drive up and the boys will quickly wash your car for 5 cents," laughed Jim.

"Car wash? Wow!" I snapped another picture.

"Be careful taking pictures as most Liberians don't like theirs taken. Spirit or something. Often you must pay for the photo," explained Jim.

I loved the noise and confusion. By United States standards this was a slum neighborhood in a third world country, but to me it was a country just teeming with life and adventure!

"That's Sinkor Supermarket where many Firestone women grocery shop and in front is a good place for buying Liberian fabrics. Someone will even make a dress for you that you can pick up on the way out of town. You can do that the next time we come to Monrovia because today we are meeting my friend Max at the Ducor Palace Intercontinental Hotel." Jim said.

We dodged the people and cars making for a crazy ride through town. Policeman stood on corners unsuccessfully trying to manage things. A small rain had just stopped and things were drying up. The humidity was intense and I was dripping with sweat. I just wanted to peel off these nylons! Why did I wear them in this heat? Never again I decided. Tomorrow my clothes and sandals. Hooray! Jim must have read my mind as he said in a low suggestive voice, "You can remove those nylons at the Ducor Palace and be more comfortable."

He burns me up being able to predict my thoughts!

We passed many large modern buildings. Jim told me they were government structures and there was the President's Mansion! It was on the beach and more than double the size of the White House! We continued to pass through the city swerving to miss people and cars. So much to see and learn! Then the car slowly wound its way up a steep hill to the International Hotel called the Ducor Palace that was situated at the top. The Ducor Palace had marvelous views of the entire city and the islands nestled in the bay. Monrovia looks like any large city from up here when you can't see the slums and trash strewn about. The bustle below moved without a sound. Just going about the daily business needed to run a city of 200,000 people. What keeps them here? What jobs do they have? A big city is fun to visit, but me; I want the peace and quiet. The quality of life that the Plantation had to offer.

"Where does that road go?" I asked pointing to the west.

"It goes to the United States Embassy and that road over the bridge goes to the shipping docks and is also a longer way back to the Plantation. It is pretty difficult to get lost in Liberia, even if there are few roads. I'll get you a map of both the Plantation and the country. Oh, here's Max."

I stretched my neck to gawk at the enormous Swiss man. He had very broad shoulders, dark brown hair and a neatly trimmed full beard. He talked and laughed with gusto as his size predicted. I instantly liked Max and felt relaxed and at ease with him. His hands and feet were wide and large. I wondered about the rest of him…hum and smiled mischievously.

Jim, Max, and I went to the bar lounge and ordered drinks. Only 1:00? I managed to slip away to get rid of the bothersome nylons but not without Jim making a comment about them and my legs. Max remained quiet…my kind of gentleman. Max told me he was the Pan Am chef for the planes that came into and out of the Robertsfield Airport. He was taking a few days off to rest at the Ducor Palace. We sat and drank for an hour or so. Too early for me to drink. So, I excused myself to wander about the hotel. The pool was fantastic with people frolicking in it and the usual sunbathers lounging around. I also wanted to jump in and cool off. The lobby was huge, contemporary furniture graced the floors. Interesting fabrics on the cushions and curtains I thought. Fabric! Oh, I remembered.

I went back to the lounge, "Jim weren't we going to select the fabric for my cushions?"

"Oh, right," he slurred. "Let's go to the German Store before they close."

"They close at 6:00," said Max.

So we continued to sit and drink until 2:30. Thank goodness for the cushions. We were rising to go when Max reminded Jim that I needed to buy a big diamond ring before leaving today and he knew a good Swiss jeweler on Broad Street.

"Diamond ring?" Why do I need one?" I said looking at my two rings-one from St. Benedict's and the other from Villa Maria College.

"This is Africa and one never knows when one might need to protect oneself. A big diamond ring does just that. Take it off for a dash to get onto a plane if trouble breaks out."

"Oh, I really don't like diamonds but I certainly don't like trouble either. Maybe I'll get a small ring."

At the Gold Art Swiss Jewelry Store, I just stared at all the incredible gold and silver. I hadn't seen such unique and intricate designs since I was a young girl peering into the shop windows in Paris and Geneva. A distinctive horseshoe shaped diamond ring caught my eyes. Wow! There were 6 tiny diamonds on each side. I liked it immediately! A perfect fit too, with a price that I couldn't refuse and I walked out of the store wearing it and vowing to return in the future. We all then drove to the German Store. I chose a medium brown fabric for my cushions. Max said goodbye as we departed the store.

"Come back for the cushions in 3 weeks," the German man said as we left.

Jim and I climbed into the car and David drove us quickly away. Whew! So much accomplished in such a short time when it had looked like we were to spend the day drinking at the Ducor Palace Lounge. All too soon we were at a beach spot on the edge of town. We managed to catch the sun setting over the Atlantic Ocean. Simple silent colors of soft reds and purples painted the western sky. Low hanging clouds reflected the rays for minutes after the sunset.

"Breathtaking!" I murmured breathing in the salty air with tears in my eyes. "I shall never forget this scene as long as I live," I choked.

"I forget how lovely it is until I am able to share the experience with someone like you," Jim whispered trying to put his arms around me. I slipped away and walked along the edge of the water as it lapped my toes.

"Hum, how cool and inviting after such a hot humid day," I said.

David stayed with the car as usual and we walked a short distance to a small restaurant along the beach.

"Oscar's is one of the finest restaurants you will find in the world! Oscar serves the best Chateaubriand!"

We entered a dark candlelit room with small open windows facing the ocean. The window and table coverings were a deep red and the ambiance screamed romance! It would be a simply perfect place to eat with just the right person. But, my boss? He was really scaring me coming on so fast.

Oscar greeted Jim by name and I was introduced. How impressive this simple man was. He wore Swiss shorts and suspenders. His white shirt was decorated with embroidery on the collar. He seated us in a corner where the lights were even dimmer. Jim ordered for both of us. The wine was delicious and I sipped slowly to make sure I remembered everything and to be sober for the long ride back to the Plantation.

I felt caressed by the warm ocean breezes that blew through the open windows. "Wow! Last week I was in Erie eating at MacDonald's! Now here I'm in this terrific place in Africa no less! How utterly incredible! Thank you for bringing me here and sharing an interesting day with me. I won't forget it ever," I promised inhaling the warm salty air.

Jim reached for my hand and squeezed it saying, "There is so much more to experience in Liberia and I want to show it all to you. I have a very special surprise I want to share later."

"Jim, this is overwhelming. I believe you are presuming a little too much about me err…us. I just arrived and really appreciate all you have done for me. But, things are moving too quickly. You are a pretty terrific man and are doing so much for me. I appreciate it; believe me and I don't want to hurt your feelings," I continued slowly and carefully, "I have a policy about becoming romantically involved with someone I work with…simply put you are my boss and I only want a friendship with you. I also have a boyfriend back home." Whew! I did it and hope I did it in a nice and friendly way. How he takes it will determine our relationship the remainder of the year.

"Ahh," he said in a low tone after a delayed time. "I believe I understand. I am a very decent and patient man. Perhaps I have given the wrong impression. I'm sorry if I have offended you. I respect your point of view and you no longer have any need to worry about me. That is if you were worried. I hope we will become fast friends and I will be pleased with this relationship." He reached for my hand to shake sealing the pact.

I did. But, I felt uneasy nevertheless about how easy it seemed to be. Did he mean it? Only time would tell. Jim ordered more wine and our meal of steak au poivre. We watched Oscar prepare it on a portable cart and as the brandy ignited, I hoped the spark set in Jim was doing the opposite.

Oscar did not disappoint and the meal was fit for the gods. I savored every last mouthful. The banana flambé was incredible, too! We sipped our wine and made lazy conversation sharing some of our past. Our meal finished, we said our goodbyes, and made our way back to David who was waiting by the car. What a terrific day, if I can get home without incident…hooray!

I silently wished ciao to the ocean and looked forward to returning. We spoke little on the way back. It was late with little traffic. We moved as smoothly as possible and I was beginning to doze when I felt the car slowing down and turning.

"I want to show you something impressive," informed Jim, "remember when I said I had something to share? Well…"

The car made its way down the narrow winding dark road. Palm trees lined it and gradually we came to the end of the road. David stopped and left the car. Oh no…I thought this is it…he was reneging on his promise and was going to pounce on me.

"Come on I want you to see this!" He said dragging me from the car. Protesting my tiredness was to no avail. Jim insisted. I removed my shoes and followed on the cool sand. It squeaked as we walked and I could hear the sounds of the waves pounding the shoreline. Jim made his way a little to the right and a large mirror seemed to be lying on the white sand reflecting the light from the first quarter moon.

"Mirror? Oh, it's the moon!" I shouted. "Wow! How beautiful!"

Jim was taking his clothes off right in front of me! Yikes! I lagged behind not wanting to see and waited until he entered the lagoon's water.

"Come on in! The water is refreshing and a nice way to cool off before returning to the Plantation. This is the surprise I wanted to show you."

"Surprise? Okay, Jim as long it doesn't include anything else. Are you a man that goes back on his word?"

He stood up in all his glory and declared, "I do not go back on my word and you are not to be afraid. I will not rape you, Kathleen. Sex is to be shared between a man and a woman. Rape would never be something I would or could do."

Gee, I am to believe that line of bull shit? He can talk all he wants but he won't be seeing me in the altogether that's for sure!

"Again, come on in and experience pleasure," he said in a lusty voice.

"Uhhh, this is quite fine for me walking by the water's edge. I have had enough for one evening and am very tired. Can't we go back to the Plantation?"

Jim continued to swim about and I to walk. I decided to return to the car where David greeted me with a laugh.

"The Missy no like to swim? It fine-o."

"Swimming is all right but, I am very tired, David, and would like to return to the Guest House."

"When Mister Smith says so."

Finally Jim returned slowly picking up his clothes and began to get dressed by the car. He chatted easily not being bothered by his nudity. Okay, I too can behave in a sophisticated way and started talking while giving him a good stare at what was between his legs.

I won! He glanced away and sputtered for me to get in. The rest of the ride was uncomfortable with only the hum of the engine to break the silence. Maybe I shouldn't have done that? Having to deal with Jim Smith came sooner that I had anticipated. Gosh how should I write this back home to my family, Tim, and friends?

> Dear friends Stop
> Greetings Stop
> Arrived being Stop
> Baptized into culture Stop
> Experiencing much Stop
> Lots to tell Stop
> Saw Boss Stop
> In nude stay tune Stop
> Hugs African kisses Stop
> Kathleen

Gee, this will go over really swell with Tim and those at home. I can only pray that tomorrow brings an opportunity to smooth things over between Jim and me. Time will tell. David dropped us off at the Motor Pool and we rode home in silence in Jim's car. Goodnight was easy and Jim drove off humming, *You Sexy Thing*. I entered my room and surrendered to sleep in my bed at the Firestone Guest House.

My Ford Zephyr 49 D parked under my bungalow

Chapter 4

49 D

I awoke to a light rain tapping on the tin roof. I thought, how peaceful and serene the rains are here. Did last night even happen? Maybe it was all the drinking Jim was doing and being lonely that caused him to behave so. I wondered how things would go today. Jim Smith was not someone I wanted to anger as he could make my life miserable and that wasn't something I wanted to deal with. Why does this have to happen to me and with the person who is my boss? I had no one to discuss this matter with. How I wished I could pick up the phone and call my friend, Angie, perhaps she would know how to handle this Jim Smith fellow. Maybe there will be another teacher that will be able to assist me. They just might know how to deal with this man. I do feel sorry for him being in a place where there are few available women but I simply don't want to be tied down to one man especially one who is so much older than me. I thought, with Africa to discover and so very little time to do it. If things work out, I just might have to stay for another contract to get all my exploring done.

While showering and lathering my body with soap, it hit me-my luggage was arriving via Pan Am this morning! My clothes and personal things would be here soon....well I hoped so. How wonderful it will be to have my own clothes and the supplies I will need in my classroom. This could prove to be another exciting day. My green dress was missing from the chair and not in the cupboard. The guys were in my room again while I slept. Will I ever get use to the invasion of my personal space?

I went to the dining room to enjoy breakfast to find Jim already there talking to another Guest House visitor.

"Good morning Kathleen! Meet Charlie Lorenz, manager of Firestone's Plantation in Cavalla which is in Maryland country," Jim said looking smug as he pulled a chair for me to sit next to him.

"Happy to meet you and welcome to Liberia," Charlie said smiling and appraising me.

"Please tell me about yourself. You know it's not often we have such a young woman here to work on the Plantation. I heard a lot about you last night while dining with friends. How do you find Liberia and the Plantation so far?"

"Thank you. Well...I find Liberia to be a very interesting place so far and quite revealing too...uh...right Jim?" I said staring at him. I want to control the conversation and not be intimidated by him. Maybe it worked but looking at Jim I couldn't tell with that Cheshire cat grin as he stroked his mustache in a seductive way. Darn that man!

Without missing a beat or blushing, Jim said, "I took Kathleen to Monrovia yesterday and met Max, the chef for Pan Am Robertsfield there. I showed her around and today we'll be off to the school to get ready for the first day."

"Jim, isn't my luggage arriving today on the Pan Am flight?"

"Yes, and I will have Zanga, the school's custodian, collect it for you. He'll deliver it to your room at the Guest House. Eat up and I'll take you to school."

Now he's ordering me around…gosh darn it…hum. "That is so sweet of you to offer, but I'd like to meet you at the school and stay longer if I don't get finished before you do. Having my own car is so nice and I can't wait to drive around and explore a little bit, too." That ought to get him off my back for today at least.

"Great idea Kathleen!" Charlie said, "Exploring on your own is a good thing but, before you do any, stop by the Central Office and look up Charlie Barbel or Jerry Swanson. They will give you some maps of the Plantation."

My kind of man this Charlie Lorenz and he did this in front of Jim…nothing Jim can say now.

"Sounds like a workable plan to me," said Jim. "I'll see you over at the Staff School."

Having eaten my breakfast, I quickly excused myself to drive to the Staff School. Driving 49 D, my freedom vehicle, down the road was thrilling! Wow, to roam this place on my very own…well when I get the maps at least. I don't want to get lost in this jungle!

I found the school and parked outside my room. Jim's car was already there. My class list was on my desk as were the teacher's manuals. Wow! I will be using the same manuals that I used in the Erie School District! This is incredible! I studied my children's names and recognized some from meeting their parents at the Sunday brunch. Yep, only 13 children like Jim had said. This is unreal to have so few! Seven girls and six boys…what a Christopher and another one?!!! You've got to be kidding!

Slowly I rearranged my room and passed out the books, crayons, notebooks, rulers, erasers, and pencils. I decided to wait with the reading books until I knew what reading level the children would be in. My mind kept wandering and wondering what the children would be like. So…I continued to ready my room when there came a knock at my door.

"Hello! I welcome you to the school. I am Hil Koops and the secretary here."

Hil came into my room with a big smile. She was not tall and had short blonde hair. Hil was extremely curvy and always fussing with her light weight sweater. I thought, how can she wear a sweater in this heat? Maybe it is to distract people from looking at…but, instead your eyes are drawn to her top. She also played with her thin wire rimmed glasses. Hil said that she took care of the library and explained how a school day ran, what I needed to do for attendance, and some other school related business.

I will teach everything including art, gym, music, and library. Hil continued to tell me so many more things and answered my questions about my students. She explained that she was Dutch and has two children and her son, Cees-Jan, goes to the American school in Monrovia and daughter, Marjanne, is in seventh grade at the Staff School. Her husband Jacques is a division manager. I liked her a lot and found her to be very helpful-just like a secretary should be.

Again, I heard another knock, but this time from another door that was in the blackboard wall. I hadn't noticed it until now, but the whole blackboard appeared to swing back to make a huge room that included the next door classroom and mine.

A tall attractive brown haired lady introduced herself, "I'm Billie Darsey and I teach fourth grade. Welcome Kathleen!" She said as she hugged and greeted Hil.

Billie told me she has been teaching at the Staff School on and off for many years! If I needed anything, just ask. I could see immediately that Billie would become a great mentor. She was from Georgia with a delightful southern accent. Her husband, Darsey, has been in Liberia for 24 years! Billie came as a new bride back in the early 50's and has four children. Their three girls went to a boarding high school in England and son was in seventh grade here at the Staff School.

Billie explained about the swinging blackboard and how all of the school children can fit into both rooms for assemblies and meeting parents for Open House.

"School is good here and the parents are so helpful to us all. You are going to enjoy your stay. How do you find being here so far?"

"I am trying to establish a routine and look forward to school beginning so I can do just that. I am finding the language difficult to understand and oh yes, the houseboys keep coming into my room when I am asleep. How do I stop that?"

"Ouee," drawled Billie, "You'll just have to put an end to that. The boys know better. You must be very firm with them!"

"Well, Jim Smith did talk to them and it…"

"Ouee…now… that Jim Smith…now you just watch that man," Billie said wagging her finger at me. "Jim Smith can be so charming and then well, you'll see, just keep your eyes peeled," she said winking her eyes in a knowing manner.

Aha, I thought, someone to help me with this sticky situation with him. Perhaps I'll wait since he knows people will be telling me lots about him. Peeled…huh…and how, if she only knew!

Hil and Billie invite me for lunch at the restaurant in the Robertsfield's Hotel.

"I'd like to drive but you both have to sit in the back since there's no floor on the passenger's side."

They both saw 49 D and stopped.

"What? I never saw such a mess of a car…what is the big deal?" said Hil.

"Oh, I love it! Not another one like it around!"

"That's for sure…everyone does have to pay their dues before they get a good car. It is safe to drive?" Billie said.

"I guess…would I be given a defective car? I was told it had pieces of many other cars and that it ran well."

"Jim Smith didn't do anything?" Hil asked.

"He certainly wasn't happy, but I like it and that's that."

Instead, we piled into Billie's blue LTD.

"Hey, I have noticed that all the cars and pick-ups around the Plantation are Fords. I don't see any other types. Is there a reason?"

"Sure is…Harvey Firestone and Henry Ford were great friends and they made a deal to put Firestone tires on all Ford cars. Of course, that's why all cars in Firestone service are Fords," Billie informed me.

"Wow! That is pretty cool!"

As we passed houses, the women pointed out where some of my children lived. They explained how buses pick up the students that live out on the divisions and how some parents drive their children in. School has around 108 students first through eighth grades. Jacqueline Clough comes in to each room daily to give French lessons. My class is scheduled for 10 minutes. Any French I can speak throughout the day will be great! I told them how I lived three years in France and studied French both in high school and college. So, no problem there. Boy, I am really excited for the school year to begin and meet my students.

We passed a road on the left and Hil said, "That is the road to go upcountry. See that huge tree? It is a cottonwood and that little place is called Cottonwood. Also, it is the way to where Jim Smith lives. Wait until you see his place! It is situated on an island above the hydroelectric plant and waterfalls. It is one of the prettiest places to live on the Plantation."

Billie added, "You'll see it when Jim has the monthly staff luncheon. I agree it is a fabulous place to live!"

We continued to ride along and the women pointed out another road on the left.

"Just off the Plantation is Sammy's Place. It is kind of a Seven-Eleven where you can get supplies when the Firestone Grocery store is closed." Billie explained.

"Also, many people hang out there to chat and drink a beer after work." Hil added.

"Whoa!!!" I said inquisitively, "What is that awful smell?"

"Money!" Both women piped up.

"Money? I don't get it!"

"Wind is blowing just right and the factory is cooking the rubber. So the odor is rubber and our money! Why we are here. Don't worry, you'll get used to it and know our rubber is needed in the world some place," Hil said.

"Oh, Okay." Will I really get used to that pungent odor?

"By the way, Kathleen, we always stop at Central Office to check for mail," said Billie turning into that road. "I should have a letter from my girls, Debbie, and the twins Jan and Ann. I miss them ever so much! Oh, yes, mail comes in three times a week and we all crave news from home."

But there was no letter for either woman and their faces showed their disappointment. I knew I would be there soon. Must write a letter tonight to Mom and Dad and Angie because I know the cablegram won't be enough for them.

The women introduced me to some more people including Charlie Lokko. I had met Mr. Lokko and his wife on Sunday at Lawton's brunch. He had a robust laugh reminding me of Santa Claus! He again welcomed me and said that his wife, Isobel, was looking for me. She had been by the Guest House a couple of times to find me out with Jim Smith.

"She'll be around more now that she has her own car and is not dependent on Jim," drawled Billie.

Earlier, on the way to the Central Office, the women told me about Americo Liberians and native Liberians. The first were descendants of the freed slaves from America and the latter were native Liberians. Firestone employed about 80,000 people and most were native Liberians. The government was made up of mostly Americo Liberians. Did I know how Liberia came to be? I then explained to them about the mock model United Nations from high school. Both women were impressed that I had such a thorough knowledge of Liberia.

"But, I want to learn more about these delightful people who are always laughing and smiling around me. I also want to go exploring on my own. Oh, yes, this morning at breakfast, Charlie Lorenz told me to see Charlie Barbel or Jerry something to get maps. Do we have time?"

"Sure we do, all the time in the world for you," said Charlie Lokko, "Let's go to the Personnel Office."

So, he led us around the building to the office where I met the two men. A slender black hand was extended to me as Charlie Barbel introduced himself to me. He was a small man with a quick smile and pleasing eyes. Jerry Swanson was also small, but stockier with searching eyes framed by thick black glasses. Both men were happy to meet me as they had heard all about me. Gosh, I must be the new "toy" in town to discuss.

"I understand that you are the men who can give me maps of the Plantation," I said.

"Maps, why yes, we have them but, you don't want to go driving around this place by yourself. We don't want you getting lost on the Plantation!" said Jerry.

"That's precisely why I'd like the maps," I smiled and flirted.

Charlie handed me many maps, one of Liberia and the others of Divisions 1, 40, 42, 43, 44 and 45.

"The factory, Central Office, Grocery Store, and other office buildings along with Harbel City are here in Division 45. Many homes, the Staff School, church, and Guest House are in Division 44," Jerry added.

"Oh, then, my house is in Division 44."

"Yes," Billie answered. "I would stay in these two Divisions and not venture into the other Divisions alone as we just can't be having you lost on the Plantation!"

Everyone agreed and so I pretended to take heed.

We said our goodbyes and Charlie Lokko explained the unusual way the Liberians shook my hand after I asked why they were trying to shake in such an odd manner.

"First you take the hand firmly; shake, and then you both slide back slowly readying your fingers to snap off the other's fingers at the ends. Like this," he demonstrated.

"Ah, I see…I had wondered what was up with this handshake. Thanks for explaining it to me," I said laughing and repeatedly trying to get it correct.

Everyone was laughing, too, and said mastering the handshake took time. Time…there was that word again. So much to learn about my new country.

We climbed back into Billie's Ford and headed toward the Robertsfield Hotel which I now realized was just off the Plantation.

I glanced over at the long low cement building on the right and recognized it as the place where I had sat waiting for my adventure to begin. It seemed like years ago when it was only three days ago! I then proceeded to relate the story of my arrival to the women.

"Ouee…that Jim Smith and his drink! Many times he is just plain out of it. So glad that it all worked out for you!" Billie huffed. "You just watch that man now you hear?"

I said, "Jim did tell me he thought I was to arrive on Wednesday and was so surprised I came in on Sunday." Now it seems like I'm defending him...gosh, I wonder what else I need to know about Jim Smith. Is this the time to tell about last night's lagoon swim? No, not yet, I decided.

The Hotel was a two story cement block building on the left with a large wide lobby in the middle and the one story restaurant on the right. We walked through the lobby and then through sliding glass doors to an enormous size pool and lounge area on the right. The pool was a cool refreshing sapphire blue with a permanent roof.

"Wow! This is really nice! But why cover the pool?" I inquired as I took my place at a table. The sounds of children and others went up in a roar when they saw Mrs. Darsey! Our table was quickly surrounded by them as Billie introduced me to all. Yes, indeed, two were in my classroom. Susan Johnson and Leonie Witteveen were so bubbly and thrilled to meet their new teacher before school started. I had met their parents at the brunch on Sunday. A Liberian waiter came with menus and Hil said only order by number as they usually couldn't write English. The entire menu was numbered-even a glass of water! We placed our "numbers" and continued chatting.

Billie explained why the pool was covered, "This is the rainy season and it isn't too hot but, come the dry season…ouee…it is so lovely to come down here and submerse your body in the cool water and get out of the tropical sun. During the rains, you can swim."

"Are there more pools around?"

"Well, some people have little wading cement ones and they are nice to cool down and of course the children love them!" Billie added. "But, no, this is the only pool close to Divisions 44 and 45. There is an inground pool at Center Site. Usually Sunday after church, everyone goes to the beach. It's about an hour from here. We barbecue and enjoy the ocean, beach, and lagoons rain or shine. It doesn't matter."

Oh yeah, I know all about the lagoon…I thought.

Our "numbered" food arrived and soon it was time to head back to school and continued getting set up for Monday.

Back at school, Jim told me that my luggage had arrived on the flight and was now in my room at the Guest House. Yes, sir, things were looking up.

I worked in my classroom until 6:00 and drove 49 D carefully back to the Guest House and my baggage. Words can't describe how wonderful it was to shower and put on my own clothes.

I ate dinner with Charlie Lorenz and told him about my day and he spoke of his. He also invited me down to the Cavalla Plantation. He went on to describe it as a much smaller plantation with only a few ex-pats running it. There wasn't a school there either; in fact, Harbel Plantation had the only school in all of the Firestone Company. We continued to chat and I quickly grew very tired. I said my good night and went back to my room.

I will miss this companionship once I move into my own house. This will be the first time that I will live on my own. Another fear to conquer.

I sat at the desk in my room and poured over my maps. They were easy to read and the Divisions were huge with many secondary roads for me to explore. Looks pretty easy to get around and tomorrow after working in my classroom, I'll go exploring.

Before going to bed, I wrote a quick letter to Mom and Dad trying to explain this wonderful place. As I slowly dropped off to sleep, I sent a mental telegram to Angie.

Dear Angie Stop
Met secretary Stop
Fourth grade teacher Stop
Pool here has covered roof Stop
Luggage arrived Stop
All is good Stop
Hugs African kisses Stop
Kathleen

Covered pool at the Robertsfield Hotel 1973

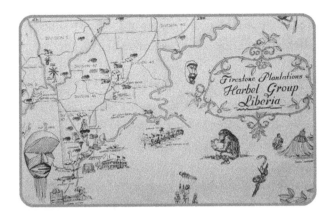

Some Firestone Divisions near where I lived and worked.

Chapter 5

Exploring Divisions 1, 40, 42, 43, 44, and 45

I awoke on day five to the sound of rolling thunder. Still in my nightgown, I quickly went out onto the veranda and watched the rain pour down. The scent in the air drove me to stretch and inhale deeply.

"It rain all day, Missy," someone said to me causing me to jump a mile high!

Wow! I understood him! I hadn't seen him before and he said his name was Pencil.

"Pencil?"

"Ya Missy, I Pencil," he said with a huge grin on his face. He was very proud of his name. Perhaps I didn't understand him as I had thought.

"Zanga here. He say you need something?"

"Zanga? Oh yes, he is the janitor at the Staff School. Right?"

"Ya, he work school. He says things okay? Mr. Smith want know."

"Tell Zanga to tell Mr. Smith that I am very fine indeed. I don't need anything today. Please thank Zanga for me." Great, now I have Jim Smith taken care of well, for the time being.

Charlie Lorenz was already eating when I came to the table all dressed for the day.

"How did you sleep during the storm?" Charlie asked.

"Pretty well, thank you. In fact I practically slept through it. I find that sleeping here is no problem at all as I am usually exhausted by night time."

"What are your plans for today?"

"Well, work at school and then do some exploring with the maps provided by Charlie Barbel and oh, yes, I do want to check on the work progress at my home."

"Sounds like a good plan. I will be leaving for the Cavalla Plantation this afternoon. So, I'll say goodbye. Remember to come down for a visit anytime!"

"I am looking forward to it and to see more of Liberia. Perhaps at Christmas? I understand that we have three weeks of vacation."

"Sure, anytime…just send a cablegram ahead of time via Gail Ruef."

"Okay, I met Gail on my first day here and so I know where the radio building is."

Driving to school was so fun in this crazy car. My car was absolutely the coolest car going! I stopped at my bungalow on the way and the place was swarming with workers. Most were standing watching others paint the walls. They all were laughing and talking very fast. I told them that I liked the colors and they were doing a great job. I drove to the school.

I recognized some of the cars as I parked and entered the office. "Good morning!" I said to everyone where they had gathered to get their mail and perhaps a cup of coffee.

Jim introduced me to Elaine, grade 1 and Bessie, grade 2 and they welcomed me. Both told me that if I needed any assistance to see them. After visiting, I went to work in my room and it was still before 7:00! Good thing I was an early riser.

By noon, my room was in great shape and just about ready to receive my students on Monday. So, I decide to explore Divisions 44 and 45 after lunch. Slowly, I wandered about trying to not get lost…I found the Community Church high on a hill, parked, and walked around it. It was a simple church with white pillars holding up a roof that overhung the entrance. Peering inside, I saw the wooden pews and Firestone brick walls. Someone had told me everyone attends the Sunday service here or at Du Side Chapel. Since this chapel was so close to where I'd be living; this would be my church.

Next, I noticed another large brick building and the sign said it was the Firestone Golf Club. Entering the Golf Club, I was instantly greeted by a man called Mr. Willie Stanley Livingston and he showed me around. He introduced me to Mr. Johnson who bartended behind the long shiny bar.

"Missy, you want a Coca Cola?" Mr. Johnson asked.

"Yes, please." And taking my drink, I passed the square tables on this side of the room and headed to the huge windows where lounge sofas were placed for people to relax and enjoy the view of the golf course. Mr. Willie told me that this was a nine-hole course. He also explained about the greens which were oiled sand so people could play in all weather. Not knowing anything about golf, I nodded and smiled. Mr. Willie invited me to play golf and would get me a caddy to carry my bag.

Laughing, I explained, "I don't play golf but, perhaps one day I'd take you up on the chance to learn. You know, Mr. Willie, my father plays golf and would be envious of me playing on a Firestone Golf Course!"

Outside and standing by an oiled green, I admired the beautifully landscaped view with many flowering bushes and trees. Firestone brick houses on pillars were perched amongst the trees spaced far apart. How perfect it would be to live on this golf course! After saying goodbye to Mr. Willie and Mr. Johnson, I continued driving around looking at these houses which were gigantic compared to mine.

Leaving this area, I drove to Harbel City in Division 45. The Plantation and city were named for Harvey and Idabel Firestone and again the buildings were made of the Firestone brick. Street after street, house after house, hundreds, I guessed knowing the city had hundreds of people.

Turning back, I headed down to the factory passing the Firestone grocery store, Motor Pool, and other buildings. When I saw it was close to six, I headed back to the Guest House for supper. Tonight was the night to write my many letters home. No one will be happy with just the cablegrams I had sent.

After another wonderful dinner and thanking the cook, I sat down at an unset table in a corner of the dining room. I wrote my letters trying to cram in all that had happened to me in the last few days when, a very tall black women entered.

"I see, I finally found you!" she boomed grabbing my hand in the Liberian handshake. "Remember me? I am Isobel Lokko and I met you on Sunday at the Lawtons."

"Hello," I said, hoping I could still use my hand! "The stewards and your husband told me you had stopped by to visit. I am pleased to see you again!"

Isobel continued to pump me with the usual questions and then she proposed she wanted to take me into Monrovia to see it "proper".

I told her I had been shown around by Jim Smith and Isobel promptly poo-pooed that and said, "only, a Liberian can show you Monrovia!"

She would hear of nothing but my agreeing to go with her tomorrow. It was a good thing that my classroom was ready as I could clearly see there wasn't any way that I could be released from the whims of Isobel Lokko!

It was agreed that I was to be ready by 7:00 and to be prompt! There was much to see and do. And with that Isobel Lokko departed.

Guess I am going back to the "big" city again. I wonder what adventures awaited me with this happy woman.

    Once again the time has come to go to bed. Today has been good and at least I gotten some letters written. Then there is tomorrow, I mused as sleep overtook me…

        Dear Mom Dad Stop
        Routine falling Stop
        Into place Stop
        Drove around FPCo Stop
        Didn't get lost Stop
        Back to Monrovia tomorrow Stop
        Hugs African kisses Stop
        Kathleen

Road to a beach

Chapter 6

Isobel Lokko

The day looked to be promising as it wasn't raining. I quickly dressed and went out to eat and wait for Isobel Lokko to take me into Monrovia. I was ready before 7 and no Isobel. I waited and waited. The Guest House stewards didn't know how to reach her and so I decide to drive to the school to get her phone number from Hil.

"Isobel said she'd be there by 7:00?" Hil just laughed. "You don't know the Liberians. She will come by sometime. It is a Liberian way. They follow no clock. Do you know how to work the phones?"

"Of course I know how to use a telephone!"

"The Plantation phones?" Hil asked "They are different to operate. I'll call her as their bungalow is on the same party line as the school. Watch how our phones work," Hil said and went on to demonstrate how to dial and hold the button down. "Count to 10 and lift the button to see if the phone was answered. If not, continue holding the button and count again to 10. No answer, they aren't home or the houseboy is out. This is the party phone system."

Hil did get an answer and laughing told me that Isobel was coming but would be late. "Pick her up at school."

Boy, was Hil ever good! A secretary was worth so much! Using my latest class list, Hil told me about my thirteen students. I have only one American, one Canadian, one British, four Dutch, four Liberians, one Indonesian, and one Filipino. Hil said that not all students will be here on Monday because their parents go on leave at different times. Nine will be here on the first day of school. Gosh, 13 students are certainly better than the 36 I had last year in the Erie School District! With my updated class list in hand, I headed to my room.

When Isobel hadn't shown up by 8:15; I headed back to the office. Jim told me laughing. "It's the Liberian way to come when they come. She'll be here some time. Just go back to your room and I'll get you when she comes."

Sometime later, I heard the screeching of tires and looked up to see a white LTD parking in front of the office. Isobel came tearing down the hall to my classroom, "Hurry, hurry, we must go," she said gasping for air as she ordered me to hurry up as she had things to do! Whoa, Isobel had turned it around so instead of her being late, I made her late. What gives? I only hope she isn't the driver to Monrovia as she tore out again and in "two seconds" we arrived at the Motor Pool for our driver. What a relief when I saw that David Sharwillie was our driver today.

I decided to stand and wait until told what to do as Isobel was quite demanding, bossing David and anyone near her. Maybe this wasn't such a good idea to be traveling with someone when I barely understood their English. Somehow, I ended up in the back seat with Isobel who just talked the entire trip into town with me bobbing up and down trying not to throw up. David drove like a wild man-must be he wanted the trip to end also. Amazingly, we safely made it into town.

Isobel told David that he was to drive us to a place called Cooper

Town, a suburb of Monrovia. We arrived at her dear friend's for lunch. Introductions were quickly made and we sat down at a long wooden table. Isobel raised her drink and toasted me, welcoming me to their country, and insisted that I try everything placed in front of me.

"Fufu?" I asked bewildered. They had their fingers in a dish, swirling the thick white soft stuff around and dipping it into a gravy-like liquid and swooping it into their mouths.

Isobel laughed and said, "Mr. Smith no show you this food, eh? This is Liberian food made from the cassava plant. Liberians make many dishes from cassava," she continued to swirl, dip, and drop. Everyone did the same from the communal dish. Oh well... I swirled, dipped, and dropped, and almost choked from the spicy heat.

Gasping, I choked in a weakened voice, "Water, water," I gulped the water and was horrified that it might the local water and not boiled and filtered. Who told me to only drink boiled water so as not to become sick? At this point, I would welcome sickness to get rid of the burning sensation spreading throughout my digestive system. Oh godddd...

The women were laughing at my pain and telling me to eat sweet food to cool my mouth. Using my fingers, I grabbed and shoved pineapple into my mouth. Miracles of miracles! It was working! My burning mouth and throat were beginning to cool down. Are these people nuts or what? They continued eating and I stuck to the sweet foods like pineapple, coconut, banana, papaya, and surprisingly peanuts. I managed to taste most of the food presented to me but avoided the brown liquid stuff and the hot peppers. I did like the fish soup and a peppered chicken dish, well at least I hoped it was chicken!

The women chatted and I tried to keep up, but this Liberian English was spoken so quickly that I could only pick out a word here and there. My eyelids grew heavy and the noises continued to buzz around me when before I knew it, Isobel awoke me to usher me back to the car and we headed to a place called Water Street and shopping.

As we crawled our way through the traffic, I swear everyone was honking their horns when Isobel jumped out of the car pulling me with her onto the crowded street. Next thing the skies opened up and we were caught in a hard downpour. I now saw why this place was called Water Street as the place became flooded yet, no one seemed to pay any attention to the rain or the water up to their ankles. The urge to shop prevailed and that's what we did, soaking wet, with Isobel saying never mind the rain no hurt anyone and there are things to see and buy. My kind of woman! We went in and out of the many stores, checking out their wares from bolts of brightly colored fabric to clothes-western and Liberian, to household items. I even saw small jewelry shops and shoes, oh the shoes! So many people pushed and shopped. To my dismay, I wasn't able to shop for me but I did buy a couple of presents for my family. Isobel had things to purchase and other places to cart me. Back to the car and by now the rains had stopped only to serve up hot and humid conditions. The air conditioning felt heavenly and I was exhausted but no time to sleep as somehow we made it through Monrovia, Sinkor, and to another friend's home. This incredible place was called Sugar Beach and was it right on the Atlantic Ocean. The house was huge and the floors were a cool glistening white marble with beautiful simple furniture and the views were magnificent!

Mrs. Cooper invited us to the veranda and I drank in the warm ocean breezes. A steward served us drinks of sweet pineapple and rum and that's all I needed as I slumped in my chair fast asleep. I just couldn't stay awake with all the stimulus I had had the past few days and I guess jet lag was kicking in. Luckily, the women let me sleep until it was time to head to the Plantation.

"I'm so sorry that I fell asleep," I said stretching and yawning.

Mrs. Cooper laughed, "I understand Isobel's need for speed and her zest for life. Don't worry. I am happy to meet you."

Mrs. Cooper introduced me to her daughters who had arrived home from the ACS School in Monrovia. They explained to me that it was an American school and some of the Firestone students in high school were bused there daily. Think I knew this already...?

We said our goodbyes and David practically flew back to the Plantation. I did manage to stay awake and knew that someday I would laugh about this most unusual day spent with Isobel Lokko.

Isobel dropped me off at the Guest House where Pencil was waiting for me with my dinner.

Quite lovely, I thought back, as this strange day came to an end. Later, I was in my bed listening to the pinging of raindrops on the tin roof and being lulled to sleep as I mentally sent home my telegram.

>Dear Mom Dad Stop
>Wonderful day back in Monrovia Stop
>Spicy hot time. Stop
>Chicken food? Fufu? Stop
>Hugs African kisses Stop
>Kathleen

View from Jim Smith's bungalow at Hydro Falls

Chapter 7

Faculty Meeting ala Jim Smith

I awoke to a noise. A steward was gathering my clothes. I screamed, he jumped, dropped the clothes, and ran screaming from my room. Off to a brilliant start, I thought smiling with satisfaction. Maybe he will cease entering my room while I am still asleep.

It's Saturday, only two more days until I meet my class! I dressed, ate, and drove to the school to work on a *Welcome to Grade Three* bulletin board. Slowly other teachers arrived and soon there were the sounds of the teachers readying classrooms for our students. How I loved this noise!

Billie Darsey came into my room to remind me of the luncheon at Jim's home at the Hydro. She told me I could ride with her as it was tricky to get there. At 11:00 a group of excited teachers piled into Billie's white LTD and off we went catching up on each other's news. A shiny tomato red LTD loaded with more teachers followed Billie's. The drive took us by my bungalow in the bachelor compound and then further on down the road where it branched off to the left. This road led to Cotton Tree. We turned here and passed a small gas station with a cement block store. This store had a hand-painted sign saying Cotton Tree and another huge primitive painting of a leopard adorning the white-washed wall. Many local men were gathered talking, laughing, and smoking. These cotton trees were enormous! Spreading protective branches that seemed to be endless. It had stopped raining and the leaves glistened in the hot sun.

Hil explained, "There is a Liberian camp just past Cotton Tree store called Ten Dollar Camp."

"Ten Dollar Camp?" I questioned.

"The camp is called this because you can rent a woman for $10 a month," someone in the back remarked.

"Gee," I mused out loud. "The house boys get paid a dollar a day to cook, clean, and do the laundry. I think I'll get a $10 woman to work for me."

Everyone howled at my comment and clarified that a $10 woman only provided sexual favors and didn't do housework.

Of course, I mused, this had been a set up to fool the new girl and it had worked. So, I laughed along with them. I guess a house boy will be doing my housework after all.

The rest of the drive was filled with constant chatter as the scenery whizzed by. Palm, rubber, and poinsettia trees, and thick colorful bushes; how will I learn all the names? Billie slowed and we turned down a narrow one-lane wide road that grew even narrower until there was water on both sides of the road or was it a bridge? Then, there it was! The loveliest picture-perfect one-story bungalow nestled amongst the trees on a small island! Jim's bungalow wasn't on brick pillars like most of the Firestone homes. I half expected the seven dwarfs carrying picks and shovels to come out of the bush singing "Hi-ho, Hi-ho!" His place was planted with magical blooming flowers in so many colors.

Someone had taken much pride in landscaping this piece of Eden. Billie parked and we piled out, stood, and took in the incredible sight of the Firestone Hydro Falls! The noise was loud and the spray cooling! I guess being headmaster had its merits. Our group joined the others walking around enjoying the colorful bougainvillea and other perfumed flowering shrubs. What a place! I looked around at the group and saw that they were also drinking in the scenery proving that this doesn't get old. Jim came out of his home followed by four stewards carrying glasses of champagne on silver trays. They were dressed in white jackets, black slacks, and even wore white gloves!

Wow! What a way to start a new school year! We chatted, enjoying the view while the stewards passed out hot and cold hors d' oeuvres and refilled our champagne glasses. Someone announced that lunch was ready and we quickly moved to the back under a wooden gazebo that had palm branches woven together to make a roof. Colorful Christmas lights were hanging from above. The long table was set with beautiful white china, silverware, and many crystal vases filled with purple flowers arranged down the middle. We sat and ate a delicious meal of French onion soup and shrimp sandwiches. By now, we had switched to white wine and again there was plenty of it. Jim certainly knew how to impress and entertain and his teachers all took this in stride. We enjoyed a flan and Jim conducted the faculty meeting. Who would believe this back home? No one, that's for sure, and maybe I had misjudged Jim. He was full of charisma, funny, and knew how to get and keep everyone's attention. I wondered if they also had seen the Jim Smith I had seen at the lagoon the other night. Time will tell. Meanwhile, I sat back and savored the sights, smells, and tastes this afternoon meeting held.

When the meeting was over, Billie, Myna, Hil, and I walked around the bungalow. What I thought was a bridge, was the top of a dam.

Billie explained, "The Hydro controls the water flow which turns the turbines to produce the Plantation's electricity. Our homes around the church and school are on this grid. The Hydro Lake is full during the rainy season and during the dry season, the water will completely dry up."

"Gosh, I find this impossible. All dried up? What do we use for electric power then?"

Myna Butler was the sixth, seventh, and eighth grade English teacher and she said, "My dear, the factory will always have electricity. If hydro doesn't power the generators then they run on diesel fuel. But know this; the bungalows, schools, stores, and most other places on the Plantation won't have any electricity. That's when this place gets to be the hardship that we yearn for!"

Billie and Hil joined in laughing with Myna.

"Are you kidding me? We won't have electricity? How will we manage this hot humid climate? How do we cook, run the washers, take showers, flush...?"

"Girl," interrupted Billie, "This is the tropics and you'll learn to adjust and find ways to compensate. Everyone takes it in stride although some just go completely nuts!"

"Living in the tropics puts hair on your chest, sets you apart from the weaklings! Where will you fall?" Myna questioned but not really wanting an answer as she slowly wandered away.

"Oh, great, something to look forward to," I laughed.

Hil offered, "Myna is pregnant and due soon so, forgive her if she sounds off."

"Pregnant? She doesn't look pregnant! Will her baby be born at the John F. Kennedy Hospital in Monrovia?"

"Oh no," Billie informed. "She will go to the Firestone Hospital on Division 11. I had my four children there. We are so fortunate to have this wonderful hospital on the Plantation!"

"I had my daughter, Marjanne there but, my son Cees-Jan was born back in Holland," piped up Hil.

We walked around the front of Jim's bungalow and entered into the living room. It was quite large with floor to ceiling windows overlooking the waterfalls. Jim had a huge set up of stereo equipment on one wall. His collection of records was impressive as was his Atari tape deck system. His speakers were huge and similar to what my brother

Bobby had back home. Must be a guy thing as he had few books. However, the most impressive thing was Jim's wall to wall, white shag carpet! So sexy! Soon we all were sitting on the shag rug while Jim put on music and the stewards continued pouring us after lunch drinks. I had been here almost a week and discovered alcohol to be part of most gatherings. I was not accustomed to this much booze. I asked about this custom and Billie just laughed.

"Ouee! You will see that there isn't much to do other than work and party which, of course, does include alcohol. It is up to you to decide how to occupy your free time. Play poker, bridge, golf, tennis, someone is always running some kind of class that you could get involved with. Many parents help out with Girl and Boy Scout groups. You could even offer to teach one of your hobbies. But get involved otherwise you could be in for a difficult time here in the tropics. Some can't make it and return home."

The others agreed.

"Well, I know I will get involved with something and it will benefit me and others."

"That's wonderful!" said Billie. "But we need to get going if I'm to get you back to get ready for that dinner party you told me you were going to tonight."

"Oh, right!" I rose to say thanks to Jim for the lovely unorthodox faculty meeting and soon others were doing the same.

Now that I know we were driving on top of the dam, I held my breath anticipating it collapsing and us tumbling down the falls. From the sound of releasing breaths, the others were thinking the same thing. I wonder how Jim did this daily.

Back down the Cotton Tree Road, turn right, go past the bachelor compound, turn left at the church on the hill, and weave our way back to the school. I believe I had this down as I said thanks and see you on Monday and retraced the car's path to return to the Guest House which was past the church on the hill.

Once at the Guest House I wrote a letter to my friend Angie recounting the faculty meeting. I know the teachers back at Diehl School will enjoy hearing about the meeting. A small Liberian named David came by with a vodka and tonic and I asked him to wake me in 1 hour. Neat alarm clock I thought as I stretched out on the wicker sofa and sipped my refreshing drink. I needed my quinine to prevent malaria…ah, I love this place, I thought, as I drifted off.

However, I was softly awakened by Jim Smith who was offering to take me to the Hunters' bungalow for the dinner party. Wouldn't you know it, Jim was also invited.

"Okay, I need to get ready…err could you give me about an hour?"

"Sure, I'll be back to get you. Don't be late."

True to his word, I was back in his LTD on the way to my first dinner party on the Plantation. I wore a pale yellow mini dress and my white shoes. And nylons. Got to find out if women wear these things here. My girdle was killing me. I don't want to wear my special panty nylons as I only brought a few here and haven't seen any in the stores. Jim continued to make me feel uncomfortable staring at my legs whenever he gets a chance.

I had received an invitation from Dorothy and Richard Hunter a couple of days before to come to their dinner party. We drove through Harbel Knolls, a subdivision by the Staff School, and Jim pointed out peoples' bungalows to me. Yes, it was starting to fall into place.

The Hunters greeted me warmly as I climbed the stairs to their bungalow. Their place was enormous! The rooms were three times the size of mine and so beautifully decorated. Long cream-colored curtains adorned the floor to ceiling windows and the table was set for a party of twelve. I counted eight people here already, so we weren't late after all. I recognized Dick and Polly Hugg and Ron and Mae Gillian. Steve and Gail Ann Lawton arrived after us.

Next to arrive were John Francis and Franz De Roos. From their accents, I knew John was Australian and Franz from The Netherlands. John had burnt red weathered skin and bleached blond hair with a huge curl on his forehead. A cigarette hung from the side of his mouth which was twisted from holding too many of them. He was dressed in a bright orange, yellow, and purple Liberian design shirt and white pants. He also wore about three pounds of gold chains under his one buttoned shirt. It must be a macho thing to wear your shirt this way with gold chains.

Franz was much taller with strawberry brown hair and wore a loose-fitting white golf shirt and navy pants. He also smoked and had a weathered look. Could the tropics be causing the skin to look this way? These men were characters and the life of the party as they were joking and teasing everyone.

Two stewards, dressed in white, took drink orders and passed out hors d'oeuvres. The group was lively enough without any alcohol as it seemed everyone knew one another quite well.

I slowly took in how Dorothy had decorated this room. It was in warm rich browns and creams with red as an accent. Lots of fantastic African artifacts enhanced walls and tables. I loved how she did this and couldn't wait until I could decorate my bungalow! I excused myself to the restroom and had to pass through the Hunters' bedroom and I was shocked by the decorations. The walls were painted red and the king-size canopy bed had a black fur bedspread with tons of red and black pillows. Black curtains hung long covering the windows and the corners of the canopy, but to my surprise, there were mirrors on the ceiling over the bed! Who would ever think of decorating like this but, more to the point, why? Nope, I decided not to ask…could be like the Ten Dollar Woman. Yes, best to leave this alone!

Richard Hunter rang a small dinner bell (got to get me one, too) and we were seated. I sat between John Francis and Jim Smith. Franz sat across from me and got a conversation going about his upcoming trip to the United States. He was flying KLM out on Monday to The Hague and then he was flying into Toronto, Canada. Franz then said he was catching a bus to go to Akron, Ohio and then on to visiting retired Firestone friends in Florida.

"You will be passing through my home town. Could you call my parents and tell them you met me and a little about the Plantation? They are waiting for news from me and you will beat my letters home!"

"Ya, sure, I could also bring something small for your family,"

Franz said in a thick Dutch accent.

And so it was planned that Franz would carry a couple of rolls of undeveloped film and small gifts for Mom, Dad, Bobby, Marie, and Therese. Yes, Franz did indeed call my parents on Wednesday when he arrived in Toronto. My parents were thrilled to get first-hand news of me and invited him to stay a few days in Erie. They showed him around and grilled him about life over in Liberia. And for the next three years, Franz also managed to insert in conversation about how he had slept in my bed. People would then yell back, "Ya, ya, but there was also an ocean between you and Kathleen!" And everyone would laugh at this joke. I, however, was always grateful to Franz for doing this small favor for me. He also visited my parents many times over the next two decades.

The rest of the dinner party was uneventful, but I knew that these wonderful people were becoming fast friends. Someone said that sometimes at these dinner parties, they played cards, showed slide shows of family and vacations, and just plain share themselves. I liked this.

Jim managed to get me home with no awkwardness and simply said he'd pick me up tomorrow after 9:00 church to go to the beach.

"Beach? During the rainy season?"

Jim simply answered, "It doesn't rain at the beach-never does!"

He drove off leaving me exhausted. How can I continue at this pace? Everyone seems to go, go, go!

I fell asleep in my pink nightgown and planned what I would take photos of and small gifts to pack for Franz to hand deliver to my family. I stretched and fell into peaceful slumber as the rain fell on the tin roof.

    Dear Mom Dad Stop
    Dutchman Franz calling Stop
    Bringing gifts news Stop
    Hugs African kisses Stop
    Kathleen

God's Little Acre near Caesar Beach, Liberia

Chapter 8

Mr. and Mrs. God

After a quick breakfast, I drove 49 D to the church up on the hill for 9:00 Mass. The church was large enough to house about 100 people and yet intimate enough to feel in touch with the other churchgoers. The outside was white with a New England tall spire and a slanted roof. White pillars stood on either side of the front door and that's where I met Father Michael Rooney. Father Rooney was a robust red-faced Irishman with a quick roaring laugh and deep thick Irish brogue and I liked him immediately!

"What part of Ireland do you call home, Father?" I asked excitedly.

"The town of Galway," he said with a far off look in his eyes. "How I miss dear old Ireland and…"

"Father Rooney," I said, practically attacking him, "my mother is from Athlone, Ireland and her Dad's side of the family resides in Galway. I have many fond memories of visiting family there with my Uncles Jack and Bertie Murray."

"Please call me Father Mike. Murray, yes, I know the family and Jack, the baker, he courted my older sister. Yes, I still have some family in Galway and make it back every few years. I do believe the world is truly a small place."

"Small world indeed," I said. Inwardly I felt much more at home here in Harbel after meeting Father Mike and I knew a strong bond would be created.

I met more people before going into the church, taking a seat, and waved at a little girl I had met earlier in the week at the hotel's pool. Susan was so beside herself seeing me, that she paid little attention to the mass. She just smiled and waved to me the entire time.

Even with the windows and doors open, the huge oscillating fans at full speed, the air was so sticky, steamy and slow. I checked and yes, all the women wore nylons. Why? Was this some silly rule? I met many people after Mass and then made my excuses to leave. Many people said, "See you at Caesar's Beach." I would soon learn that indeed most of the Staff and families went to Caesar's or Marshall's beach every Sunday- rain or no rain.

True to his word, Jim was waiting for me when I pulled in front of the Guest House drinking a coffee and chatting with the house boys. I quickly changed and grabbed a beach bag I had prepared last night.

"Can we go around a few places so I can take some photos? I want to have everything ready for Franz De Roos to carry to my family."

We did exactly that. I took pictures of the Guest House, my bungalow, and Staff School both inside and out. I took more of the factory, Central Office, and even the Firestone Plantation sign. More were taken on the way to and again at the beach. I was so excited that Franz would be in contact with my family in a few days and beating my letters home. Won't they be surprised and relieved that where I live was a nice and safe place!

Jim drove off the Plantation without a driver and we headed towards Monrovia. This is my third time there in a week. I have a feeling I will be going there a lot.

"What's that?" I asked seeing the small handwritten sign for the first time. "It says 'Smell No Taste' what does that mean?"

Jim laughed, "During World War II, the United States Army built the runway which is now the Robertsfield Airport. The Army had temporary housing for the soldiers and this town sprung up near the kitchen. The locals could smell the food but couldn't taste it. So the little village was called 'Smell No Taste'. However, on the other side was another small village called 'F_ck No Pay' and well, the soldiers didn't pay for sex. Both villages have great local bars and good dancing. I'll take you there sometime."

"You have got to be kidding about these names. I find it hard to believe that's what these villages are called."

All of a sudden Jim swung the car around and we were headed back to "Smell No Taste". It was small with few houses, a store, and a bar called Simon's and there it was another small handwritten sign declaring this town to be called "F_ck No Pay". A repeat of the other town buildings but this one had a pharmacy.

"Unbelievable!" I sputtered. "No one would believe this back home."

Jim told me, "This pharmacy was used for getting medicines you can't get back in the States as there is no law banning any drug being used here. Of course, most of the Staff go to the Firestone Hospital for medicines and so this pharmacy is for emergencies."

Jim swung back onto the road and we continued to the beach. Even though we were about 15 miles as the bird flies to the beach, it took us about an hour to get to where the road branched. The right branch went to Monrovia and the left to Caesar's Beach. During the entire drive, we drove in and out of torrential downpours.

"Are the slash and burn fires along the roadside a permanent item?" I asked as we repeatedly drove through streams of smoke.

Jim told me they do this only during the wet season. In the dry season, the rice or cassava grows and then women or children sit in the fields pitching stones at the pesky birds. He turned down the left branch of the road and I could at last smell the salty air. The terrain was flat with few dunes, tall grasses, and palm trees waving in the breeze. The closer we got to the ocean, more palm trees appeared. Just before getting to Caesar's Beach, we stopped at a small hut with a thatched roof proudly displaying a sign stating, "God's Little Acre".

    This place was properly named as it was a little piece of heaven! It was close to the beach and surrounded by many different types of palm trees and colorful flowers. We stopped to buy some charcoal made by a man called Mr. God. Who knew God lived in Liberia on a beach making charcoal for us to burn on Sundays! Mr. God said he collected and burned pieces of wood to the charred state. He sells the charcoal to people who gather at the beach every Sunday. A nice little operation he has going on. Mr. God also sells fresh fruit and Jim picked out a handful of bananas and four pineapples.

    Back in the car, we continued the drive on the potholed dirt road to Caesar's Beach having left the pavement back at the road branch. Graceful palm tree branches danced in the warm winds off the Atlantic Ocean as we parked by the edge of a huge lagoon. The Atlantic Ocean was to the right with huge six-foot-plus waves surging and crashing on the shore pleading for me to come on in.

    "I can't wait to swim in the ocean!"

    Jim explained, "That would be deadly because the continental shelf is close to the shore. There is a terrific undertow which makes it dangerous to go into the ocean." He demonstrated by throwing in a piece of driftwood and very quickly the wood was taken out to sea. To the left and some distance from the ocean was the lagoon and a more safe way to cool down.

    Dotted along the edge of the lagoon were small thatched-roof huts with no walls, called palava huts. Underneath were picnic tables and lots of small children running about and Liberian boys chasing them. Adults were putting out tablecloths and dishes.

    I could smell charcoal burning while helping Jim unload the car.

His house boy had packed a cooler full of Heineken, Club Beer, and Coca Cola. He had also packed a basket with goodies. I hadn't even thought about bringing food. I came with some magazines, baby oil, and a blanket. Looking about I saw there weren't any concession stands. Everyone there had huge coolers and picnic tables were laden with all types of food.

    Jim moved to one of the palava huts and began to arrange the food while I went and talked to a group of people I knew. Children came running up to me to say hello and say what grade they were in. Some were in my class and were anxious for school to begin. They began pulling me to the lagoon to swim when I jumped or rather hopped screaming ouch, ouch, ouch! The sizzling sand was burning my feet! Quickly, I put my sandals on and followed them to the lagoon. Removing my sandals, I hurriedly entered the crystal clear water which was warm like a bath. I walked out further to get to cooler water. I floated and found I was practically lying on the surface as the water was so salty. The further out I went, I found I could sit as if in a chair, float, talk to others, and drink a warm Coca Cola someone gave me. Ah, this was the life!

    Scampering back to get under the shade of the palava hut and Polly Hugg offered me a Club Beer and some Brie cheese. I took a Coca Cola instead. The Brie had lost its shape and oozed onto my cracker as I scooped it up. The flavor was tantalizing and I followed it with another and a piece of warm fresh pineapple. Yep, they had stopped off at God's place too. I noticed that Polly was reading my magazines and as were three other women. They were devouring them as if they had never seen one before. All the women wanted news from the States. Me. Giving news to these older women. So, we exchanged information about Stateside and Liberian news. I noticed when I got another's magazine; there were many names in columns on it. Mae Gillian told me that most newspapers, magazines, and even personal letters were passed around for others to enjoy. All you had to do was scan to see if you already read it. I like this system and I can see how any news was savored and gratefully appreciated.

"Ralph Welsch, happy to meet you! I guess we are neighbors," said a sunburnt man with dark glasses, lip hanging cigarette, and holding a Club Beer. Moving the beer to his other hand, he shook mine and added, "I live in a bungalow down the hill from yours in the bachelors' compound. Glad to have a woman move in. There are only men in the other bungalows except for two empty ones. One is for the new guy in my computer department and he hasn't arrived yet. Oh, yea, there are three empty bungalows in the other part of the bachelor compound."

"I think I met him while Firestone was processing me in Akron. Could he be Joe Ward?" I said while noticing his beer belly ball resting on skinny spiky legs.

"Yes, that's the man. Some mix up with his shots, but he is due to arrive later this week.

"Wonderful!"

Ralph and I continued to chat. He was really a nice man, divorced four years ago and had three children back in Ohio. I got the impression that he would keep an eye on me like a father. Good. Perhaps he could help keep Jim in tow.

After another warm Coca Cola, I decided to explore the beach and surrounding area. A couple of children joined me. They were Susan, Leonie, and Regan who I felt were going to be great helpers in my classroom. I noticed black patches of tar at the water's edge and some places on the beach. The girls warned me to stay away from it as many times their house boys used butter or baby oil to scrape it off their shoes and feet.

Susan said, "If it gets onto your suit, you have to throw it away."

Good warning, I thought, as I avoided a blob of it. Leonie ran ahead to another place with palava huts. As we approached, I came to realize that the ex-pats were in "the altogether" as my Irish mother would say. My dad would state, they're just plain naked! This didn't faze the girls as they were Dutch and English. It seems, only Americans were the prudes. I was introduced to the group of KLM and Swiss Air crews. After a bit, we said our goodbyes and headed back to the clothed section of Caesar's Beach.

The smell of grilled hamburgers met our noses before we spotted the palava huts. Gosh, I was hungry! Racing back, we found the long connecting tables had been set and food arranged. People were eating and drinking. Jim came up to me and gave me a huge pineapple with the top removed and a straw sticking out.

"Drink this Mai Tai," he said.

"Um, Mai Tai, I love this drink! When I visited Hawaii last winter, I had a Mai Tai and enjoyed it." Even though it was warm, the drink was extremely refreshing.

The rest of the day was spent eating, talking, lagooning, and Mai Tai-ing. This life, I could get to love!

All too soon, the beach-goers were packing the cars and heading back to the edge of the jungle. Jim and I followed, too.

Riding back in the car I could still feel the heat of the African sun on my body. I had a little too much sun and then I realized that I was burned! The closer we got to the Plantation, the more I knew I was in deep trouble. I had stayed most of the time under the palava huts, wore a hat, but still not enough I guess.

Jim also noticed my burn and told me an old tropical secret to take care of the sting.

"You're kidding," I said in surprise, "that's all? Just lightly wash with a damp cloth to remove sand and then slather oil on me?"

"Yep, don't even take a shower for 24 hours as this removes the oil and layers of skin exposing your newly burnt skin to oxygen. Then you'll have pain with blistering and peeling."

"Thanks, I learned something…being so fair, I burn first and it usually takes a few exposures to get a good tan. I hate the pain of the burn in the meantime."

We continued on the road occasionally passing through charred fields and rain until the flat grasslands turned into the rolling hills and finally the edge of the jungle. At last the Plantation. I declined dinner at the Robertsfield Hotel. I just wanted to clean up, get my clothes ready for the first day of school, and sleep. And yes, I had to quickly grab the few gifts I had and the three undeveloped rolls of film for Franz de Roos to carry to my family. Jim said Franz was staying at the Guest House where everyone stayed a day or two going and coming to Liberia. Jim asked a guard what room Bossman de Roos was in and he delivered my gifts for me.

Jim made a low bow as he bade me goodnight. "See you tomorrow!"

"Ah, tomorrow!" I thought as I got ready for bed, what does tomorrow hold for me?

    Dear Mom Dad Angela Stop
    Met God Stop
    On beach selling Stop
    Charcoal pineapples
    Been to Smell No Taste Stop
    F_ck No Pay Stop
    Hugs African kisses Stop
    Kathleen

Firestone Staff School

Chapter 9

First Day of School

My bed shook and I about fell out. What a way to wake up on my first day of school! Another boom of thunder. Was this an omen? I hurried and dressed in my lucky green dress I had worn on the flight here. Did the usual dress routine when I realized my sunburn didn't hurt. Wonders of wonders, Jim's trick had worked!

More booms as I headed out into the dark and then to the dining room for my breakfast. The house boys were bustling about and talking to me. Already sitting with a huge breakfast of pancakes and steaming hot coffee was Franz de Roos. I said my good mornings to everyone and again thanked Franz for carrying my gifts. Franz was pleased to accommodate. The house boys were chattering to me and I shrugged and pointed to my ears.

"I don't hear them yet. Wish I could understand their Liberian English. Someone told me it can take a couple of months to hear their English."

Franz nodded in agreement while gulping coffee and did the translation for me. So, I ate, pointed at food, ate, and pointed, Helen Keller I could do. Suddenly the boys' voices grew high and shrill and one grabbed my arm to take me outside. The others followed, clapping, and chanting to celebrate my first day of school. I guess they don't want me to be late. Hum, don't let mothers of the world know this trick! I shouted goodbye to Franz and to have a wonderful trip in the States.

Driving through the predawn in a torrential downpour, I made it to school and entered the office where a group of teachers had gathered chatting excitedly. Hil was pouring coffee and welcomed me with a stack of forms to pass out and collect from the students tomorrow. The day begins at 6:45 am with students arriving and in their seats by 7:00. I had been instructed to teach reading, math, and language arts before 10:00. Snack and recess went from 10 to 10:30 and then we covered the other subjects finishing up by 12:45 p.m. My day ended at 1:00. The Firestone School operating time was so different from the time in the States.

"By the way, Kathleen, you have another student added to your list," Hil said updating me with her information.

I followed the elementary group down the open air hallway and entered my classroom. Even though it was still raining cats and dogs, the air was thick, damp, and close. I got the oscillating fans running, cranked the windows open on both sides of the room, and checked my plans. Billie came in and remarked how nice and inviting my room looked.

"I'm so excited that I tossed and turned all night with the yearly start up nervousness. Will I ever get over these first day jitters?"

"Guess not, as I still feel this way every year. I believe you wouldn't be a good teacher if you didn't have these feelings," Billie remarked and hugged me for good luck.

One bus pulled up in the driveway and then two more along with many cars. Students poured out and ran screeching to the protective covered hallway to escape the rain. The screams and high pitched laughter continued until Jim Smith loudly rang an old fashioned large hand bell. The noise eased as the students lined up outside their classrooms. School had begun!

My class entered, found their named seats, and sat with their hands folded. Wow! I was impressed as their behavior was akin to Catholic schools. I looked around at everyone, introducing myself, telling a little about who I was, and what I expected. They all sat perfectly still-all ten of them. Not like the 36 students I had last year.

One by one the students stood and introduced themselves and told something interesting they liked to do. Christopher A., a Filipino, was born in Liberia and had three sisters and one brother. He loved puzzles and playing soccer. I noticed he wore leg braces but, I guessed that didn't hold him back. Chris J. and Walter both Dutch, loved soccer and had huge sunny smiles. Edwin, Liberian, only liked playing soccer and difficult math problems. Leonie, Dutch, with silky blonde hair, loved to read chapter books. Susan, English, was interested in all school work and wanted to be a nurse when she grew up. Regan, Canadian and English, loved learning French. Markavee, Liberian, said she enjoyed reading and soccer. Mona, Liberian, was the new student coming from the District of Columbia. She was very nervous and quiet. Finally, Andrea, Liberian, who just loved school and wanted to be a teacher when she grew up. The group was an interesting lot and the year looked to be promising. Next, we looked over our new books and their excited chatter was encouraging. It looked like we were off to a brilliant start and I knew I had to learn what this soccer game was!

Nine of my students knew each other having gone to school together since kindergarten. Three students were still on holiday and due back in late September. Every two years the staff members received three months of leave. Depending on the department, the leaves were staggered and this caused a disruption in their children's education. Thus, there was summer school. Jim had already told me that I would be teaching that six week program and then I could take my leave.

The children were eager to learn and so we dove into lessons, breaking for snack at 10:00 with recess following. The rain hadn't let up and so the children played in the open air hallway. The rest of the morning went smoothly and all too soon the first school day was over.

Billie came over and relayed that she had also had a good start. She invited me over for lunch and I accepted providing she make the phone call to the Guest House telling them not to wait lunch for me. She did.

I followed her to her huge bungalow up on a hill past the church and golf club. The rains were going strong as I ran into her house. Billie said sometimes it can rain like this for two to three days. Many areas flood and make traveling difficult on the dirt roads on and off the Plantation. She still loved living here as she had come as a young bride and had her four children at the Firestone Hospital. What an interesting home she had. African art was displayed everywhere and Billie went on to explain most of them. I really liked the masks with the feathers and sea shells embedded. Others had pieces of tin cans. Huge pieces of ivory tusks were carved with such precision and detail; this was amazing work! Where ever I looked, there were beautiful colorful African lappas draped on chairs and used as tablecloths on the dining room table and other end tables.

I asked, "Billie, I have some letters to mail. Where is the post office?"

"You can buy Liberian stamps from Hil at school. Your letters can be dropped off in the school's office and Zanga will take it to the Central Office Mailroom. Once there, it is sorted, bagged, and delivered to Robertsfield Air Terminal. Mail to the States goes out when Pan Am flights return to New York. Gee, you've been here one week and shouldn't expect mail for another two weeks. That was providing people have written to you," said Billie

Now I understand why mail and magazines were all shared; people were starved for outside information.

After leaving Billie's, I drove down to the radio building to send a radiogram to my parents announcing that Franz de Roos was arriving in Toronto, Canada and would be calling them. After my radiogram was sent, I remembered that they were radioed to Akron, Ohio. Once received, it was typed out, and sent via the US Post Office. The letter would arrive in one to two days. Bummer, I should have thought about sending the radiogram yesterday…oh well.

Back at the Guest House, I ate dinner, did my school work, and read before calling it a day.

> Dear Mom Dad Stop
> Good first day Stop
> Expect visitor Stop
> Hugs African kisses Stop
> Kathleen

Central Office

Chapter 10

The Nazi Problem

How quickly the daily school routine kicked in. The children were wonderful and eager to learn. My students, whose native language was not English, also had lessons in their language when they went home after lunch.

Week one became week three and still I had no mail even though I drove down to the mail room on the designated days. Three weeks and I had not received any mail of any kind from anyone. I was anxious to get mail from my parents acknowledging that Franz de Roos had visited them and they had developed the rolls of film. I needed to know they understood that I was living and working in a safe environment.

Once again my hopes rose as I drove down to the mail room. Maybe today would be the magical day. Driving up and parking, I said hello to the men that had the same intentions as I. I had gotten to know the men who congregated at the mail room and it was a few days ago that I learned a valuable lesson. Be careful playing into their silly pranks.

On that particular day, the men were bugging me to ask Willham Schmitt what he was doing and why, that is, if he showed up. I had seen Willham on one other occasion and I was curious about an odd thing I saw him doing. Kevin Estall explained to me that Willham had been in Hitler's army and everyone on the Plantation was afraid of him. They had heard many terrible stories, but they had always wanted to know why he did that strange and curious thing. Kevin thought that Willham wouldn't attack a pretty young thing like me. He and the others pleaded for me to ask him why he did what he did.

Earlier, I had seen an ancient Ford pickup come to the mail room. A large burly blonde-haired man got out of his truck grabbed one of the hundred or so hand-made-witch-like brooms from its bed and proceeded to sweep the ground in front of him. Vigorously sweeping he swore and swore and swore. "F_ck, f_ck, f_ck!" He collected his mail and swept his way back to the pickup and drove off. Very strange and something I wanted to know also. So, I agreed to ask Willham.

A short while later, the old green beat up Ford pickup turned into the lot. Yes, Willham Schmitt was making a visit for his mail. Again, he got out, selected a broom and began to sweep and swear in a low almost inaudible tone. Some of the men said hello to Willham but, he just grunted and continued with "f_ck, f_ck, f_ck!" I watched as John Chapman gave the Hitler salute and quickly clicked his heels and the other men followed suit. However, Willham had his head down and hadn't notice.

I walked up to Willham and sweetly said hello. I stuck my hand out and introduced myself as the new teacher at the Staff School. Willham froze! His eyes grew the size of saucers. He stared at me with my outstretched hand. Then with fear in his eyes, Willham slowly backed up and began his sweeping around me. His f_cking chant became much louder. Out of the corner of my eye I saw Ron Gillian and John Chapman motioning me to ask again. And so I obliged, even more curious to find out why this man was obsessed with sweeping.

In a strong voice, surprising even me, I asked "Willham, why do you sweep as you walk?"

Suddenly and with the gusto of the wicked witch of the West and twirling his broom over his head he shouted. "Why, why, why, I sweep, I sweep, I sweep? Got to clean this f_cking COUNTRY, got to CLEAN this f_cking country, got to clean this F_CKING country!" Willham slowly lowered his broom and with renew fervor; he swept to clean the country.

Behind me the men were howling, grabbing their sides, and jumping around. John Chapman rolled on the ground, hysterically. I felt really used and didn't like how I had treated Willham. However, he appeared oblivious and climbed the steps to the Mailroom, collected his mail, and drove off in his pickup. He had places to clean. I, on the other hand needed to get these men back with something good…hum.

That was yesterday and so today, I walked up to the mail room door and asked the Liberian mailman if I had any mail. John Chapman greeted me with a sheepish smile.

"Hi Kathleen, I really am sorry about the prank we played on you. I'd like to make it up to you by taking you out for a coffee. We could get it at the Robertsfield Hotel."

I said, "Thank you, but I don't think so".

Then a chorus of men's voices coming from around the corner said, "We are also sorry and we want to join you and John for coffee."

I thought about what they said. Perhaps, after all, the men were trying to apologize and show their kinder sides. So, I agreed.

With that said, a line of assorted Firestone vehicles followed by 49 D, paraded to the restaurant at the Robertsfield Hotel. The group followed me into the bar, sat, and ordered coffee. I was surrounded by this group of men who were laughing at some inside joke of theirs. When I stood to go to the restroom, they all stood, tipped their imaginary hats, and slowly bowed as if I was royalty. I just knew something was up and upon exiting the restroom, I found that John Chapman had placed himself between the barroom and me. He spoke hesitantly, "I am sorry about the prank. Please, please forgive me. I really think you are beautiful and don't want you angry with me! Um...can we go to a room to discuss this matter further?"

"Okay, I accept your apology John but, what else do you want to discuss?"

"Uh...that you and me uh...Oh I am just going to say it. Can we get together for a quickie?" he asked in his cute British accent.

"Oh, a quickie? A quickie? Hum...how long do you think it will take?" I said in a demure way but thinking of a way to set him up.

With enthusiasm and a pretty please sound in his voice; John spurted, "Five or maybe ten minutes!"

"Well," I sashayed to the bar room and waved for John to follow. He followed like a puppy dog on a chain with his tongue hanging out. When I was close to the other men, I said in a sugary sweet voice, "Make it four hours, honey, and we have a deal!"

John fell to the ground in shock. Two men jumped up and pulled him to his feet asking, "Well?"

Ah ha! I knew this was another set up! So, I said to John, loudly enough for all the men to hear. "Dear, dear Johnny, get back to me when you can deliver...okay... sweetness?" With that said, I kissed him on his fire-red cheek while the others sat, staring and not believing their eyes and ears.

In one gulp, I finished my coffee, collected my purse, and stood. Speaking in a sultry voice I said, "Boys, I'm willing to do coffee anytime and yes, dear John, I'll be waiting for an answer from you!" I blew kisses to them all and made sure I walked slowly and sexily out of the bar. The men were hooting and cheering. I am now one of the guys! I thought.

When I arrived at the Guest House Jim Smith was sitting in one of the white wicker chairs and sipping a martini while he waited for me.

"Great news, all the painting has been completed and the kitchen cupboards were installed today in your bungalow. Looks like you can move tomorrow," he said.

I asked, "Where can I shop for fabric for drapes, dinnerware, and other household items I need."

"I knew you would want to do some shopping and I planned to take you to the Harbel open-air market on Saturday morning. It has most everything you could need without having to drive into Monrovia."

He asked me out to dinner at the Hotel. I declined as my soon-to-be neighbor Ralph was taking me but, he was more than welcome to join us. To my surprise, he agreed.

Ralph picked me up at the prearranged time and off we flew to the Robertsfield Hotel. He really puts his foot to the metal as we skidded into a parking place having done the drive in what seemed like seconds.

Ralph remarked that the President of Liberia or some other dignitary was at the Hotel upon seeing the limos and many motorcycles. It was President Tolbert and his wife enjoying dinner. We passed by their table and wished them Bon Appetite. Jim had a table for us and as we sat, a waiter poured the champagne he had ordered.

"Here's to your newly painted bungalow and moving in!" He toasted.

With raised glasses, we clinked, and drank. I told them that this would be my first time living alone and I was excited to begin this new phase of my life and indeed I was. Ralph assured me that he would look out for me and anyone messing around would have to deal with him. I was happy that this was said in front of Jim.

A waiter dressed in white with a black bow tie set the menus down. He stood and waited for us to order. I had thought ordering by numbers was akin to painting by numbers…I ordered 4 for my appetizer, 9 and 14 for dinner, and declined wine as I had the lovely champagne to finish. I was getting to be a pro at this process and liked the attention being lavished upon me. Life in Erie, PA seemed so very far away and boring.

While eating, I talked to the guys about meeting Willham Schmitt and his sweeping matter. They said there were many rumors about him but, he was a loner and did his job well.

"If he didn't, Firestone would have sacked him," Ralph said.

Later, sitting at the bar, I reminded Jim about school tomorrow. I needed to get back to the Guest House. Ralph and I said goodnight and he drove me back to the Guest House.

"Hey, I'll stop over at your bungalow after work. Say 3:30? I am anxious to see what they did at your place." Ralph asked.

"Deal!" I answered as the sky opened up with a deluge and I made a run for cover.

>Dear Mom Dad Stop
>Think I am one Stop
>Of the boys Stop
>Took care of Nazi problem Stop
>Moving in bungalow Stop
>Hugs African kisses Stop
>Kathleen

Standing on my bungalow's steps

Chapter 11

Moving In Day

Today is moving day! I have my very own bungalow! Mine to decorate and decide everything without having to consult anyone else! I liked staying at the Guest House, but I really wanted to be in my own place. After school, I drove 49 D over to my place to find that Jim was already there with yet another bottle of the bubbly and pouring it into two tall thin glasses.

"Surprise! A toast to your first place!" he said as he handed me my glass.

"What is this? Whose things are these? Who did this?"

"This is the surprise I was telling you about. Hil and Billie came over and unpacked the loaner boxes from the Company."

"Wow! They are so sweet to do this." I said as I looked around. My home looked great.

"Remember, the company wants the loaner items back when your shipment arrives. But, in the meanwhile, you can use everything. If you need anything, let me know."

I hurriedly checked out the kitchen and loved the new white cabinets. They looked even better with dishes, pots and pans, and things on the cupboard shelves. It was wonderful! Next I dashed to my bedroom and yes, the twin beds were still together making a king bed. The bathroom had towels, soap, and a small mat on the floor. I could tell the women had taken time and put much thought into setting up my bungalow. Looking in my walk in closet, I saw my clothes hanging and suitcases stacked up on a high shelf.

"Who brought over my things from the Guest House?"

"I drove Zanga over this morning and the house boys had everything packed and ready for us to deliver here," Jim replied puffing out his chest.

"Well, I am pleased and thank you for helping me with my bungalow. Principals and teachers at home would never do something like this and especially for someone they just met."

"Things are different over here. We are one giant family."

Sitting on my new cushions, "I hope this doesn't mean we aren't going to the Harbel open-air market tomorrow?"

"I had intended to take you and also Ralph. This reminds me, some of the bachelors are coming over for dinner at my place tonight. Care to join us? Ralph is also coming. Usually we play poker after dinner."

"Sure. I'll call Ralph and ask for a ride."

Jim coached me on the dialing procedures via the party line. It was set that Ralph would pick me up about 6:00 and not come over at 3:30. I again thanked Jim for his help and said goodbye.

I went over my bungalow room by room and made a list of things I needed to buy and then got ready for a night with the guys. I wondered who would be there.

On cue, Ralph banged on my door. He was totally surprised by how my place looked.

"Gee, I've been here three years and my place doesn't look anywhere near this furnished. Perhaps you can help me."

I explained that Billie and Hil had done this for me but I would be more than happy to help him out.

Ralph did ask if I planned on getting a dog being single and all.

"Dog? I hadn't thought about that. Isn't it safe here?" I asked.

"No, you are safe here and besides all the bachelors in this compound will keep an eye on you. No, I just thought you looked like a dog person. I had a dog but forgot to keep the "juju" active on him and he was stolen."

"Juju? Stolen? Please explain."

"When you have a pet, you need to go to the witch doctor in Ten Dollar Camp and pay for protection. The witch doctor makes sure everyone knows this animal has a "juju" on it and the people won't bother it. No "juju" and your pet will go into someone's pot for dinner."

"Dinner? Oh, my goodness! I had thought about getting some pets, but would hate to lose one because it became someone's meal."

"Just remember to keep the "juju" up on the pet," Ralph said closing my door. We sped off into the darkness to Jim's.

Cotton Tree flew by and I saw lights coming from Ten Dollar Camp.

"Ralph, do you have any suggestions on how I should go about hiring a house boy and night watchman? I don't talk Liberian English and understand very little. I don't think I will be able to do this. Could you help me?"

"Sure thing, Jeremiah is my house boy and he just told me he has some friends you could interview. I'll set it up for Monday after work. Usually, the night watchman is related to the house boy but anyhow, you need to get the oldest man to be your night watchman. The older, the better."

"Oldest? But how can he protect me?"

"Oh, he won't, but his extended family will do the protection for you. That's why you need an old man since he will have a large family."

"This is an unusual custom but I can understand the reasoning.

Old man it will be!"

As we were turning onto Jim's road, I remembered the water on both sides of the road getting to Jim's island and bungalow. Ralph told me how about seven months ago Earl Loucks sped off the road and into the lake! Luckily he went into the lake rather than over the waterfalls. Ralph also slowed. Thank goodness for Earl's help on this I thought as we parked and went up to Jim's front door that was lit with a string of Christmas lights.

As before, Jim's place looked wonderful and scrumptious smells perfumed the air. As I was enjoying his home and his choice in jazz music, a group of bachelors smoking and drinking martinis entered the living room from the beautifully lit patio. I noticed the Vodka bottles on the bar along with an ice bucket. Ice! Great! Maybe I can get a cold Coca Cola I thought as a vodka martini was placed in my hand. I took a sip and was instantly hooked! I liked this drink! Introductions were made and we then sat at the long party table set for the group. Conversations spun around me as I continued sipping a second martini and eating fresh cold shrimp with hot sauce. More sipping required. Gosh, I was enjoying martinis a little too much!

A dinner of Beef Bourguignon with homemade flat noodles was served. It was delicious! Jim told us that his house boy Charles had learned to cook from a former employer. Meanwhile, I was scheming how I could become Charles' new employer. Paul De Longchamp echoed my thoughts. Now, I was even more determined to hire a good cook as my houseboy. Our meal and lively conversations continued until a flaming Baked Alaska arrived to thunderous applause. I wanted to dance around as this evening of food from heaven and the vodka martinis was incredible.

The group adjourned to the living room for brandies and coffee while the stewards cleared and dismantled the table setting it up into 3 tables of four to play poker. Game on. This was when I realized that I didn't know how to play poker well, especially when the men took out wads of cash and check books. I was in big trouble as my college-Union-Hall-poker wasn't going to cut it with these guys. Pros? I believed so.

I sat at a table with three guys who looked like sharks, puffing on cigarettes and gulping martinis. Cards dealt, bids set, game on.

Unbelievably I won the first three games. Being nice to me... however, the next three games went to the men. What I had won was now gone. I excused myself and went into the kitchen to talk to the cook...well, I tried.

Charles greeted me as "Missy" and I asked if he knew a house boy that cooked as well as him did as I was looking for one.

"Ya, Missy, my friend he good good cook. He called Benjamin. I send him to bungalow tomorrow."

"Benjamin? Okay. Send him tomorrow." I answered reentering the living room. I checked out Jim's record and eight-track collections. I was tired or wasted, I don't know which, but next thing I knew, Ralph was waking me to take me home.

"Home?" I was confused as I was dreaming about my parents. I asked again. "Home?"

"Yes, I lost all my money and taking you home is a good excuse to leave," said Ralph.

So once again I sat in Ralph's car and headed home when he told me that Basjaan, a Dutchman, living out on a division, had moved into the house between his and my bungalow. We'll be including him in our adventures if he wants to join.

"Oh, wow! That sounds great and tonight is my first night sleeping in my own bungalow!" I remarked as I got out of his car and then thought. "Yikes! I don't have any food!"

"Come down tomorrow to my bungalow around 8:00 for breakfast. Jim is picking us up at 10:00 to go to the Harbel open-air market. Then we will go to Marshall Beach via my boat. Some of the guys and Jim are coming along also. So, pack your suit and a beach bag."

"Great! Thanks!" I yawned and climbed the stairs to my home.

I showered, packed for the beach, climbed in bed, and quickly fell asleep.

Dear Mom Dad Stop
Slept in my bungalow Stop
Want pet need juju Stop
Hugs African kisses Stop
Kathleen

Fanti fishermen near Marshall Beach

Chapter 12

Marshall Beach via SNAFU Bay

The next day as promised, Jim drove into Ralph's driveway, parked and sprinted upstairs for coffee. I had just finished my breakfast that Ralph's house boy, Jeremiah had prepared. Simply put, the best pancakes ever!

"Hey Kathleen, there are some men under your bungalow waiting for you. I recognize one as a friend of Charles who works for me. I guess they want to be interviewed to be your house boy," Jim remarked.

After finishing our coffee, the three of us drove over to my place where I let Jim and Ralph do the interviewing for me. They read the resumes and questioned the four Liberians while I stood trying to make heads or tails of the conversation. Once interviewed, Jim and Ralph suggested two candidates that could hold the position of my house boy.

However, I made the final selection by choosing Benjamin, Charles's friend. My reasoning was he'd be as good a cook as Charles. Benjamin said he would start tomorrow, but I told him to come in the late afternoon knowing we were going to the beach after church.

I felt great that this chore was done as we drove off to Harbel City and its market. I was excited that I had hired a house boy to do my cooking and cleaning. My dear Irish mom will be green with envy when I write and tell her this. Mom always wanted someone to do the heavy cleaning once I had moved from home. Little did I know that having Benjamin as my house boy would pose some trying times for me adjusting to having hired help, the language barrier, and his "sticky" fingers.

Suddenly, the skies opened up and it poured. We passed by an unusual sight where there was a small group of naked people and sitting on their folded clothes. I gasped and asked, "What's going on?"

"Might as well get a shower and cleaned up with the free rainwater," Ralph responded with a giggle in his voice.

"Oh, I think that's a good idea."

I told the men that a few days ago I had driven through Harbel City and was amazed that it was so large. I was excited to go to this market now that I had moved into my bungalow.

Jim warned me, "Hold your purse tightly because sometimes in large crowds like this, there are rogues with sticky fingers. Be careful about displaying money. And barter, barter, barter. It's all part of the game and if you are good at bartering and even entertaining the seller, they will show you their appreciation by giving a lower price and maybe even a dash!"

"Dash?" I inquired.

"Yep, dash. A dash is a gift and can be given by one or both parties and is usually small," Ralph explained.

By now the rain had stopped and Jim was parking his car near the market place where there looked to be thousands of people crowding into a large rectangle! Many small boys came scampering up to Jim and begged to watch his car. He chose two boys and bartered the car-watching-price to ten cents. This must have been a lot of money as they were jumping up and down and were extremely happy. The area was packed with people searching for treasures or selling some. We slowly walked up and down the rows of sellers examining their wares. What an array of bright colors, rhythmic sounds, loud haggling voices, and appealing smells in the market with mostly women doing both the buying and selling. We saw an assortment of fresh fruit and fish. Many of the fish were smoked. There were peanuts, raw, roasted, or still clinging to the roots of the peanut plant, huge bunches of cassava leaves and roots, and other foods I had yet to learn about. Everywhere I looked there were baskets of bananas, pineapples, papayas, coconuts, grapefruits, oranges… well, at least I thought they were oranges and grapefruits.

"Are these oranges and grapefruits?" I questioned pointing to round green fruits with some yellow splotches on them.

Ralph answered, "Yes, all fruit usually grows wild here. Citrus fruits are juicy but very stringy. Most people just cut the tops off and suck on their juice."

"Oh, yes, I saw some children last Sunday at Caesar's Beach sucking on what I thought was candy but now I guess they were oranges."

I saw beautiful lappas of every color you could imagine. Some in printed patterns and others colorfully tie-dyed.

Most goods were placed on small pieces of paper bag or in tin bowls on the ground. Some merchants had wooden stalls with roofs of woven palm leaves. Other goods were in vividly colored enameled tin bowls or handwoven baskets. I instantly fell in love with these bowls and baskets! I bought a set of enameled bowls that were decorated in red and medium blue and painted in a repeating square pattern. It was a set of three with lids to match. The men laughed at my bartering technique and they quickly jumped in to seal the deal for me. Another attempt had an old woman laughing at my pitiful efforts to barter and she patiently coaxed me along when I was buying some lappa fabric. I thought I could use it to make throw pillows for both my bedroom and living room.

"This is fun!" I said struggling to make my way through the

crowd carrying my purchased goodies. "Is this market where I come to grocery shop? Billie told me there is a store around here. Where is it?"

Ralph answered, "We usually shop at the Firestone Store for our weekly groceries and sometimes go to the Sinkor Supermarket in Monrovia. To grab forgotten things, we go to Sammy's when the Firestone Store is closed. Also, your house boy will shop at the market if you want to have native food for some of your meals. The house boys are very good at getting the best prices for food."

"Sammy's is similar to the Stop and Go or Seven-Eleven back at home. But forgotten items or not, many people stop by Sammy's for a Club Beer or Heineken and to catch up on local news," Jim added.

"Yeah, and a place to find out the latest gossip," laughed Ralph.

"Yes, Billie Darsey told me about Sammy's," I said. "And I bet a lot of juicy gossip originates there also," I said thinking about my previous experiences and wondered if I was involved in any of the latest gossip.

"As with any gossip, some is true and some is made up. The latter is usually the case at Sammy's when the men have had a little too much to drink or were completely bored and wanted to embellish a story."

We continued to explore the marketplace and I enjoyed walking around and admiring the people dressed in wonderfully colorful fabrics. A light mist began, but few people seem to notice when out of the corner of my eye, I saw something unusual. Slowly, I walked over to this area and the items came into a clearer view. I abruptly stopped and gasped; oh my goodness, I felt sick to my stomach. I started sweating. Then my head began to spin and I struggled to stay standing. I had heard and read that in parts of West Africa cannibalism was still practiced. Could this be? Jim came up behind me followed by Ralph and I turned to them and said, "I'm going to be sick… I can't believe what I have seen."

"What? What's the matter?" Jim inquired.

"Look!" I barely managed to whisper, "Is that what I think it is? Is it?"

"What are you talking about?" Jim said taking my shoulders and trying to help me stay on my feet. "Is it the heat? Do you feel faint?"

"No, no, I think I have seen small dead African babies over there that someone is selling," I whispered trying to point without drawing too much attention to us.

Both men's eyes followed my pointed finger. Ralph and Jim smiled.

Ralph spoke softly and said, "Those are smoked skinned monkeys and not African babies. Most people have the same reaction as you when they see this. Don't worry, it's okay. Remember when I told you about having a "juju" on pets? Well, just as there are tribes that eat cat and dog, there are also many that eat monkey."

Jim added, "I have eaten monkey meat and liked it. I probably have eaten cat and dog, but wasn't aware that's what it was. You will be exposed to many different things when you eat local foods. I also like goat soup and lamb soup."

"Oh, goat soup, I had some when Isobel Lokko took me to Monrovia and I did like its spicy flavor, but I don't know about monkey meat. The verdict is out on that subject."

We slowly moved away from this section and headed back toward the car still exploring the foods and merchandise.

"Hey, are we done shopping? I am eager to crank up my motorboat and do some fishing," said Ralph.

"I'm done for now, but do need to get to the Firestone Store to do major grocery shopping," I said feeling relieved that it was monkey meat and not what I had imagined.

With a goal in mind, we hurried back to Jim's car, paid the car-watching fee, and drove off to go fishing. We left the Plantation and turned on the road to the Robertsfield airport and hotel and continued, passing some houses again in the Firestone brick.

Jim said, "That's the compound where the airport personnel live and LITM is located there."

"LITM?"

"Liberian Institute of Tropical Medicine," Ralph answered.

"What do they research?" I inquired.

"Tropical diseases," Jim responded. "The section of houses on the left are where EX-CHEM families live. EX-CHEM is a Canadian explosive company that works closely with LAMCO. LAMCO is the mining company in the Nimba Mountains. You will meet many of the people working for these companies at the BYOB parties."

"We're close to SNAFU now," said Ralph.

"SNAFU? What's that?" I quarried.

"It's an acronym for Situation Normal All F_cked Up," Ralph said.

Jim added, "In the 1940s, the US Army built the runway and named the area SNAFU."

"Gosh, I have heard this acronym over the years and it is kind of neat to see where it originated. Wait till I write and tell my friends back home."

We continued to bump along the dusty road when, there it was, a sign saying SNAFU Bay, where Ralph's boat was docked. We parked and unloaded the lunch basket of goodies, cooler of beer, and fishing gear. There were other cars parked, when Jim remarked, "Looks like we'll have company at Marshall Beach."

Ralph's boat was a nice six to seven-seater with an outboard motor that purred as we trolled along. Every so often Ralph would stop and cast his line hoping to snag a grouper.

"Grouper is the sweetest meat you'll ever eat!" said Ralph. "I love it and the sport of catching it!"

We continued boating along the Farmington River headed to Marshall Beach. I kept putting my hand in the water scooping some up onto myself to get cool when Jim said, "Keep your hands inside the boat."

"Why?" I asked pulling my hand back.

"Well, you never can be too careful in regards to water snakes or hungry fish."

"Okay!" Enough said on that topic. "I will remember to bring a container to dip into the water the next time I'm on a boat."

We soon arrived at our destination. A few boats were anchored near a large long sandbar and we followed suit. We unloaded the boat and Jim and Ralph set up a small tent or cabana as they called it because Marshall Beach did not have permanent palava huts as they did at Caesar and Cooper Beach. The cooler and basket of food were set inside.

Ralph said, "This sandbar is constantly changing so setting up permanent huts wouldn't work."

One boat was pulling a water skier and it sure looked like a lot of fun. I decided to walk on the long sandbar along the Atlantic Ocean collecting a variety of seashells. The ocean loomed and the waves were unusually high and strong. Looks like the tide was coming in I thought as I turned and headed back.

I didn't realize I had been gone over an hour and a half. The men had started to pack up the boat and we were soon on our way back to SNAFU Bay with a good boost from the incoming tide on the Farmington River. The sun was hanging low in the west behind us and the sky showed an array of reds and oranges. I thought I'd hate to be on the boat on this river in the dark with absolutely no daylight to show the way back to SNAFU Bay. Creeping along, we finally got back to SNAFU Beach as night fell. We hurriedly loaded the car. While heading back to our bungalows, Ralph told me how a tribal custom had impacted them last year.

"Last year around Christmas, a group of us had gone to Marshall Beach for the day. Many families brought their small boys to watch their children. The sun had set when we arrived at SNAFU Beach and while we were packing up our cars, the boy watching the Hangartner's children, was taken! We never heard or saw anything! We searched and searched. Three days later his body was found floating near the Firestone dock. Some tribal rituals had been done on his body. After that, we decided to return with plenty of daylight whenever small boys were with us."

"Tribal beliefs are difficult to understand and I don't think I will ever understand them," Jim said in a soft voice.

We rode in silence thinking about this young boy whose life ended so tragically.

Dear Mom Dad Stop
Sobering day discovering Stop
Tribal beliefs Stop
Life delicate balance Stop
Hugs African kisses Stop
Kathleen

Little collared fruit bat

Chapter 13

Bat Man, Stewards, Leopold, Ah Ha!

Wonders of wonders! I slowly pulled my 49 D into Sammy's parking lot avoiding the chickens and goats. This was the first time I noticed an ape was chained to a nearby tree. He had been in his "ape house" when I was here before. I approached him cautiously with my hand flat and extended. Someone inside Sammy's hollered to give him a banana. Turning to go get one, I saw the strangest sight! There, waving and wrapped in white sheets, were the "boys" prancing around in circles.

Dick Hugg squealed in a high-pitched voice, "Help me! Help me!" while tip-toeing in circles waving his white sheet.

"Oh, no! Is it a man? Or a bat?" teased Kevin Estell, "Help me! Help…Me!"

But the best reenactment of last night's episode was John

Chapman with the white sheet wrapped around him, his left hand clenched holding it under his chin while pointing his right hand, "He's in there! It's a Man-Bat! Or is that Bat Man?" John Francis pretended he was the giant Basjaan with a stick (his make shift gun) shaking it all around saying, "Where is he? Where is he?" Sammy's German Shepard ran around everyone barking and barking. John rolled on the ground holding his sides laughing while kicking his legs in the air.

Even I had to laugh at the men's silly antics. Looks like the word was out that Basjaan had rescued me from a little fruit bat. Boy, news travels fast here and it's a wonder with such poor telephone service.

Clapping, I congratulated the group, "Okay, guys, great job! You all have earned an Oscar!" That's when I saw Basjaan coming out of the building carrying a case of Club Beer for everyone. He shyly smiled and asked if I managed to get any sleep.

"Slept like a baby bat clinging to its mother!" I grinned and took a Club Beer. My Mom never told me there would be days like this or did she?

Getting the supplies I needed, I left and returned home driving in and out of downpours. The cardboard box on the passenger side was soaked. I needed to keep a stash of cardboard in the trunk and back seat I thought. Still have another two and a half months to go before dry season and be rid of this rain. Little did I know how beastly and unbearably hot that season was.

Under my bungalow was a group of men who immediately queued up as I parked my car underneath.

"Benjamin!" I called, "What are these men doing here?"

"Eh Missy, they want job of night watchman," he answered.

I looked over the men in line and not one of them was under 60 years old. They all had white hair and some had a staff to hold them up. Great watchmen I thought. Yes, someone did say I needed to get the oldest man to watch my house in the evening and during the night. One by one I read their recommendations. All explained the terrific job they did at their last employment. I asked each one why they left their job. Whoa, the answers were mostly that the people they work for flew away.

Even I couldn't believe that seven staff members had left Firestone leaving these old men jobless. I told them I would think about their many qualifications and that Benjamin would contact the one I selected. I went upstairs and finished up my schoolwork when Benjamin came in to set the table for my dinner.

"Missy, the men not my friends. I no like them."

"Okay, who do you recommend?"

"My good good friend, Ezekiel. He come soon."

"Umm… Ezekiel? I will read his recommendation and thank you for your input." I thought that would be that when I noticed the "redecorating game" had begun again as there were many items that had been moved around in my living room. I remembered what Ralph had told me when my bras and underwear went missing back a couple of weeks ago. Benjamin had said I had given him my clothes. It took 2 days to get my things back. So, I asked Benjamin, "Why are these things moved? Move them back now!"

"Ya, Missy, Benjamin like things here."

"Ya, I hear you Benjamin but this is my home and I want my things where I put them. Okay? Now do what I told you to do."

Grumbling under his breath, Benjamin did move every item back to its original place. Interesting, I thought, he knew exactly where they belonged. Yep, Ralph was right about keeping eye out. I quickly went into my bedroom and counted my bras and underwear. All present. No repeat of the previous disappearances. Thank goodness.

During my supper, Benjamin came in to refill my wine glass and told me Ezekiel was here.

"I'll see him soon, when I finish eating."

Ezekiel was not an old man as I was expecting but more youthful like Benjamin. I did however read his recommendation letter and told him I would let him know. I then walked down to Ralph's house for a visit. Ralph had gotten a letter from his daughter and read it out loud to me. Ralph's three children were coming at Christmas for two weeks and he was very excited to have them visit at the holiday. It had been over a year since he had last seen them in Akron. He asked me to help him buy jewelry for his daughter's Christmas present.

I agreed and told Ralph about meeting Basjaan's girlfriend, Ellen, who was a KLM flight attendant. She stays with him every couple of weeks and was the real reason why he moved to our compound from an outer division. Just then, Basjaan knocked and entered with Ellen, carrying a bottle of wine to join us for a visit.

After the introductions, Basjaan and I recounted the "play acting" done by the men at Sammy's today. Ralph roared and Ellen did once Basjaan explained it in Dutch to her. What a diverse group we were I thought. Since I had forgotten to bring a flashlight, Basjaan and Ellen walked me home before returning to their bungalow.

Over the next few days when I came home from school, I continued to interview potential watchmen. Finally, I met a tall, thin, strong-looking, and dignified man named Joseph Free Man. He kept saying, "I Free Man. I no freeman."

Even though he didn't have a letter of recommendation I decided to hire him as my night watchmen. I applauded his stance on being a "free man". And thus began one of my most enduring friendships while I was in Liberia.

Joseph was a man of few words. I soon discovered that he was once the Paramount Chief of his village which was about one hour upcountry. When I asked Joseph how old he was he answered simply, "I have no paper palava. Paper palava bad-o."

Ralph figured out approximately how old Joseph was because he said that he was born when President Barclay was in office and there wasn't any Firestone. President Barclay's term was from 1904-1912 and before Firestone began in Liberia in 1922. So, that placed him from 61 to 69 years old. I found it interesting that the Liberians placed little value on age like we did celebrating birthdays with parties, gifts, and the like. I paid Joseph 10 cents a day, a 100 pound bag of rice, a bungalow in camp, and a room under my house.

I soon discovered that he would not use his bathroom to take a shower or use the toilet. This caused many heated discussions. Joseph won one battle. He would do his toilet business in the rubber out back and my win was that once a week he would take a bath in the huge laundry tin tub with me supervising. He felt that water coming from the wall (a shower) was bad-o and the thing making noise with water (a toilet) more so.

"What's this?" I practically screamed at Benjamin when I saw him under my bungalow scrubbing my little frying pan. My parents had given me the pan with the new surface called Teflon. I loved my little pan and how nothing stuck to it when cooking. Now, I find Benjamin removing the Teflon coating from my pan.

"Missy, pan dirty. Benjamin clean and clean it. All day," he said proudly thinking he was helping me.

How could I explain this new technology and oh well, it was done and I just had to accept it. "Okay, Benjamin, thank you for helping me." Benjamin beamed and skipped away to prepare my dinner.

About four weeks later, I came home to find Benjamin asleep on the dining room floor and lying in sudsy water. He had apparently fallen asleep while scrubbing the floor. I woke him up and discovered he was drunk! And on my liquor! My vodka bottle was now empty and in the empty upside-down bucket.

He began explaining, "The people, they come and make me drink vodka. I beat them," he showed me punching the air, head nodding, and eyes rolling. Benjamin claimed that it was not his fault. I just nodded not saying anything out loud, but this was the final straw with this man. I called Joseph to help me get him downstairs into his room and onto his bed. Benjamin had passed out and Joseph mumbled under his breath, I knew he wasn't pleased with Benjamin's behavior.

He said, "Benjamin, he no good man for Missy."

I agreed with Joseph's wise insight as I had felt something was not good with Benjamin over the past couple of weeks especially when I discovered my bras and underpants missing after laundry day. Benjamin had argued with me saying I gave them to him. I made him go and get everything or else I'd call the PPD. It took 2 days to get most of my stuff back and I also placed him on a behavioral program.

I told him, "One more mess-up and you will be sacked."

"Sack him now!" ordered Joseph once we had Benjamin on his bed.

"Yes, I will when he sobers up. Joseph, I want you to put your eye on him," I said thinking now my night watchman was bossing me. However, Joseph was 100% accurate in his judgment of Benjamin's behavior. I just hated to be back to square one in hiring a houseboy when Joseph recommended someone and I decided to hire that man. His name was also Joseph and he came from Joseph's village upcountry. Joseph said that he was, "A good good man!" That is how Inside Joseph became one of my household employees and my watchman was now called Outside Joseph.

Two hours later Ralph pulled into my driveway and we were off to a dinner party at Max's, the Pan Am airlines chef. We arrived at his bungalow and joined Paul and Colette Vuillaume, Werner Schaub, his girlfriend Christine, Jim Smith, Paul De Longchamps, Earl Loucks, and Dick and Polly Hugg. Max's bungalow was ground level with the back facing the Farmington River. He had Christmas lights wrapped around the many palm trees and others draped in bushes. Max had a long table set up underneath a palava hut with Christmas lights adding to the ambiance. I do love how Christmas lights were used around the bungalows. Got to get me some strands I thought.

Soft music was playing from his reel to reel stereo system as his house boys circulated serving drinks and hors d'oeuvres. I learned that Paul and Colette were from Paris and had two daughters named Veronique and Sophie. Paul worked for Mobil Oil and they lived close by. Werner was Swiss-German and Christine was English and Swiss and the rest of the group were American. What an interesting group Max had gathered. Dinner was a variety of Indian foods and this was my first experience eating this food. The variety of flavors, subtle yet powerful spilled into my mouth. I had never tasted anything like this before. I found Indian cuisine wonderful, but avoided any hot, spicy dishes remembering my experience with Liberian food when I was with Isobel Lokko.

Drinking black tea after our meal, I heard a strange cry coming from the side of the bungalow and I went to investigate with Max following. Max said that his houseboy today had discovered a baby cat that was about 3 weeks old and he was looking for a home for it. I stooped down and picked the kitten up only to see that it weighed about 3 pounds.

"This can't be a kitten. It weighs too much," I stated and the kitten instantly grabbed my finger and began nursing. I was hooked. I fell under its spell and I loved its warm body nestling by my neck all the while sucking on my finger. The kitten was a dirty orange in color with white fur on its sides, belly, throat, and chest. Pale brownish spots were blended on the white belly. His tail was really much shorter than cats at home. He was simply beautiful!

"I'll give it a home…please let me take it with me! Okay, Max?" I pleaded.

"He is a Golden Cat, a Liberian Bush Cat, a killer, and wild," Max explained and continued to warn that they were difficult to domesticate knowing that's exactly what I wanted to do.

However, I knew, we were bound together by a magical spell and that little bush cat was now mine! "How big do bush cats get?"

"Well, some are around 30 to 35 pounds and about foot or more in height. These are wild cats and can't be tamed like the cats you are thinking about," Max added still trying to persuade me not to adopt the cat.

No matter what he said, the cat was mine and I knew he had chosen me also. Max got me a cardboard box and lined it with a towel. Ralph and I left with the kitten in the box and before we pulled out of Max's driveway, the kitten was back in my arms nursing on my finger. His purr was extremely loud and comforting. Ralph voiced his opinion that he thought this was not a good decision on my part. A wild animal does not belong in house and I should keep it under my bungalow. I chose not to listen to him and once home the little bush cat quickly became the king of my bungalow.

Joseph simply stared at the cat and me and shook his head when I carried it up stairs. Joseph followed carrying the cardboard box and said,

"Missy, he cat!"

"I know he is a cat! He is my cat and my friend."

"Joseph, no like cat!" And with that he plunked the box down and marched downstairs.

I decided to name him Leopold as he did resemble a leopard. So, Leopold was his name! I rehydrated some powder milk and heated it. Dipping my fingers in the warmed milk, I fed Leopold. He really did not know how to lap milk. I knew I had my work cut out for me in teaching this kitten how to eat and drink. Before going to bed, I took Leopold down the back stairs and tried to show him how to loosen the soil so as to go to the bathroom. Leopold simply sat and stared at me. I set the alarm for a couple of hours later to repeat the feeding and bathroom procedures. Once in bed, Leopold snuggled by my chin and his purring lulled me into sleep.

I awoke to noises coming from the kitchen where Inside Joseph was working and the strong smell of coffee drew me into the dining room. Leopold wobbled along on shaky legs after me. Inside Joseph jump back and said, "Missy…what that thing?"

"Joseph, this is Leopold, my cat! Please help me find something for him to eat."

"Missy, that thing, he bad-o!" Joseph repeated many times shaking his head. Oh well, we shall see how this "thing" works out I thought going into the kitchen's dry cupboard in search of food. Something will have to do until I get to the store. Eggs! I broke one, scrambled it and he sucked it off my fingers along with warm milk. Hooray!

I got ready to go to the airport with Ralph as we were going to meet the Pan Am flight carrying Firestone's new accountant, Joe Ward, who would be working in Ralph's computer department. The plane was late due to turbulent weather but it finally landed. So different to the day I arrived when no one was here to meet me. Ralph helped process Joe through customs and collected his luggage. We went over to the Hotel for brunch and to get acquainted. Joe came from Detroit, Michigan and was single. He stood about 5'10' with medium brown hair showing more head skin than most men wanted to. He was easy to chat with and relaxed with Ralph and me. I had met Joe in Akron when we were processed. It was great having another bachelor in our compound.

    Joe was anxious to see where he would be living so, the first stop was his bungalow. His was across from me and next to Ralph's. His place was freshly painted and in better shape than mine. There were already cupboards in both the kitchen and bathroom and even the cushions were in pretty good shape. After Joe saw my place, he decided he wanted to have his painted in colors of his choosing before he moved in.

    I fed Leopold and told Joseph I was eating at Ralph's and not to cook supper for me. Joseph agreed to take care of Leopold while I was gone. I think he is beginning to like him especially when I gave him $20 to go to the Chief to buy a "juju" for Leopold. Joseph could keep the change for helping me out. Okay, so I bribed him, however, I looked at it as a business arrangement.

    Joe and I piled into Ralph's car and continued the Plantation tour visiting the important buildings, my school, Firestone grocery store, Sammy's, and where he would be working in the computer department. We kept him awake and headed to Ralph's for a barbecue with Basjaan and Ellen. Jim joined us and a fun evening was had by all. Basjaan and I reenacted the bat skit and I could see that Joe was sleepy and nodding off. So, Jim took him back to the Guest House on his way home.

    I must say that both Josephs served as surrogate parents for Leopold while I was gone, but I knew the cat was mine when he came stumbling into my arms to again suck on my finger. For a few weeks the routine continued of feeding, scratching dirt, playing, and sleeping for Leopold. He learned to lap then to eat food but, the toilet business was not very successful as he wouldn't dig; he just did his business on top of the ground.

    As he became stronger, we would walk the perimeter of my property and he sprayed marking his territory. It was funny to see the Liberians walk on the other side of the road when passing my place. I don't know what stories the Josephs told about him in the camps or perhaps the "juju" was keeping him safe because the Liberians were terrified of Leopold!

Leopold grew quickly and after a month and a half, I never knew what condition my place would be in when I came home. He had periods of being crazy, racing through the rooms and knocking things over. By the middle of month three, I made the decision to keep him outside or on my porch as he began to shred my sheets, curtains, and had started on the new cushions. Leopold was now about 15 pounds and gaining daily.

Inside Joseph was beside himself with the constant straightening up from the cat. He threatened to quit unless I put Leopold outside where Outside Joseph also had his strong opinions of where this cat belonged and he would mumble…in soup. Increasing both of their pays made amends with the men.

Before I put Leopold outside, I had the carpentry shop make a little house for him which I kept under my bungalow. Surprisingly, Leopold liked the security of it; however he really enjoyed humbugging both Josephs! Many a night Outside Joseph would bang on my front door begging me to take the cat away so he could get some sleep. That was how I learned that when I was home, he went to bed even though he was my night watchman. His explanation was that I was home, the cat was on guard duty. And when I was out, Joseph sat on his chair with his gun on his lap, wrapped in his blanket, and his hat covering his face. I kept reminding myself that Joseph's old age kept danger away from my place.

Life was indeed good.

> Dear Mom Dad Stop
> Had bat white-sheet caper Stop
> Sacked Benjamin hired Stop
> Two Josephs Stop
> Joe Ward came Stop
> Wild cat guards me Stop
> Hugs African kisses Stop
> Kathleen

Memorial headstone in the Liberian interior

Chapter 14

Upcountry

I awoke to the soft pattering of rain on my tin roof. I had hoped that the rains would hold off as today was the day I was going to the town called Sanoyea in Bong County. I had hired Willie (a Firestone driver I often used when going into Monrovia) to drive me to Sanoyea and also his village which was near this town. I was super excited to see jungle life and hopefully some animals on this my first trip "upcountry"!

I had heard that back in June of 1951, a Pan Am Clipper plane departing from Accra, Gold Coast (Ghana today) had crashed into the mountains near Sanoyea. There were many stories going around about what caused that doomed flight; from a terrible thunderstorm, pilot error, or even mechanical troubles with the plane. I had decided to visit there and say prayers for the 40 people who died that day. Willie had told me about the plane crash site being near his village and so here we were today…going to do both things in this trip. Apparently he didn't get home often and was very happy that I asked for him to be my driver to Sanoyea and also letting him visit his family. Willie said I could stay with his parents. They would be honored to have me be their guest since I was bringing their son home to them.

Parents are alike everywhere, I thought, remembering how my parents welcomed Franz De Roos to their home. Franz stayed with Mom and Dad for one week and they showed him all over Erie and the surrounding area. My parents were thrilled to do this since Franz was able to talk about the Plantation and life in Liberia and answer their many questions. Yep, parents were alike everywhere.

Driving in and out of patchy, dense fog, and soft rain, I arrived at 6 am on the dot at the Motor Pool where Willie was loading up a green pickup that I had signed out for our excursion. No way would my 49 D make this trip! Willie was talking to Jerry Elam. Jerry came to my car and greeted me as the sun was beginning to rise and light the dusty gray sky. It was still cool and foggy…yes this was good weather for the trip.

"Morning," Jerry smiled broadly. "Willie tells me you are going upcountry to his village. This is good!"

"Yes, he's taking me on my first upcountry trip. I am excited to see deep jungle and hopefully some bush animals. We are also visiting the Pan Am plane crash site. Have you been there?"

"Yes, the crash happened a few years before I started working with Firestone. A terrible loss of life," Jerry bent to help Willie load some gas cans into the pickup bed.

"Hi Missy! Ya ready?" Willie excitedly greeted me with the Liberian handshake.

"Yes, Willie! I see you have supplies to bring to your family, but why the gas cans?"

"Missy, I get gas for truck. Sometimes, no good place to get gas upcountry. Best be safe."

"Okay, good thing you are driving," I said looking at my folded Mobil road map of Liberia which I had gotten from Paul Vuillaume. I had remembered that he worked for Mobil Oil and said he would supply me with maps if I decided to venture upcountry. If? I had been planning to travel upcountry since I was a little girl. This excursion would be the beginning of many adventures.

"Map? Missy, I don't need that thing! I go home to my village Totota and know the way. Put map down," Willie laughed as he loaded two more gas cans in the back while I climbed into the cab. Willie had more things here making it impossible for me to put my feet down.

"Willie," I said, "this will not do. Please put some things in back. I need room for my legs." Jerry and Willie did just that and still added more stuff to the back as I got somewhat comfortable.

"Missy, I bring Club Beer, Coca Cola, and water. No stores for long time. I got food too."

Interesting that he named beer first and food last. I knew that Coca Cola was made on the Plantation at the bottling plant by Coca Cola Lake. I, however, found it to be very sugary and didn't like it as well as the coke back home. Many people told me that drinking this Coke was an acquired taste-just like drinking the warm Club Beer which I tolerated and in fact, was beginning to like. I was glad that Willie knew what to bring as I only carried a change of clothes, my camera, several rolls of film, my journal, and most important-toilet paper. I had learned to always have toilet paper with you when my family lived in Europe. I also made a mental note to pack better when traveling upcountry in Africa.

We said goodbye to Jerry and pulled out of the Motor Pool and headed back toward my place where we then turned onto the road to Cotton Tree.

The road went from paved to red dirt and was extremely dusty. I sputtered and choked. I guessed it hadn't rained here and I put a red bandana over my mouth and tied it in back. Yahoo! Giddy up…I felt like a bank robber in an old western movie. This trip certainly made me feel like I was in a movie traveling on some desolate back road but, this wasn't a back road as we were still on the Plantation.

Along the road we saw tappers hurrying to cut the bowing-west-towards-Akron rubber trees using special hooked knives. The tappers would slash the bark on the tree and then shake some drops of ammonia into the little cups hanging on the tree trunk. All morning the white latex sap dripped into the cup and the ammonia prevented the latex from coagulating. Later in the afternoon, the tappers would return to collect the liquid latex, pouring the latex into large metal pails. These pails were then dumped into an even larger container on the side of the road. This container would then be delivered to the factory via latex tanker trucks. The tappers also pulled the coagulated string rubber from the slashed area of the tree and collected the spilled latex from the ground and stuffed this into bags crisscrossed on their bodies and hanging on their sides. All rubber was collected with nothing being wasted. Once at the factory, the liquid latex and dried rubber was processed. I asked Willie to stop so I could take some photos.

He urged, "Ya, Missy, we must go now to make it in light."

"Okay, I'm ready," I said climbing back into the truck's cab.

We continued heading east through the Plantation passing through Division 41 and Division 38. Everywhere rubber trees were planted in beautiful avenues. We passed through miles of the Plantation and I spotted small roads branching off calling to be explored. "Soon," I whispered, "soon".

"Willie, how much longer? Are we near yet?" I inquired.

"Missy, it one hour one hour."

"So, you mean it is two hours away?"

"No, Missy, I say, it one hour one hour."

"Willie, I find this Liberian way of talking strange. We have driven almost one hour to here, so, it must be one more hour. Right?"

"Ya, Missy, it one hour one hour," he restated with a huge grin on his face.

I just shook my head and said, "Never mind," And a few minutes later we pulled up at 26 Gate and signed off the Plantation and headed to the town of Kakata. Off the Plantation there were no longer the avenue of rubber trees but, many different kinds of trees. I asked Willie, "What type of trees are these?"

"Missy, they cotton wood, queen ebony, cam wood, and mahogany. Other trees, I don't know. Here old President Tubman's farm and there a good good restaurant called Coo Coo Nest. The food-it fine-o!"

"I see the sign for President Tubman's zoo. Have you been there?"

"Ya, Missy, I go. Fine things to see there. We don't have time today for zoo," Willie apologized turning right and continuing to drive now in an east south east direction. "This is Monrovia Road upcountry."

"Monrovia Road? So, then if we went left back there, we get to Monrovia?"

"Ya, Missy, it is the old road to Monrovia and the Freeport. Firestone boats come to Freeport from United States."

"Wow, is Free Port an interesting place to go to?"

"Ya, Missy. Many big big boats there. Many things go on big boats and come off. The place it good to see."

"Thanks Willie, you have given me more places I want to visit and soon. I want to start with the Tubman Zoo. Are there many animals there?"

"Ya, many kings and presidents from African countries give animals to President Tubman. He make zoo. Zoo have pygmy hippos, big-o turtles, ostriches, deer, snakes, and many more. The place, it fine-o!"

"Zoo, someday soon I will visit you!" I said as we left the town of Kakata and headed toward the Samuel Cooper Farm. The road became noticeably rougher to drive on. We swerved all over avoiding huge potholes and ruts in the road. Many Liberians were walking on the road carrying an assortment of items on their heads. Mostly baskets of food and even a case of Coca Cola! Then, I shouted, "Watch out! Don't turn!" Ahead was a man carrying a twin bed on his head! If he turned, the bed would slam into the truck on my side! Fortunately the man didn't turn as we passed him.

People after people we passed put out their arms-hands flat up-flip to palms down. Willie yelled, "Ya, man there no room to carry you ya."

"Why do you say that?"

"The people, they beg for ride. I no can give them ride in Firestone truck."

"Oh, I see. So this is the Liberian way to hitch hike with turning hands up and down?"

"Hitch hike? American word. Ya, loco chicken!" Willie hollered and tooted the horn as we plowed through a group of chickens, goats, and sheep. "The animals, they crazy and foolish. They want to be killed. I no kill chicken. Missy, you no kill chicken, goat, or sheep. The people be vexed plenty-o! You go to jail and plenty palava."

"Jail? For killing a chicken or goat? Are you serious?"

"Ya, Missy, you pay for chicken, the children of dead chicken, the children of the children of dead chicken…it big palava!"

"Wow! How can people know how many children the dead chicken will have? This is really a serious matter, eh?"

"Missy, the Paramount Chief, he judge and he tell you money you pay to the owner of dead chicken."

"I will try not to kill any animal and thank you for the information Willie!"

We continued bouncing all over the road and I kept checking the truck's bed to make sure we didn't lose anything while trying to stay in my seat. Even with a seat belt on, it proved to be quite strenuous. Every so often we would pass some houses on both sides of the road. Children came running up and along side the truck laughing and begging for the horn to blow. Willie accommodated and the children squealed! This brought back memories of my brother and I doing the same thing with trucks, ah…this must be a universal thing.

We stopped at both Samuel Cooper Farm and Parker Farm where Willie brought some things for his friends. At the village of Parker Farm, I found a bathroom to use and drank a sweet warm Coca Cola while eating some bananas I had picked. Small children came running to me to look at my short blonde hair. A couple of little girls tried to plait it but couldn't. They giggled and showed me how to plait. Amazing! It really is a French braiding technique but done in geometric circles and knotted in the center. I told them no way would my hair plait like that as it wasn't the right texture. Needless to say, they didn't understand me because I didn't know how to talk Liberian English very well. We laughed and giggled and I snapped some photos while waiting for Willie to finish his business. I walked around and found a large pool in a nearby stream with women beating clothes against the rocks. Laundry day. Many washed clothes were draped over rocks drying in the sun. Three small children were playing in the water. It was a peaceful scene.

Walking further, I spied a painted wall scene on a cement block home. A lion and a leopard were confronting each other under a tall tree. I loved the primitive art style and bold colors the artist had used.

Willie called me and we went back driving on the dusty road. While we traveled, I noticed that the vegetation became denser and closer to the road. We passed fewer people and mud huts. Definitely upcountry now and I tried to take pictures but doubted they would come out due to the constant bouncing. Giving up the camera, I tried to doze off which was a near impossibility as the air was heavy with heat, humidity, and dust…then finally, the skies opened and pelted fist-sized rain drops. Never had I witnessed rain like this! Lightening jerked streaks across the dark cloudy sky. This was a full-blown thunderstorm which had been building for the past hour finally releasing us from the oppressive jungle heat. The deluge was typical of the rainy season, I learned.

Suddenly, we stopped and there in front of us was a make shift bridge of tree trunks placed close together across a small creek. The bridge had been washed away and not been repaired and thus this temporary one was all we had to cross the creek.

"Ya, Missy, we go over bridge. You must get out to help me drive across bridge. Tires must stay on tree, ya."

"Or, Willie, I could drive and you direct or show me over the bridge. Okay?"

"Missy, you know how to drive truck?"

"For true, I do. I learned to drive on pickup trucks on my grandfather's farm. Just lead me over."

So that's what we did. I drove and slowly steered the truck with Willie's guidance over the make shift tree trunk bridge.

"Hurray! We made it!" I shouted, as we switched places and continued on our way.

After another two hours on the road I asked, "Willie, are we there yet?"

"No, Missy, it one hour one hour."

Yep, here we go again I thought he must be like my father when we went on trips and kept asking, "Are we there yet?" Dad always gave vague answers or told some insane joke that only he would get. Must be a man thing I decided.

We drove through Kopakata, Gbarnja, and were entering Totota when it suddenly dawned on me that most of the towns we passed through ended with a 'ta' and I questioned Willie about this.

"Missy, 'ta' means 'town' in many Liberian languages. Totota is my town. We will stay here and go to Sanoyea tomorrow. There is a Lutheran Mission church in that town. My family go there every Sunday. The people will know about plane crash."

Soon, some people recognized Willie and came yelling and chasing the lime green Ford pick-up. Willie laid on the horn and more people came to welcome their friend. Totota was as large as Kakata however, I didn't see any restaurant or zoo. We pulled up to a large cement block house with a tin roof that belonged to Willie's parents. Parking, he was mobbed by family and friends.

Willie's mother, a large woman with coffee colored skin, warmly greeted me while thanking me for bringing her son home. She then led me into her home showing me around. I was pleasantly surprised with how large and cool the home was even though it was sparsely furnished consisting mostly of chairs similar to the Firestone ones. Wide arms to hold drinks or small plates and the cushions were covered in many different colored cotton fabrics. On one side there was a large long table and many dining room chairs under it on all sides. No oscillating fans were suspended from the ceiling and then I noticed that there wasn't any electricity. The room was very large and open with lots of light flowing through the windows. There were metal shutters on the inside that could be closed when needed. I could see that rooms branched off this main room when she led me to the room I would be staying in. No screens… or curtains to block bugs or other critters from entering however, there was a mosquito net suspended from the ceiling over the bed I was to sleep in. Glancing behind, I really expected Humphrey Bogart or Dr. Livingston to casually walk into the room that had one electric lamp on a small table near the bed. No electric outlet-just the lamp and the hope that someday there would be electricity in that room.

    After putting my bag down, we went back outside to join the group and I decided to walk around the town snapping photos. I watched a woman sitting on the short stool in front of her house with what looked like a spinning top. She was taking puffs of cotton from a hand woven wooden basket and twisting it onto the string and spinning it into a thread which she then twirled onto a piece of wood. Fascinating, I thought, snapping pictures. The woman beamed. She was wearing a purple and white tie dye lappa around her waist and a green and yellow one on her head. She had the widest smile with a Lauren Bacall gap and when I indicated that I would like to try this spinning, she giggled and eagerly stood up letting me sit and try spinning. A crowd gathered to watch me do this and they were surprised to see me succeed. All the knitting and crocheting I had done, had given me the skills I needed to take cotton puffs, and spin them into thread. Luckily, there wasn't a tall spinning wheel to prick my fingers I thought, searching the crowd for a wicked fairy godmother.

    The crowd cheered at my success and drew me to another woman. She was behind the house using a large wide flat wood stick stirring something in a huge black kettle that was suspended over an open fire. I discovered that she was dying thread using an indigo plant. I also saw two other kettles, one ochre and the other black. They used bulbs to get the yellow color. I didn't understand the explanation of what they used for the black dye. There was also another pot where a piece of woven fabric was soaking in what smelled like ammonia. Someone explained they used urine to bleach white to really white. As a child, my family and I had visited Pompeii, Italy. There, we saw a restored Roman laundry building that had also used urine to bleach their clothes. I found this whole process of dying thread and fabric truly fascinating.

I was led around to the back of another cement block home where a country weaver was shuttling white thread back and forth and stepping left then right, on the pedals of his loom, weaving a long narrow piece of fabric. The width of the fabric was only about six or seven inches and he worked very quickly with a rhythmic beat. The strip of woven cloth stretched about 15 feet from the man and the loom's pedals. This loom was so different than the ones I had seen before in my travels.

Of course, I wanted to try weaving and I went slowly but never was able to get the speed or beat the weaver had developed that was second nature to him. I thanked him and asked to take his photo. He stopped weaving and went inside to get an outfit he had woven. It had long sleeves, a round neck, and came down past his knees. It was in stripes of white, brown, and black and all the strips stitched together. It was indeed a very beautiful piece of work. He even put on a hat he had woven. I quickly snapped photos of the weaver wearing his wonderful tunic as he resumed his weaving.

I bought a large blanket he had woven using only white strips. These strips were sewn together and then painted with many different

Country weaver wearing a country-cloth robe he made.

animals. The animals were painted in deep black ink and told a story about snake and spider tricking goat and chicken. These animals were used in many Liberian folk stories.

I walked around about 30 minutes more and headed back to Willie's home where his mom told me to rest. She would get me when it was time to eat. I did just that falling asleep before my head hit the pillow. All too soon someone was shaking me awake. As my eyes focused in on the single candle light I remembered where I was. Straining to sit up, my body moaned. I ached all over. How do people travel like this I wondered? We had been on the road for about six hours only covering about 100 miles but, I still felt like I had been beaten. It's the heat I said to myself as I quickly freshened up and joined the family outside under the thatched hut. I remembered that this was a country kitchen. Many women of various ages were preparing the meal of goat soup, rice, fufu, chicken and peanut gravy. Fresh fruits, coconuts, and peanuts were included as Liberian condiments. One young girl stirred the goat soup which was in a pot suspended over the open fire. This image conjured my Irish grandmother working over the open fire that was in my grandparents' main room of their house back in Ireland. My brother and I usually were on turf detail and always kept some turf bricks by the fire to add when needed. I smiled remembering the warmth of that room and my family. Not much different here except for the outdoor kitchen. It was just too hot to cook inside.

"Wow! What a feast! Please tell me what I can do? I am so sorry I fell asleep and didn't help before. Please what can I do?"

The women simply laughed and told me to sit and one lady thrust a bowl of fufu in my hands. They indicated for me to eat so, I put my two fingers in it and scooped; then popped it into my mouth waiting for the explosion of heat as before when Isobel Lokko took me to her friend's home in Monrovia.

"Not hot! Wonderful!" I smiled and swallowed. One young girl wearing a green tie dye lappa gave me a plate of cut up something. Yep, it was cut up hot peppers.

"No way!" I jumped back grabbing my stomach and exclaiming,

"I had that before and almost died! I can't eat it, I'm sorry. I feel terrible as my parents had always encouraged us to eat what a hostess presents. Please, please forgive me."

Willie's mother said, "Ya, no problem, peppers are hot. Liberians like. No problem. No problem."

I wandered over under a large open porch where the men were crouched down and loudly playing some kind of game. I watched and saw a long narrow board with small holes carved in it. Two holes side by side for a total of 12. Reminded me of a carton of eggs but, instead of eggs, they used small round pebbles and the strategy was to move and keep your opponent from moving on the board. Confusing to me but the men seemed to be consumed by it and then I saw the money. They also were betting on the game. Lots of laughing and finger snapping and the game was over. I later learned that the game was called Mancala. Everyone moved and sat at the long table with a purple tie dye tablecloth. Candles and kerosene lamps were everywhere. Food was passed and I drank my first palm wine. Not bad if you overlooked the little things moving in the glass and the wine being warm. I passed on the cane juice as it smelled like kerosene and I remembered someone had told me that I could go blind drinking it. The meal was delicious and the company charming. I could see that the family enjoyed Willie's return especially when he passed out presents. Much jumping, clapping, oohing and aahing when they were opened.

Next, the group moved away from the table and started a rhythmic dance movement to the beat of drums. Most were chanting, clapping, and moving to the beat under the starry ebony skies. I joined in and felt kindred to the beat. I think we could have danced all night except that the sky quickly clouded up and rain poured. Fleeing inside and seeing the time, everyone adjourned. Once in my room, and under the mosquito netting, I fell into a deep contented sleep.

All too soon, I was awake and dressed for services at the Lutheran Mission in the nearby town of Sanoyea. I joined a group of women dressed in beautiful matching lappas on their heads and bodies. They also were wearing the most beautiful gold and silver jewelry. And so, with umbrellas in hand, we climbed into the truck's back and Willie drove us the two miles to the Lutheran Mission. All along the way, people came walking out of the bush and were equally dressed-to-the-hilt. There were women, in special lappas, and men wearing full morning suits complete with black tails, top hats, swinging carved walking sticks or umbrellas. What a group they were singing, one song after another to quicken their walk. Our truck was full so there wasn't any room to carry more people. The sun was quickly climbing into the sky as was the heat and humidity with no relief in sight when we finally arrived at the Lutheran Mission and the minister approached.

"Welcome all! Praise to God!"

"Amen!" The group chorused and many began to enter the stone chapel. I was introduced to both the minister and his wife as we were led into the church. It was much cooler inside due to the thick stone walls. We filed into the rows, found seats, and the service began. It was said in three languages. The singing and clapping was robust and happy. Many people jumped up with arms flailing shouting "Hallelujah to God". I felt a rising fervor of religion all in the name of Jesus when I remembered as a young teen curiously peering into the Southern Baptist Colored Church when we lived in Thomasville, Alabama. The parishioners in Alabama had sung and moved in the same manner.

When service was over, we filed outside under an open palava hut to eat a brunch of fresh fruits and drink coffee-warm strong coffee. I ate and drank while the group caught up on local news. I asked the minister about the Pan Am plane crash so long ago. The minister and wife walked me over to the memorial site. How sad to see in the background the low mountain that had a dip in the middle where the plane crashed through. The jungle was returning after the fire that burned for days and this was about 22 years later. I was told it had taken a runner five days to report where the plane was to Pan Am at Robertsfield Airport. I bowed my head in reverence and said my prayers at the memorial site.

Having said our goodbyes to the Minister and his wife, we headed back to Totota with me carrying some mail to post for them. I promised to return in the future and would bring some items they always needed.

When we returned from church, Willie quickly loaded things onto the truck and we were ready for our return trip to the Plantation. We said our goodbyes and left Totota facing a grueling six hour trip over the dusty red dirt roads. I had really enjoyed my time upcountry and had a better idea what to bring when I made a solo trip. Then, I could stop and go at my whim and see and do what I wanted. A good plan I thought as we pulled into Gbarnja only to find about 100 people shouting and blocking the road. We stopped and exited the truck to see if we could help thinking there was an accident.

No accident that we could see as we moved through the loud, chanting mob. I didn't like this at all and felt very nervous listening to the wild chants. Finally, we approached the center of the group to find a ring of fire burning in the red dirt. Frantically dancing around inside the circle of fire was a scorpion! The crowd was going crazy whenever the scorpion came near the edge of the inner circle. The trapped scorpion couldn't see how deep the fire was and if it could hop over. Instead, in desperation, seeing no way out of the fire, the scorpion chose death by stinging itself!

I was aghast! How could these people think this was entertainment? But they did. There were more scorpions in jars along with gasoline filled Coca Cola bottles and then, I saw money, a fist full of money in a man's hand. I backed up, my head was spinning, and I almost threw up but, Willie grabbed my arm and led me back through the crowd to the truck.

"Ya, Missy, don't talk! We go fast. Get out now!"

Once inside the truck, he ordered me to close my window as he did his. Slowly he drove into the crowd honking the horn. People moved but did so slowly until we were upon the ring of fire. The man with the money was yelling and telling us to stop. It was then that I realized that some people were betting on this torture of the scorpion like it was a cock or dog fight.

Willie did not stop and continued honking and yelling in his language. Thankfully, whatever he said made the crowd turn on the crazy man with the gasoline bottles, scorpions, and money. They began pushing him off the road as we drove through the fire. I prayed that we would escape the fire and the mob. Would the truck blow up driving through? Thank goodness we safely drove through the circle of fire. Willie hit the gas pedal hard and we sped out of town and back on track returning to the Plantation.

"Willie, why do they do that to the scorpion? They were betting on the scorpion to kill itself."

"Missy, some people do stupid things. They like to hurt animals. My people does not do this. I no like to see. Liberian people are not bad people. Some people crazy."

"Okay, I see. Even in my country there are crazy people who hurt animals and also people. Americans don't like it either."

We drove thinking about what had just happened and how fortunate we were to get out of there unscathed.

Willie broke the silence saying we were going to stop in Kopakata to eat something and put more gas in the truck.

"Okay, I hope there won't be any problems there."

"Ya, no problem, Missy."

We continued traveling in and out of rain bursts and dust…dust… and more dust. I was beginning to get a feel of what dry season was going to be like and I didn't like it. No time to ponder this as we pulled into Kopakata. It felt good to walk about and stretch my sore muscles. Then, back in the truck headed for the Plantation.

We repeated the tree trunk make shift bridge caper and continued to Parker Farm. We stopped as Willie had some things to drop off at his friend's house and I found a bathroom-well, it really was a hole in the ground that I squatted over. Good thing I had my toilet paper!

"Willie, I thank you for driving me upcountry! I have learned much about your country and people. Your family and friends are great and made me feel comfortable and very welcomed!"

"Ya, Missy, my people are good! God is in them! They see God in you and you can go back to them any time. I will drive you, Okay?"

"Okay, you can drive me however, I think I can drive upcountry myself in some places like Kakata, Tubman Zoo, and Tubman Museum. I want to go there soon!"

I rode enjoying the vine encrusted trees along the edge of the red dirt roads and could now pick out Queen Ebony and mahogany trees. I must learn the other ones I thought, fighting sleep, as we drove through the Samuel Cooper Farm. The air was so heavy with humidity that the only relief would be rain. But there was no rain, only dust and more dust. I put my bandana back on as breathing grew more difficult. Willie told me in dry time, the winds come from the great desert and not the great ocean.

"You mean the Sahara Desert?"

"Ya, Missy, the sand is heavy and every where and it is too hot to work or move. Then the winds change back. Much better."

"I think I am looking forward to experiencing this sandy weather."

The sky changed to vivid reds and oranges reflecting off the tall trees as night slowly fell. I marveled at the star encrusted skies. This was a beautiful end to my first upcountry trip.

We continued to ride passing through Kakata and the Bright Farm when Willie said, "Missy we soon come to 26 Gate and back on the Plantation."

"Wow, I am relieved that we are almost back! I say this has been a very good experience for me and I thank you!"

"No problem Missy."

The rest of the ride was quiet with both of us reminiscing about our two days of travel.

After getting my car, 49 D, and saying goodnight to Willie, I headed back to my bungalow where Joseph was waiting for me. Leopold was stretched out on the bottom step and also greeted me as Joseph carried my bag upstairs telling me that, "That cat, he humbug me too much!"

Yep, back home and the tenuous relationship between Leopold and Joseph hadn't changed. It's good to be home!

Dear Mom Dad Stop
Upcountry trip fine Stop
Stayed out of heated Stop
Spot with scorpion Stop
Hugs African kisses
Kathleen

Entrance to the US Embassy in
Monrovia, Liberia

Chapter 15

Big Palava

I was wearing a yellow sun dress, famished, waiting on my front porch for my neighbors Ralph and Joe to pick me up. We were going to eat dinner at the Hotel. This had become our routine after spending the day at the beach. I love these Sundays of rest, sun, sand and surf, and being with my new friends. But now I was starving and they were late. I saw Joe under his lighted bungalow and waved for him to walk over. Oops, I forgot, Joe was squeamish about walking and potentially stepping on a snake or a scorpion. Then I saw Ralph's gold LTD pull into Joe's driveway, collect him, and speed over to my place. I climbed in and off we flew. Food and drink awaited the baby oiled, sunburned trio when the sky once again burping huge splattering raindrops...ah, the rainy season.

As we entered the restaurant, shaking ourselves dry, we said hello to other Plantation staff who had had the same idea. Ralph ordered a bottle of wine-number 25 from the wine list. Of course, the list only goes to 20, but Ralph never tired of playing this prank every week.

After a small amount of time, Isaiah the waiter returned and stated, "I say Bossman, number 25 it fini-o but number 20 is good-o."

So, Ralph ordered number 19. The rest of the meal was pretty much the same. Giving the wrong numbers to the waiters, who were running back and forth and finally, after a fashion, the desired food selections were made. I can tell Ralph has been in Liberia way too long as he thought this was a hoot! After dinner, we stopped in the bar to have a brandy. I was seated at the bar in the middle with Ralph on my left and Joe my right. Sipping our second brandies, we heard sirens in the distance approaching closer. Someone said that the President of Liberia was coming to either the Hotel or the airport. Within a few minutes, we knew it was the hotel and that it wasn't the President. Ralph recognized the Liberian strutting in wearing a white Liberian Swearing-in-Suit, African turban, supported by an ivory walking stick with a huge gold lion's head. He was A.B. Tolbert and the president of Liberia's son.

Before A.B. had entered the bar, gun-toting soldiers ordered people to vacate their seats. One half of the bar was cleared, furniture moved, and one table was left in the far corner. Most people left and I later wished that we had been in that group. However, the patrons sitting on the bar stools were allowed to remain. The atmosphere had changed drastically. The room felt hot and smoky and stale with an element of danger.

Ralph whispered to Joe and me that we were to be careful as the man was A.B. Tolbert, the President's son, and a bad character. Ah, we gasped as we both had heard the stories. Next thing I knew, Joe excused himself to spend a penny. I smelled him before I felt him. A.B. Tolbert was pressed up against me. I leaned closer to Ralph while the pushing on my right continued.

I turned and spoke, "Excuse me, sir, you are hurting me."

The large Liberian demanded that I come to his table and drink.

I politely declined.

He then grabbed my arm and yanked me toward him saying in a gruff manner, "Do you know who I am?"

"Yes," I managed to stammer, "Please leave me alone. I don't want any trouble."

My Irish rose as he rudely fondled my breast saying, "I want to f--k you, come now!"

"No!" I practically screamed but trying to remain polite not wanting any trouble with this drunk man.

Slurring and spitting in my face he said, "Don't you want to f_ck an African man who is President of Liberia's son?"

Somehow I blurted out, "I don't care if you are purple and the Catholic Pope's son, get your hands off me or I'll…" I left the rest to the imagination of the drunk man.

I felt myself being pulled to my left and off the bar seat. Ralph was talking in a diplomatic way to A.B. Tolbert while ushering me out of the bar. He grabbed Joe returning from the men's room and led us out into the steamy night and his LTD.

"We got to get out of here before there is a big palava! Don't say another word," Ralph barely whispered.

I listened, as Joe was brought up to date as to why the quick departure from our half-emptied brandies.

Screeching onto the Plantation, Ralph explained what had happened and added a prayer that A.B. Tolbert was too drunk to do anything about us. He warned both of us not to speak of these past few minutes to anyone.

"Keep a low profile!" warned Ralph.

So, low we kept and Sunday rolled into Monday and became Tuesday. I was teaching my class when we heard quickly approaching sirens in the distance. Teachers, students, Jim Smith, and I poured out into the long open-air hallway of the school to see who was coming.

A light rain was falling as Jim walked up to the long black limousine led by two motorcycles with their sirens still blaring.

A door opened and we all watched a small Liberian step out

carrying a letter. Some Liberian handshakes and greetings were exchanged. Jim turned to the quiet group and called, "Miss Mobilia, come here please."

I wanted the ground to swallow me but I did walk to the limo, Jim, and the Liberian with 120 or more pairs of eyes glued to my back.

"Yes, I am Miss Mobilia," I said in a steady voice surprising myself. "May I help you?"

"Missy, my Bossman give this to you," he then reached into the limo and brought out a huge basket of enormous Florida oranges. The crowd gasped knowing what an expensive package this was while I tore open the letter. I quickly scanned it, ripped it up, and told the messenger that my answer was…

"No, and take the oranges back to your Bossman!" With that, I turned and walked back to my class wishing I was anywhere but here.

I heard the limo and the motorcycles starting up and pulling away from the school's parking lot. Teachers once again took charge and students returned their classrooms when I heard Jim asking to speak to me. I knew that I would have to explain the past few minutes. I told my class to start reading while I talked to Mr. Smith.

"Jim, let me explain…"

"What's going on? And the note? Who was it from and what did it say?"

Okay, here it goes, sorry Ralph I thought. Then I recapped. "It was an invitation to dinner at the President's Mansion by A.B. Tolbert. You heard and saw that I refused to accept it."

"A.B.Tolbert? What? How?" Jim stammered, "Explain."

I explained all that had happened on Sunday night at the hotel while Jim listened disbelievingly.

"I see…I'll look into this matter. For now, return to your class."

I did. Nothing more was said.

Wednesday was a repeat of Tuesday's caper, more sirens, motorcycles, limo, Liberian messenger, invitation, and a large wrapped gift from the Swiss Jewelry Shop.

Again, I refused by tearing the invitation up and we all tried to get back to normal. However, it was now Thursday and the entourage happened again with the usual response from me. Billie Darsey looked at me with a small smile. Yes, I had also shared the situation with her and she had given me her wise motherly advice. "Stay true to your convictions."

Jim, on the other hand, had relayed to me this morning what my response was to be. This response was from the Firestone bosses. Yes, Firestone was also in on the problem and their decision was not to my liking.

Friday came and my stomach was lurching. I knew that stepping through the red door at Firestone Central Office would be a major step in either solving my crisis or making it worse. The event that I had given so much thought to was about to be resolved but, I wasn't sure how. My decision to stand by my convictions could get me fired. I had wanted to come to Liberia to work and experience all I could. Yet, this meeting with my bosses at Central Office concerning the palava with A.B. Tolbert might be the end of my dreams.

I truly believed that I was right in refusing A.B.'s invitation to be wined and dined by him. And dinner was to be at his father, President Tolbert's Executive Mansion. So what if his father was the president of Liberia! His crude, obnoxious, and drunken behavior last Sunday at the Robertsfield Hotel was unacceptable.

My headmaster, Jim Smith knew that for 3 days I had been refusing his lavish gifts delivered by a representative using the President's limo. No matter what, I swore I would not buckle under to A.B. Tolbert's demands and how dare he contact Firestone, my employer!

Jim had reported to me that the bosses wanted me to act as an ambassador for both the company and the United States. He said, "The company believes I could be a positive link for them in these times of negotiations."

Yes, Firestone was in the midst of friendly talks with the government of Liberia. Positive link or not, the guy was a loudmouth using his father's name and position to advance his desires. Yes, my mind was made up to declare that I would not be dictated to by Firestone as to how I was to spend my free time even if this meant me giving up my lifelong dream! Yes, indeed, I decided, I would be on board the next Pan Am plane home. Taking a deep breath, I gathered my dreams, my dignity, and entered the room to face my future. Will I be staying or flying home?

Closing the door behind me I thought was akin to closing the door on my dreams, but what awaited me was a complete surprise. Seated in a semi-circle on couches with tables well supplied with coffee, tea, and small cookies sat an unusual array of top Firestone executives. Some I had met before, but most not and oddly enough while most were in western business attire, one Liberian gentleman was wearing the traditional Liberian Swearing-In suit. He looked oddly like a university professor puffing on a pipe emitting the best smelling smoke I had ever experienced. He also leaned with one hand on an ivory walking stick with a gold lion head on top. A little too similar to what A.B. Tolbert had used.

The meeting didn't take long to get to the point. Already the executives including my principal Jim Smith had recognized that as a teacher I was just what they had hoped for. They indicated that they also understood my reluctance to play the "Liberian game" as they called it. They said they were going to do their best today to keep me at my school and happy, but they also wanted me to understand that living and working in a foreign country was not like living and working in the United States. My dear neighbor, Ralph Welsh, proceeded to explain how he was there the night that A.B. Tolbert made some extremely rude comments to me and accosted me by grabbing me in a very private area. Ralph spoke how Mr. Tolbert appeared to be drunk and made no attempt to apologize to me when Ralph ushered me out of the Robertsfield Hotel and away from the toxic situation.

That's when the professorial gentleman took over. He stood and paced the room and what he said next was to change my life forever. The gentleman introduced to me as Mr. Brown spoke clearly and distinctively.

"Miss Mobilia, I am so pleased to meet you and understand why Mr. A.B. Tolbert is interested in you. Please bear with me and know that

I represent many friends of yours," he said this with a twinkle in his eyes as he blew sweet-smelling smoke circles about his head.

Friends, I'm thinking, I've only been in this country for 6 weeks and know only people from Firestone. But, wait, could this be the person that the Third Secretary at the American Embassy told me he would contact? After school yesterday and not telling anyone or hiring a Firestone driver, I secretly drove off the Plantation and went to Monrovia. Once there; I parked my car at Sinkor Supermarket on the outskirts of the capital. I then hired a taxi to take me to the American Embassy. Thirty minutes later I was at the impressive tall black wrought iron gates of the American Embassy asking for admittance and ushered inside to wait. I wanted another egg in my basket just in case Firestone would not support my decision. I hoped the Embassy would offer me refuge if I needed it and a ticket back home.

Upon entering the Embassy, I explained my predicament and the fact that I hadn't seen my passport since the day I arrived in Liberia six weeks ago. I had no legitimate way to prove that I was an American citizen other than my Pennsylvania driver's license. The person led me in to see the Third Secretary to the Ambassador, Mr. Paul Fuci. After explaining the nature of my presence, Mr. Fuci assured me that I was correct in coming to the Embassy as they had been watching the activities of A.B. Tolbert for some time. Mr. Fuci said he also worked with the other embassies in Liberia as their citizens also had reported trouble with A.B. Tolbert. There were complaints of him beating and raping women especially stewardesses.

"So, why would my boss, Firestone, pressure me to go out with this character?" I asked.

Mr. Fuci did reveal to me that the relationship between Firestone and the American Embassy was strained. Firestone was being forced into opening their 99-year contract with the Liberian government and renegotiating its terms. Firestone had been operating for 47 years in Liberia and Mr. Fuci thought that perhaps Firestone believed they could use me as a go-between that would sweeten the talks. He told me that he would see to it that I would not have to do anything against my will, not to worry, go back to the Plantation and wait for someone he would send. He had a plan and would meet me tomorrow. Did I know a Firestone employee named John Francis? Yes, I had met him a few times and I had heard of his wild reputation and wilder yet parties but I had never attended one. Mr. Fuci said he usually went to the Pan Am crew parties that were held at John's Plantation home on most Friday and Saturday nights. He would meet me there tomorrow to see what happened to me on Friday. He was also going to check into what happened to my passport. And so now, I looked around the Firestone conference room and wondered, could this Liberian, Mr. Brown, be the person Mr. Fuci had in mind to aid me? So, I listened to what Mr. Brown had to say.

Mr. Brown asked me how I found Liberia and her people before the episode with A.B. Tolbert. I answered honestly that I was enjoying my weeks here and learning so much about the culture and the Liberian people. It was so much more than I had imagined and Liberia hadn't disappointed me! I want to stay, work, travel around the country, and learn as much as I could about Liberia. He smiled, liking my response. He then explained his position in the government. He was the head of the Liberian National Security Agency which protected the President and his family and other high ranking government officials. Mr. Brown officially stated that President Tolbert was deeply concerned that his beloved son, A. B., was humbugging me and to accept his sincerest apologies. He would like me to come to a dinner dance next month where many foreign embassies would be attending. Unfortunately, his son would be on business in England and was saddened that he would miss seeing me.

Whoa! What is going on? Is this for real? Was a President apologizing to me? Could this be? A dinner party at the Mansion and my problem would be many thousands miles away! I calmly stared at every man in the room. All were smiling like Cheshire cats and nodding while Mr. Brown wore a hopeful look, almost a plea, on his face. This was it. My decision was being demanded now. I didn't have any time to ponder. Again, my heart took flight and I answered that I indeed would be honored to represent the United States and Firestone by attending this dinner dance next month at the Liberian Presidential Mansion. Did I hear breaths being released? Given the body language and sudden smiles, I guessed the compromise was agreeable to all. So, yes, it looked like I was going to stay in Liberia and continue teaching at the Firestone Staff School thanks to my new friends, a Liberian government official, Mr. Brown and the helpful Third Secretary, Mr. Paul Fuci. Yes indeed, friends in high places. Now home to prepare for the wild Pan Am crew party at the legendary John Francis' bungalow. I wondered what this adventure would hold for me.

> Dear Mom Dad Stop
> Met the Devil Stop
> Mr. Brown and Fuci Stop
> My angels Stop
> Hugs African kisses Stop
> Kathleen

Pan Am jet and crew

Chapter 16

The Legendary John Francis

Later that evening as Ralph drove us over to John Francis' bungalow; I explained what had happened at Central Office to Joe. I had kept both of my friends updated all week long but hadn't told them about my excursion to the American Embassy in Monrovia.

Ralph said, "I was surprised to see Mr. Brown at the meeting. I liked how he turned everything around into a favorable result for you."

"Absolutely," I said and continued to explain how I had driven to the American Embassy and sought out their help. I went on telling the guys about Paul Fuci and his promise to help me. "I believe that Mr. Brown was sent to assist me in this situation, at least I hope so! Now, let's have a fun relaxing evening and put aside the palava of the past few days."

The rain had slowed as we pulled into John Francis' driveway. His back yard had many small palm-covered huts with Christmas lights strung around the edges. Already people were partying. Some were dancing and others were clustered by the barbecue pit. The smell of steaks grilling on the open charcoals teased our senses. Gosh, I was starving!

Wearing a bright yellow and blue flowered shirt, heavy gold chains around his neck, white shorts, and carrying a large drink with a tiny parasol. John Francis said, "Welcome to my humble abode, grab a drink, introduce yourselves, and start to party! There's plenty of food and drink!"

John Francis didn't have to tell us twice. We headed to the bar for drinks. A steward made our drinks from a well-stocked bar as dance music blared from outside speakers fed by a very sophisticated reel to reel tape set up. Something akin to Jim's but larger. Groups of people were scattered about eating, drinking, or dancing. So far, the party looked to be like other parties I had attended. We chatted with many Firestone friends including John and Carol Chapman, Dick and Polly Hugg, Aldo and Ingrid Holzl, and Jack Van Dam, who was John Francis' good friend.

We then wandered over and introduced ourselves to some Pan Am pilots and stewardesses who were in Robertsfield for a two-day layover. Jim, a pilot, told us that the crew stopped here before flying their next work leg down to Kinshasa, Zaire for another stopover, and then Johannesburg, South Africa. After yet another stopover, they flew onto Nairobi, Kenya with two days there before returning to Robertsfield with another two-day layover and then headed back to New York City. "Two weeks on and two weeks off," Jim told us after his explanation of his job. "Only the most senior crews have the African flights. You'll hear people saying that we are Pan Am's Kings and Queens," he continued, "hey, if you need anything from home, let me know and I'll bring it to you next month. We always bring in the steaks for John Francis' parties. It is nice that he opens his home to us for dinners and parties."

I told him that he had an interesting job with all the places he gets to explore and also about my job teaching for the Firestone Company.

"Where is Jim Smith? He usually comes to these dinners."

"Speaking of Jim Smith, here he comes and I know he is ready to party," said Coco, a Pan Am stewardess. "Need nail polish, shampoo, or whatever you can't buy here, let me know and I'll bring it to you. If you could help me buy gold and silver jewelry or Liberian wood carvings at your prices. I believe, that would be a fair exchange."

"Deal! Gosh, this would be great because I already see that there are things I can't buy here. And it is nice to know you are willing to help. Oh, I see a friend I want to thank…see you later," I said as I made my way over to Paul Fuci.

After thanking Paul and explaining how Mr. Brown made a potentially painful situation disappear I again voiced my great appreciation for his intervention.

"No problem. Glad to have been able to help out. Come, let's get our steaks and eat."

I introduced Paul to Ralph, Joe, and Jim. I know Jim was wondering how I knew Paul or where I had met him, but he didn't say anything. House boys passed among us offering huge shrimp, fresh fruit, and took drink orders.

Pilot Jim asked me to dance and the rest of the evening continued to be interesting, meeting more Firestone people, and those that worked at the Robertsfield Airport or Hotel. Someone told me about the beautiful pristine white beaches near Buchanan a little over an hour from here. One beach was near a small village called Little Bassa. Also, if I timed it right, I could buy fresh fish brought in by the Fanti fishermen. I was intrigued and found out more about the nomadic people that fished the Atlantic waters. Someone told me the Fanti were from Ghana and traveled up and down the West African coast following the schools of fish, netting, bringing the haul into the shore, and selling to the locals. This sounded really fascinating to me and I mentally put it on my list of things to do.

Soon the party got louder and the dancing…well…a bit too

risqué for me. Some of the women were now topless and men were clapping and whistling well, you get the picture. Here and there were couples in deep lip locks and it looked like the party was changing course.

I averted my eyes and went in search of Ralph to have him take me home only to find that someone had a can of whipped cream and was decorating Ralph's bald head while another girl was licking the whipped cream off his beer belly and moving below his stomach. Ralph was almost passed out with the biggest grin on his face. Yep, time to leave and quickly! Joe approached me with the visual signal to get Ralph out of here and fast. We did. I drove his car home and we managed to get him up the stairs with some added help from his night watchman and then got him into his bed.

I thanked Joe and told him I know that Ralph would be sorry in the morning if we had left him at the party.

"Glad to have left when we did," replied Joe. "Don't know if I want to be involved with that particular group if you know what I mean."

"Yes," I agree. "I, too, didn't like the direction the party was going in. I noticed many of the crew left just before we did."

"Glad I did go to the party so at least I know what people are talking about when they mention these 'crew parties' that John Francis has," Joe added. "See you in the morning for church and then the beach. I bet Ralph doesn't leave his bungalow tomorrow."

"I decided I'm going to Buchanan tomorrow. Want to go there instead of Caesar's Beach?" I asked.

"Sure! I'll pick you up around 9:00," replied Joe.

But, the next morning I drove to Buchanan solo as Joe also didn't feel well enough to accompany me and, as expected, Ralph was calling it a recovery day. No sunlight for him! Passing through the two cotton trees and just after the road to Jim's bungalow, I turned southwest. Traveling to Buchanan I remembered my history that this town was named after Thomas Buchanan the first Governor of Liberia who was also a cousin of James Buchanan the fifteenth President of the United States. Groups of freed American Negroes that were from a black

Quaker's group called the Young Men's Colonization Society of Pennsylvania returned to West Africa in 1835. They settled 90 miles south of Monrovia at the mouth of the St. John River. The harbor was perfect for commerce and the community grew. Passing by the usual scenery of low grasses and palm trees with small farms sprinkled here and there, I bounced along enthralled to be here and exploring. I passed through small villages avoiding hitting small animals and honked my horn as young children squealed. Kids were alike everywhere!

  The towns of Barclayville, Boyequee, and Takpa rolled by and I decided to go to Little Bassa and the beach instead of Buchanan. Maybe I'd be lucky to see the Fanti and their colorful painted canoes. Little Bassa was indeed quite small and very rural. I parked, grabbed my towel, camera, and beach bag and began walking to the beach outside of the village. Of course, many children came up and chatted happily even though I told them I didn't understand Liberian English. Nevertheless, they sat down next to my towel and acted like I was their good friend. The sand was white and glistened and there were few clumps of tar. One young boy brought over some cut up pineapple and shared it with us all.

  I relaxed in the warm sun and listened to the waves lapping the shore, I must have fallen asleep as I awoke to boisterous shouts and loud clapping. Jumping up I realized that a Fanti canoe was breaking the waves and headed to shore. Somewhere drums were setting the rhythmic beat for the canoe paddlers rowing into shore. The excitement was rising! I ran and started pulling in the net along with most of the villagers. Rest, pull, rest, pull; it seemed like an hour of this procedure before the total effort was rewarded as the net full of fish made it onto the shore. People came with huge enameled colorful bowls collecting the fresh catch. I had a teenage girl take my photo surrounded by the Fanti and fish. The excitement was incredible! I couldn't believe my luck in participating in this simple activity. I left with several lobsters, a hammerhead shark, and grouper.

  Arriving back on in the bachelor compound, I gave the fresh catch to Inside Joseph to prepare for supper. I phoned Joe, Bastian, Ellen, Jim, and Ralph to join me for supper. Our little group feasted, drank, and laughed as I shared my day's adventure.

> Dear Mom Dad Stop
> Thanks for Catholic upbringing Stop
> Am good girl Stop
> New career hauling fish Stop
> Hugs African kisses Stop
> Kathleen

Showing off Clorox-killed snake

Chapter 17

Great White Hunters?

Rain stung my face, drenched my hair and clothes, lightning flashed and thunder boomed. However, I managed to get to Basjaan's and Ellen's bungalow thinking that I should have driven down. Ellen was in for 2 weeks and I was helping her with English after how she misunderstood what I was saying over the phone in what became known as the Man Bat caper. She heard man….instead what I had said…bat. Oh well… As I went to place my foot on the bottom stair, I watched a snake strike a large frog! The frog jerked and flopped as the venom flowed through it and the snake stared at me probably wishing he still had a good dose of venom left to bite me. Instead he slowly and silently slithered away into the plants between the house and carport.

Ah, my first close encounter with a poisonous snake, I thought, as I climbed the steps to eat lunch with Ellen. We were going to the Hotel pool afterward for the afternoon-rain or no rain-as it would be nice to swim in the covered pool. Entering the living room, I told Ellen all about the snake and frog I had just seen and we looked out at the bottom of the stairs. The frog was lying there dead with no snake in sight. We went back in and ate our lunch and when we were headed out to the pool, we saw that the snake had returned for his prey. The snake had already unhinged its jaw and had started to take the frog into its mouth. The head of the frog went in first and Ellen and I sat down on the middle stairs to watch.

"I wonder what type of snake this is," I asked Ellen.

Ellen hopped up, "I will get book of Basjaan and look it up."

"Great!" I said and Ellen went inside and came back with the book.

Thumbing through the pages, I realized the book was in German and not English. Fortunately Ellen reads German, unfortunately, Ellen's English was poor. She located a picture that resembled the snake we were watching and tried translating the information to me.

"It says this snake only found in central Africa, the Congo area. This not be a snake from Liberia,"

"Go get your camera, Ellen. I think this will make a wonderful picture," I said thinking about what she had said about the "Congo" snake.

She returned with a camera and a spool of film which I loaded into the camera. Ellen said, "I think I will call Basjaan and tell him about snake."

Ellen came back shouting, "Basjaan said to get and keep the snake. He is coming now. He want snake. Snake come from Congo not Liberia. He write for book and make famous."

Ellen and I continued to sit taking pictures and watching the snake slowly pull the frog in and all the while we could tell the snake was very nervous. I, on the other hand, dreamed of our names being entered into this book or magazine article. Wow! How exciting this is, I thought!

Their houseboy, Bohu, came downstairs and when he saw us

sitting on the steps, he asked, "What you do?"

"We are watching that snake eat the frog. Bossman is coming to take the snake to study," I explained. And so he backed up once he saw the snake and slowly kept his distance but was obviously entranced by seeing two white women taking pictures of this snake.

Bohu waved to friends passing by the bungalow to come here and see. The small group of Liberians did just that. All too quickly we had about 15 Liberians watching from the dirt road in front of the bungalow. The Liberians were chatting and laughing and taking in this strange sight when the snake started to move back towards the bush.

"No, no…snake can't go!" cried Ellen, "Basjaan say, keep snake. He come soon."

I jumped up and tried to get the snake to move back by the steps. No such luck as the snake zigzagged, avoiding me, and I continued to jump and make crazy noises to scare the snake back towards the steps. But no way was the snake going to go back by the steps. He had it in his mind to get away and back into the bush away from all the commotion.

I picked up some small stones and threw them in the snake's path to redirect it back towards the steps. Ellen helped me. The Liberians on the road started clapping and chanting. The more Ellen and I chased and threw little rocks at the snake, the louder the Liberians' chanted.

I realized that time was running out for keeping the snake by the bungalow and away from the bush. Once the snake got to the bush, it would be gone and so too our chances of being named in the article about this rare snake that Basjaan would write about for a science journal.

"Ellen, go get some ammonia so we can knock the snake out," I said thinking what could subdue the snake until Basjaan arrived. Ellen didn't understand what I was talking about.

So, I thought quickly and said, "Ammonia, ammonia. It is used to clean the floors. I know you must have some upstairs in the kitchen. Bohu, please go with the Missy and help her get the ammonia."

Two minutes later they returned with a gallon bottle of Clorox.

"Clorox? Clorox? I asked for ammonia!" I shouted.

Bohu spoke up, "Missy, I clean floors with this thing."

"Okay, give me the Clorox bottle," I ordered. Holding the brown bottle, I waited for a little hoping that Basjaan would pull into the compound and capture the snake. But luck wasn't on our side. The chanting became louder. Yes, now the Liberian group had doubled in size. I wondered how the word was traveling that there was a "show" going on in the bachelors' compound. The crowd just kept growing but kept a safe distance. The snake must have thought, "I need to get away from these people and crazy women and back into the bush," and with great effort he started to slither away.

I screamed and jumped which also caused Ellen to scream and jump and then the audience of Liberians screamed and jumped. All this commotion for a snake that perhaps would make us famous in a science journal. Was it worth the trouble I thought?

"Yes," I declared, "This is worth it!" Ellen and I formed a circle and loaded with more small stones, continued pitching them at snake, all the while excitedly dancing on our toes and beginning a feverish chant..."Snake stay! Snake stay!" We repeated this over and over. The Liberians loved the "show" we were putting on and they joined in our chant. Okay, I was hoping the snake understood English and would accommodate the soon to be famous women. The snake began making his way to the street at which point the Liberians screamed and parted like the Red Sea. Ellen and I ran in front of the snake and threw more stones at it. We got the snake to change direction and head back to the carport. We followed feverishly.

I don't know how it happened but, it did. My adrenaline was so pumped, a deep Tarzan/Jane roar sprung from my throat. With my free hand, I thumped on my chest, threw my head back and wailed, "Ahhhhaaee!" I jumped in front of the snake, positioned the Clorox bottle over its head and poured the bleach onto it. The snake halted its escape, rose up, swayed left then right, jerked and shook its head, and then in one violent movement lurched and heaved up the frog! In a slow fluid motion, the snake laid down on the ground. The Liberians screamed, either I had killed the snake with the bleach or the wild screaming had. I thought our snake was dead and lamented, falling to the ground, crying, "Oh, no there goes our chance of being published and famous."

Suddenly, with a burst of renewed energy, the snake leaped up and practically flew toward the bush. Everyone whooped, hollered, and ran in circles away from the snake. But no, not I. I took a huge breath and reached deep into the white hunter part of me and charged at the snake determined to contain it until Basjaan pulled in. More bleach was poured on the snake and into its open mouth. The snake continued its flight to the bush from its would-be captors. Ellen and I continued to scream and do an Indian-like dance, when, I saw a large washtub under the house. I yelled for Bohu to get it and bring it to me. Bohu refused. His eyes spoke volumes-I want to be anywhere but here with the two crazy women and the snake.

Dropping the now empty bottle of Clorox, I grabbed the tub and plunked it on the snake. Ellen and I pushed the exposed body part under the tub and then piled stones around the edge of the tub. I didn't trust the snake not to dig its way out, escaping into the bush and freedom. No way was he going to flee from us! Ellen dropped a huge stone on top when we looked at each other, drenched in sweat, panting heavily, but now successful hunters! We had captured the rare snake and the rest of the world would hear about how two meek and mild women dared to face this extremely poisonous dangerous snake from the Congo! I looked over at the road and there had to be about 60 Liberians jumping, clapping, and laughing. Some had cheered loudly when Ellen dropped the final stone on top of the washtub. We humbly took a low bow and the crowd went wild! They knew we were heroes and that we had saved them all from this wild dangerous snake.

Horns were blaring and the crowd once again parted and in drove two green Firestone pickups. Basjaan was here! He had come with a team of workers to take down this snake. Ellen and I ran to him so excited that he was here and anxious for him to crate the rare snake and declare us to be truly Great White Hunters!

The air was full of anticipation of the exposure of the incredibly dangerous snake. Ellen and I were both shouting at once trying to relay the amazing saga of the capture.

"Where is the snake? The snake, where is it?" Basjaan asked.

With great pride, Ellen, the Liberians, and I pointed to the washtub with the rocks trimming it holding the snake in place. "He's there!" We said in unison. The Liberians clapped and howled.

"There? Under the washtub?"

"Ya, Bossman! Ya, Bossman! He there," the group chorused.

"Why the rocks? Are you afraid it would escape?"

"Ya!" Ellen answered.

"We didn't know if it could dig its way out. You must realize that this is a wise and determined snake," I spoke up.

Cautiously Basjaan approached the washtub, silently directing his men armed with long glass tubes and looped ropes to be ready to lasso the snake when he lifted the tub. Ever so slowly and watching the movements of his men, Basjaan using a long stick reached down to remove the rocks and raise the tub. The crowd gasped as slowly the tub was lifted to reveal the snake. I was hoping that it hadn't dug a tunnel and been lost forever along with the published article. What did I know about snakes?

The world stopped. Then Basjaan pushed the tin tub off the snake and a snicker came from his lips and then a roar. Throwing his head back and with a deep belly laugh he said, "That's a common Gabon viper!"

His crew now had a good look at the once famous snake and broke out into thunderous laughter. Jumping and pointing they spoke in many different tongues but the English words stung nevertheless. That's a common Gabon viper.

"What do you mean a common Gabon viper? Look how long it is-what six feet? The picture is in the science book. We saw it!" I insisted.

Basjaan was speaking in Dutch explaining to Ellen whose once victorious face turned confused and uncertain. She was speaking animatedly and I knew she was explaining the White Women's' Hunt that had occurred. Next, she was showing the book's photo to Basjaan who continued to roar. Looking around, the once favorable crowd was now joining in with the laughter. Yep, it looked like Ellen and I had egg on our faces! Before I knew it, I snickered, then laughed fully. This really was a hilarious situation. Looking at the snake caged in a glass tube; it didn't resemble the book's photo at all. We figured it out that when the snake had dislocated its jaws and expanded its mouth, the snake indeed looked like the one from the Congo. The stretched out markings fooled us. Damn snake; damn, damn, damn!

Two days later I received a letter via the Plantation's mail. It was a coupon for a 5-gallon bottle of Clorox. The letter was signed, The guys. What no skit? I thought.

However, I was not to be disappointed. Pulling into Sammy's that same day was a sign hung across the top of the door.

<pre>
Sign up for the Field Trip with Miss Mobilia
           Supplies needed:
            Bottle of Clorox
               Machete
            Bottle of Clorox
            Book of Snakes
            Bottle of Clorox
                 And
            Bottle of Clorox
</pre>

I laughed getting out of the car. These men were a hoot! Suddenly a drumbeat rolled and sliding-almost in a slither-came Dick Hugg carrying a tin tub and whooping it up like an American Indian. John Chapman tiptoed out toting a bottle of Clorox and beating on his chest crying, "Ahhae, me white hunter! Beware, I am armed with bleach! I am ready to hunt snakes!"

The entire group roared and pranced around thoroughly enjoying themselves. Having no TV does this to grown men I thought. Yep, these men needed me for their entertainment!

Later that night resting nude on top of my sheets, I reflected on the day's adventure and how close Ellen and I had been to being famous and perhaps even making it onto the Ed Sullivan Show.

Ah, sweet dreams took hold as I mentally sent off a cablegram.

>
> Dear Mom Dad Stop
> Me hunter Stop
> Captured snake Stop
> Lost notoriety Stop
> TV career? Stop
> Hugs African kisses Stop
> Kathleen

Le Monze's bungalow

Chapter 18

Calling via Ham Radio, Banana Mama, Green Mamba Visit

"Bonjour Augie!" I called stepping from 49 D and onto his dirt driveway. Augie Le Monze waved for me to join him by some cages built on stilts. As I approached, I saw he had a collection of snakes in individual cages the he had labeled. I thought this was a wonderful learning tool. These cages were close to the building that housed the electric generators. The Le Monze's bungalow was below Hydro Lake, the dam, waterfall, and the small island where Jim Smith lived. This looks like it could be a field trip for my class in the future. Climbing through the huge tubes sans water in dry season would be awesome!

"Bonjour Katsy! This is the snake you and your friend chased with Clorox that day. He is poisonous but would only make you very sick," Augie said with a laugh in his thick French accent. He continued to point out and give me details about each snake.

"The Rhinoceros Viper is the most deadly. The Liberians call it the Three Step Snake because you would go three steps and die! Be careful of this snake!" He warned. "It is not very aggressive and very slow moving, but very, very dangerous."

"Boy, it seems that everyone has heard about the once famous snake and the Clorox episode. I have been marked for life about that snake caper!" I remarked laughing.

"Oui…oui, however you are not here for a lesson on snakes are you. Let's go into my radio shack and try raising your father on my ham radio."

"Yes, I am excited to radio my father, but what can you tell about this sailboat here?"

"It is a hobby of mine to build boats and sail. I hope when I retire from Firestone, that this boat will carry me to Brittany, France. It has always been my dream to have this adventure."

"Wow! What a great thing you are doing and I envy you having the skill to build and sail the boats. What an adventure you will have sailing along the west coast of Africa, Portugal, and France!"

"Maybe someday I will take you and teach you to sail on the ocean. It is a wonderful experience to have," promised Augie.

"Deal!" I said, "Wow! What an intriguing tree…what is it called? I haven't seen one around here."

"It's a Norfolk Pine that I planted as a small seedling. Annick and I saw one on a trip to Florida and brought it back here. There are some around but not many. It's a beautiful tree," I made a mental note to find one for my yard as I followed him into a room under his bungalow- Augie's radio shack. (When home on leave I did find this tree and brought six seedlings back and planted them in the bachelor compound.)

Last Saturday night at the Big Club, I had met Augie and Annick Le Monze and he was the ham operator that Gail Ruff had told me about my first day in Liberia. Augie and Annick were French and were impressed that we had lived in France from 1961 to 1964. Dad was the first American to earn a French call sign after WWII. Augie had invited me over today having told me to cable Dad what band width to locate him on. Augie's shack was filled with radio equipment and books and on one wall was a large map with pins stuck in showing his many radio contacts around the world.

Presently, my Dad's ham shack was in our finished basement but, growing up, he always had a shack somewhere in our home. I remembered listening to Dad tapping away on his key pad communicating to hams all over the world. Hearing the sounds and rhythms of Morse code lulled me to sleep many a night. Dad also had a huge map with pins and a bulletin board that displayed his recent QSL confirmation postcards that the amateurs exchanged after a radio contact had been made. Dad enjoyed this hobby and it also was something he did while in the Air Force. Today, Augie was going to try to raise Dad and we would talk over the radio waves!

"Augie, I am so excited by the opportunity to talk to my parents and I hope the weather will let us make the connection. I sent a radiogram to him on Monday telling what band width you would be using and the Zulu time. (Zulu was the radio transmission articulation of the letter Z and was the time referred to as GMT-Greenwich Mean Time. It was the universal time used in radio communication.) I'm keeping my fingers crossed that we'll raise him."

Augie fired up his transmitter and tuned his rig (radio) and had a pencil and paper ready to begin the contact. I sat on the edge of a chair practically tearing my hair out with excitement.

"Oui, bien sur…CQ…CQ…CQ…this is EL… calling W3… CQ…CQ…CQ…this is EL… calling W3…" Augie repeated over and over tuning the radio in and even moving the antenna. QRL de El… calling W3… QRL de EL…calling W3… (means open radio line looking for ham)

But no luck. We waited 5 minutes and he repeated the call. Then another 5 minutes. And then another 5 minutes. I was sweating and almost ready to cry when the air waves crackled and a voice came through.

I about fell off my chair. It wasn't Dad's voice but it was one that was familiar...

"EL... EL... EL... this is K3S... John's the name. I know W3... and he lives near by. I know he is working band width looking for his YL" (young lady-me!)

"QSL QSL QSL (I understand you) I have good copy on you. YL is sitting here waiting for W3... contact. Do you have phone patch capabilities? Repeat. Do you have phone patch capabilities?" Augie spoke clearly into the mike as the tension gripped me and I held my breath.

"Roger that EL... I am calling Vince now."

"Oh, my goodness, I know John! He's a friend of Dad's!" I said trying to contain my excitement.

Augie asked me if I knew the protocol on using a phone patch.

"Yes, yes, I do!" and then I heard Dad talking to John.

"El... this is K3S... using phone patch with Vince here. Over."

"Roger that," said Augie. "Passing mike to YL over."

"Dad, hi, I'm here and thank you John for making the contact with my parents for me. Over."

Dad, Mom, and I talked via the phone patch for about 15 minutes. John's QTH (location) was perfect as Dad couldn't raise Augie from his rig. That was okay by me as we were still able to talk! Over the next three years Augie made many radio contacts with my dad via John allowing a little bit of home to come to me here in Liberia. I was happy.

A cottony fog wrapped the school and the humidity beaded up on our sticky bodies. We were having reading group in school when a Liberian lady shuffled by our classroom carrying a huge oversize enamel basin on her head. She was dressed in a purple and green lappa around her waist and an orange and brown one around her head. She wore no shirt or bra and stood by the door calling one word, "Banana."

We paid no heed and she raised her voice repeating, "Banana," and this time much louder. Edwin spoke up and said, "Miss Mobilia, that is the Banana Lady and all the teachers buy fruit from her."

"Fruit? Edwin, I don't think so right now," and turning towards the Banana Lady, I said, "We are busy now and it is not time for our snack break. Please come back later," I told the children to get back to reading.

We all jumped as a louder command thundered into the room-the Banana Lady had moved down and was now pressed against the screen door to our classroom. "BA na Na!" she screamed at the top of her lungs.

My students giggled and Leonie spoke up, "Banana Lady won't go away until you buy something from her."

"Let's read and forget about the Banana Lady. Jimmy please continue..." I couldn't finish the sentence as Banana Lady shook the screen door with fierce determination and began to chant.

"BA NA NA," boomed her voice and then came a low, deep, and evil guttural rolling demand, "BAAA NAAA NAAA! BAAA NAAA NAAA! BAA NAA NAAA!" Banana Lady continued to repeat over and over and I realized I had lost control and couldn't regain it with her chanting. By now, my class was laughing out loud and I joined in. So, I finally asked, "Who wants to barter with her?"

"Edwin speaks her dialect, let him," piped up Regan.

I got up, fetched my purse, and gave two nickels and one penny to Edwin stating, "Edwin, you must buy as many bananas as you can from Banana lady as I want everyone to have a banana."

With the money in hand, the chanting of "Banana" and shaking of the screen door from our guest ceased. Edwin spoke very quickly in her language and the class laughed when they saw she wasn't even selling bananas, but had four pineapples in the large enamel bowl. Edwin purchased a big ripe one and came back with six cents change. What a deal!

We made the experience a math problem and I cut the pineapple up passing it out to the class while we heard Banana Lady next door at Billie Darsey's room. Susan told me that the Banana lady only knows one word in English and won't leave until you buy from her. Many of the students living close to the school all had stories about her and yes, their parents or house boys bought her fruit. It seemed to me that she would use muscle if you didn't buy from her. Her loud threatening "banana" word sent chills down my spine thinking of what she'd do if I didn't buy something from her...isn't this how the Mafia got started? Usually once a week or so, the Banana Lady came by selling any type of fruit to all the classrooms. I loved to tease her by saying, "Look Ma, you have no bananas today!" Edwin translated the joke and so began this little weekly diversion.

Later that day, I was sharing my experience about how Mr. Le Monze made radio contact with my parents and me. I was explaining using a phone patch and his ham radio when suddenly the entire class gasped and some pointed at me while others put their fingers to their lips indicating me to be quiet.

"What's the matter?" I whispered taking their clue.

Just then the children slowly got up and without turning, backed up but still pointing at me. I slowly turned my head and came face to face with a lime green skinny snake hanging from the lights! Green Mamba conjured quickly from my memory banks. Okay, I thought-keep cool. This guy hasn't killed a frog but was looking for its dinner and no way was I going to accommodate him especially since I didn't have a gallon of bleach with me. Was I crazy? How could I make jokes when my life was in danger? Next flash, a command, don't run, when every bone in my body was telling me to do just that. Somehow, I kept myself together and ever so slowly side stepped away, keeping one eye on the snake and my other eye on the students who were now in a safe huddle at the back of the classroom.

"Children, go out the back door. Walter, go and get Zanga. Tell him about the snake. Jimmy, please go and tell Mr. Smith to come now."

The children quickly and quietly exited the classroom with Christopher holding the door so as not to slam it and startle the snake. I was following suit but still not breathing. Finally, Zanga, the seventh and eighth grade boys showed up with a long glass snake catcher tube. Some of the boys had brooms and one had a rake. Sure, take the snake out with a broom-hum...well, better than bleach.

"Miss Mobilia, we're here to get the snake, don't worry. Is everyone okay?" asked John Carmichael as they entered my room.

Quickly and efficiently, the boys holding their brooms and rake, surrounded the green mamba while Zanga trapped it in the glass tube.

"Hooray! Zanga got the snake! He's our hero!" Roared my class peeking through the windows slats as Mr. Smith came running down to our room. Soon the rest of the teachers and students were outside my room talking excitedly. Yep, apparently the visiting snake was a big to do and a pretty rare thing to happen. Just my luck that the green mamba chose my classroom to make its debut at the Firestone Staff School and get recorded in its history! Must have heard I didn't have my bleach with me.

"We got the snake and the school's bleach was spared!" shouting a grinning Andy Elam. Crazy news travels quickly I thought and would I ever live down the bleach and snake caper?

Mr. Smith asked the eighth grade girls to make snake soup and it was to be our entire school's snack for tomorrow. The girls cheered along with the rest of the school. Zanga would drive the four girls to the Firestone Store and Ten Dollar Camp to buy any supplies they needed. I was looking forward to snake soup as that and fish soup were among my favorite Liberian foods.

The teachers were trying to calm the students down and get them back into the classrooms when a piercing wolf whistle coming from Jim Smith quickly got our attention. "To celebrate that everyone is safe I am giving the whole school an extra recess!"

Anyone who has been in a classroom either as a student or as a teacher knows it is next to impossible to regain the children's attention after an exciting snake event and recess announcement. Simply put…we enjoyed the break that lasted until the students were dismissed for the day!

The teachers were lined up by the brick wall watching the students race tarantulas when Myna Butler remarked, "Only in Liberia would these races happen and we allow the students to have them."

"Well, the children have grown up with this danger and aren't afraid," Billie Darsey added.

"Yes, no one would believe this back home! Wait till I write home about the green mamba in my classroom! My friends will be in awe!" I said.

Jim joined our group and reminded us that ACS (American Cooperative School in Monrovia) had sent a letter again requesting that our students pen pal with them.

"Wonderful!" said Myna with the veteran teachers echoing their approval.

Billie explained that the schools had been doing this for some years with a picnic as the culmination of the project at the end of the year. I really liked this idea and said I'd get my class started on the letters tomorrow.

Slowly the days blended into weeks and Open House was scheduled at school in early November. My students worked very hard to make their autobiography book by collecting their family traditions and stories. Each student's book was unique showing his or hers writings and drawings. We got the classroom set up with displays of some of the activities we had done. The wall between Billie Darsey's room and mine was pulled back to make the huge room for parents and students to meet for the beginning of the Open House.

The eighth graders made a school book listing all the children that attended the Staff School for their parents. That evening, the eighth grade students were posted at the doors welcoming and passing these booklets out as parents entered the large room to claim seats waiting for Jim Smith to begin. He introduced all the teachers grade by grade and adjourned the parents to their children's individual rooms. Even though I only had thirteen students, it felt like I had a hundred as I was swamped by parents, students, and their siblings. The eighth grade boys had moved Billie Darsey's and my desks back in place for the parents to gather around. Yes, my students' autobiographies were a big hit!

For weeks, I had been anxious about meeting the breast grabbing mother-yep her son was in my classroom and so far the past few weeks I hadn't run into her anywhere. Nothing to worry about. Louise Grabner didn't seem to remember the impression she had made by grabbing my breasts that day I first arrived here in Liberia. In fact she was wonderfully sweet and happy about what her son was learning so far in my classroom. Gee, all that worry for nothing, I thought. The rest of Open House went smoothly and afterwards, the teachers went over to Billie Darsey's bungalow for snacks and drinks. Soon, the evening was over and I was back at home getting ready for bed and happy the Open House was a success.

>Dear Mom Dad Stop
>Good talking via radio Stop
>Banana lady fruity Stop
>Green Mamba dropped in Stop
>We ate it in soup Stop
>Hugs African kisses Stop
>Kathleen

The gang at Coo Coo Nest Restaurant in
Kakata, Liberia

Chapter 19

Coo Coo Nest and The Big Club

Saturday morning brought a dark gray dawn seeping through the window slats awakening me. I wasn't going to let this ruin the little trip I had planned with Ralph, Joe, Jim, and another car full of friends. We were driving up to Kakata to visit the Tubman Museum and Zoo. After getting ready, I went outside to wait being picked up. I marveled at how the mist hung in the air dancing around the trees and flowers and I moved about my garden enjoying the heavy scent of gardenia and snapping photos of the delicate blossoms of the spider lilies that bordered my circular driveway. I heard Jim's horn tooting for Ralph, Joe, and then for me. I was climbing into the back seat with Joe when Jim made a shocking revelation.

"You know guys, this will be my first time to go off the

Plantation and not be headed to the beach or Monrovia!"

"What?" I was flabbergasted! "You have lived here for ten years and never had the desire to explore?"

Ralph spoke up stating the same thing however he had only been in Liberia a little over 3 years and of course Joe was newly arrived.

"So, Jim, you are saying this is your first ever trip upcountry? What about other Firestone people, do they travel up country or is this a rarity?"

"Don't know, but I never had any interest in struggling to buy gas, food, or find a bathroom as I hear it is a challenge when traveling upcountry. I like the conveniences of modern city living."

"Challenge? I guess that's what I like about traveling. Anyhow, in Kakata there are bathrooms and a good restaurant across from Tubman's Museum and Zoo so, there is nothing to worry about."

Turning down the road to Cotton Tree and Division 41, we dodged heavy bullets of rain and then light teasing rains. Joe's camera was going at a fast clip to preserve this memory as we travelers chatted about everything. Yep, it was going to be a great trip!

An hour and a half or so later we were pulling up to 26 Gate and once signed off the Plantation, history was made for my three friends-we were now headed for adventure!

Sometime later, we parked in front of the cement stairs that lead to Tubman's Museum which was at one time his country residence. It now belonged to his family as President Tubman had died in 1971. The front of the building had a low stone wall holding a variety of flowering plants and bushes. Everything was neat and beautifully landscaped. The guards each carrying a long rifle, took our money, and let us roam around the many rooms to enjoy President Tubman's wonderful collection of memorabilia mostly given to him by visiting dignitaries. The workmanship using gold, silver, and precious gems was incredible! And the massive ivory carved tusks-I just couldn't imagine how huge the elephant had been! The rooms were decorated in simple modern furniture which allowed the items to be shown at their best. Our cameras were kept busy and all too soon we were exiting the museum and headed for the zoo.

The path that led to the zoo passed by a playground of sorts. Besides the monkey bars and swings, there were two cars cemented in a platform for children to climb all over and play "driving".

"Oh, my goodness. One of the cars is a Ford Zephyr like my 49 D!" I said.

"Yep, you could donate your car to the Tubman Farm when it goes which I believe will be soon," laughed Ralph.

"Hey, my car still has a lot of exploring left in it!"

All of a sudden, I got the idea…

"Hey, Jim, what if we planned a Firestone Staff School field trip up here? The museum is so fascinating to see and hopefully the zoo is also, but the children would really get a blast out of this playground! Once you check out the Coo Coo Nest restaurant and bathrooms, perhaps it could be done…what are your thoughts?"

"Great minds think alike, as I was just pondering the possibility of a field trip, too. Let's check out everything but, I think it could be a go." Jim added.

Ralph and Joe both agreed that students would really enjoy playing here and touring the museum. We headed to the gate entrance of the Zoo. Immediately we saw the large playful elephants lopping up to the fence in search of peanuts which we had in hand. Next we watched the pygmy hippos rolling in the muddy pond. These hippos were only found in West Africa with Liberia being their dominant habitat. They were about a third the size of the regular hippos that I had seen before in the many other zoos I had visited. Some day I hope to take a safari in East or South Africa. For now, this will do. Monkeys, apes, small deer, and snakes were all interesting to see when I saw a bush cat like my Leopold! This one was fully matured and paced around his tall fenced in area. He looked to be about 30 to 35 pounds.

"Hey, guys, look how big Leopold is going to become!" I called running up to the bush cat's area.

"Haven't I been telling you that your cat needs to be out of your home and living outside? Remember, he is a wild animal!" Ralph spoke in a fatherly tone.

"I know, I know, and he will be out pretty soon as Leopold is tearing up things and playfully scratching my legs. I know he has to be outside all the time and especially now that I see how big he will become. You must remember he is only about 14 weeks old and still needs my loving care."

We saw the huge tortoises and got to pet the lions! Inside the museum, we had seen a stuffed lion and had asked about him. The soldiers told us President Tubman had received Simba as a gift from his good friend Haile Selassie of Ethiopia. Simba was his favorite lion and that is why President Tubman had him stuffed.

The ostriches approached us in a friendly way looking for food and allowed us to pet their heads and backs. I was picking up some beautiful discarded plumes when I saw the enormous egg over by some rocks. Why, I believe it was an ostrich egg! I asked one of the soldiers if I could buy the egg and he said yes. Well, I left with three fresh eggs for breakfast! The soldier said I could feed many people. I told the guys they were invited for scrambled egg breakfast tomorrow at my place. I was going to find out exactly how many people I could feed.

Once the tour of the zoo was completed, we walked across to the Coo Coo Nest Restaurant for lunch. Jim and I checked out the bathrooms and found them to be acceptable to handle our large school group. Yes, it looked good for a field trip up here! Jim remarked that he thought sometime before the school's 3 week break in mid December would be a good time with the dry season beginning and the rains slowing down. He would set the field trip into motion on Monday morning and tell the teachers about the adventure giving them time to plan a variety of activities to do before and after the school trip. I was excited about the school's field trip!

Our warm Club Beers arrived and we chowed down on our grilled hamburgers and then we headed back to the Plantation. Once home, we had about an hour to get ready because we all were going to the Big Club on Division 16 for dinner and a movie.

"Movies come in once a month and just about everyone goes no matter what was showing," informed Jim to Joe.

"I think I read in the *Firestone News* that *Auntie Mame* is the movie tonight which is much better than the *Three Stooges* that was shown last time," said Ralph.

"Joe, I missed the last 2 movies because I was busy and I don't care what's showing. I am anxious to see the Big Club after all the stories I have heard!" I added.

"Like what," asked Joe?

"Like the incredibly wild parties there. For example one story was about a bachelor who was leaving the Big Club rather intoxicated, peeled out of the driveway, missed a curve and drove his truck off the road, tumbled down the mountainside missing many trees and boulders. Somehow he survived without any scratches and only a few dents on the truck! People said it's a wonder he lived to tell about it!"

"Hey, Jim, wouldn't be you, would it?" asked Ralph.

"No way, but I know who it was and let's say it was a good thing he married a certain fourth grade teacher as she put a short tight leash on him. Yep, probably saved his life marrying her, I believe!" Jim said laughing.

"No kidding? I could see how she rules with an iron fist as sometimes, I'm afraid to do anything wrong for fear of what she'd do to me!"

"You and me both and I'm her boss!" added Jim to my comment and dropped us off at our bungalows.

Jim returned to our compound an hour later smelling of cologne and whistling as he picked us up for the drive to the Big Club. Buckets of rain pelted down and continued for about 15 minutes. Then, as suddenly as it had started, the rain stopped.

"This rain is never ending. I am sick and tired of it!" yelled Ralph.

"Well, from what I hear, we better wish for the rains to continue than deal with no rain for months! Billie has told me that the ponds, rivers, and lakes dry up and the winds spin the dusty dirt about and it becomes difficult to breathe. We have to buy water to drink, brush our teeth, cook, clean, etc. Yep, that sounds really fun to me!" I responded and Ralph quieted down remembering the past dry seasons.

As we rode through the divisions, I commented on how difficult it must have been for those early pioneers to clear the bush and plant the rubber trees and this was all done by hand.

"We really have it pretty good compared to those people. Many of the older staff employees came here in the 30s, 40's and 50's. These men made the Plantation what it is today, successful in the rubber business," Jim reported. "They worked hard and played hard, but the work got done. Sure stories were told but, much embellishment was done for entertainment. I'm sure there is juicy stuff going around about us all being together for dinner, the beach, and now coming together to the Big Club. People just like to tell stories. We smile and do our jobs which is why we are here."

"Yes, I even have added stuff to some stories," admitted Ralph. "It was all done in fun."

"We are passing Botanical Research Department where Basjaan works," Jim told us. "This is where you can come and select trees and or plants to be planted in your compound or around your bungalow. Just walk around looking at the selections and then request what you want. The crews come out and plant it for you. That's how I did some plantings around my place," Jim said.

"Wow! I want to do something for our compound. My place was pretty well landscaped by Dick Hunter when he was a bachelor. However, I believe the compound does need some work. What do you think Ralph and Joe?"

"I'm all for something pretty and also useful, like fruit trees," said Ralph.

"Yes, me too. I'll come up here with you to make selections," Joe added.

"Done! This will be a great project for us!"

The light was fading as we began our ascent up a huge hill to the Big Club arriving in time to see the sun setting in a red orange ball. Stunning! The Big Club was made of Firestone brick and was one story high with huge French door windows on three sides. The breeze was welcoming and the scents were intoxicating as we made our entrance into the club. A huge group was either eating or up at the bar drinking while waiting for the movie to begin. Children were running all over while others were already in their pajamas ready to fall asleep once the movie started. I remember how my parents did the same thing with my brother and me. We really enjoyed the freedom of fleeting about and in our pajamas no less!

The four of us approached the bar, ordered hamburgers, fries, and Club Beer and stood talking to people who were also waiting for their dinner. I told them that we had gone to Kakata to see Tubman's Museum and Zoo. It was surprising how many people had never been there! The movie was indeed *Auntie Mame* and soon after we had devoured our meal, a bell rang announcing 15 minutes to the movie. Like wildfire, people grabbed chairs and positioned them in front of the screen and quieted their children with bowls of popcorn.

The movie began and when reel one was finished, it had to be rewound on the spool, new reel threaded through the projector, and number two reel was shown. Everyone stretched, went to the bathrooms, or got more to drink while waiting. This was repeated again for reels three and four. I thought the company should spring for three extras reels and rewind all after the show was over, but then the time would be shortened between for snacks and bathroom breaks. Oh, well, looks like this system has worked for many years without me putting in my two cents.

After the movie was over, families left and the Big Club was now for the childless couples and bachelors. Music was played loudly and we danced until we just about dropped! "Arthur Murray" Jim had the women lined up for a professional spin around the dance floor. He was one smooth dancer!

Finally, the evening came to an end and the celebrants poured into their cars and navigated with great deliberation avoiding a repeat of the "unknown bachelor" historic trip down the big hill. Somewhat inebriated, Jim jerked and braked his way down the steep winding road on the hill even though I begged him to let me drive. His stubborn streak prevailed and I prayed our way down.

Finally off killer hill, we slowly drove back to the bachelors' compound, a soft silver luster highlighted the leaves and branches of the rubber trees and the first quarter moon was breathtaking and made for a memorable end to a wonderful day with my friends.

"I am going to get up early tomorrow and meet the Pan Am morning flight from New York. I have heard that once everyone has deplaned, I can enter the cabin to get newspapers and magazines left behind. I met a stewardess last week while at the Hotel's pool. She was the one who told me I can do this. Jim, did you ever do this?"

"On occasion I have, but usually I sleep late and then head to the beach for the day. Hey, ask if they have any milk or fresh vegetables."

"Milk? Yes, great idea! Fresh milk would be a treat after making milk from dry powder and water. I can almost taste the cool milk…," I said in a dreamy way.

"Wait a minute weren't you having us over for scrambled ostrich egg breakfast?" Ralph inquired.

"Yes, of course, I can still meet the plane and get back by 10:30 a.m. and Joseph will fix breakfast for 11:00 a.m. Okay?" I said hoping this appeased the men and their always empty stomachs.

"Deal," Jim answered and Joe and Ralph nodded in agreement.

Before I left for the airport, I took some photos comparing the ostrich eggs and a chicken egg. What an enormous difference! I also drilled a small hole in the bottom of the ostrich eggs and using a knitting needle, I broke the yolk and shook the contents out. The mixture was ready for Joseph to cook for our brunch. I also used a watered down bleach to clean out the inside of the ostrich eggs because I wanted to use them for decorations.

The Pan Am plane arrived between light rain showers and emptied quickly. I hurried across the tarmac, climbed the stairs, and entered the plane. Gosh, it was only ten weeks ago I had exited a Pan Am plane on Sunday, September 2nd and entered Liberia hoping for adventure. I was greeted by Captain John and his crew. No problem in collecting the reading material and one small bottle of milk! What a treat we will have at breakfast, I thought! I thanked the crew and quickly drove back home where Joseph had the table set and the food ready.

The men arrived by 11:00 with Ralph carrying over a huge pitcher of Bloody Marys while Jim brought freshly squeezed orange juice and champagne for Mimosas. The group was in awe over the pint bottle of milk. I poured shot glasses of the precious liquid and we sipped savoring the flavor! In fact the milk was better than the Bloody Marys and Mimosas! The four of us along with both Josephs ate scrambled ostrich eggs. There was even enough left over for Leopold and Joe's dog to enjoy. We all feasted and drank and then left for Caesar's for a day of rest. We surely needed it after the fun packed weekend. The beach had a huge crowd that dove into the newspapers and magazines that I had taken off the plane. They were a big hit!

> Dear Mom Dad Stop
> Visited Coo Coo Nest Stop
> Big Club Stop
> Met Pan Am plane Stop
> Got milk newspapers Stop
> Had ostrich eggs for brunch Stop
> Hugs African kisses Stop
> Kathleen

Field trip to the Tubman Museum and Zoo
in Kakata, Liberia

Bakari painting

Chapter 20

Charlies, Mahjong, and Buchanan

I awoke to thundering rain. Rising and looking out the window slats, I saw the rain blowing in horizontal sheets across the yard and road toward Ralph's and Basjaan's bungalows. The winds were whipping the rubber trees branches low, bowing to the ground. I saw the fuchsia bougainvillea blossoms were strewn about the yard. This looked like an all-day-long tropical rain. How right I was! It continued in sheets. I was driving down to the carpentry shop to get some type of hook to use to hang the art work I had bought after dinner.

Last night, Charlie # 5 drove up to my bungalow and unloaded his many African treasures. I had learned that these traveling salesmen went from house to house selling their wares. This Charlie was spreading his goods under my place with Joseph protesting so loudly that I went downstairs to stop the heated debate before it escalated into something more. At once my eyes saw the still wet paintings done by an artist named Bakari. I just had to have them! Bakari lived in Ten Dollar Camp and his creative spurts were few and far between and so it was difficult to buy his paintings. He usually sold his work when he needed paint. I pretended to ignore the paintings and brought my attention to my anxious Joseph.

"Missy, that man come. I tell him go. Go now. He no go," Joseph was protecting me from this guy and displaying his gun which could or could not be loaded.

"Missy, I Charlie # 5. I bring my store to you to see. I have good good things to buy. See!" He waved his hands about his collection.

"I see. Okay Joseph, you stay here by me and help take care of me. Ya?"

"Ya, Missy I do," Joseph beamed. I knew he was looking for help from Leopold. Of course the cat wasn't to be seen.

"That is a different name you have, Charlie # 5? How do you come to be called that?" I inquired.

"I say, Missy, I Charlie # 5 and many many Charlies come see you. I, the best Charlie! Please, I beg you to keep my name to your breast and no one else. I give you good good prices," he said thumping his chest enthusiastically.

"Hum, I think I hear what you say to me. The Charlies are moving stores…right?"

Laughing, he said, "Ya, Missy, ya, you be my good good customer! Come come see my good good things," Charlie began by pointing to some very large carved elephant tusks.

"I see the elephant tusks are beautifully carved depicting a typical day in Liberian life."

"Ya, Missy, you see here are, the carvers, the weavers, the gold and silver workers, the women cooking, and the farmer digging. The work is the best in all Liberia! I only show the good good work," Charlie #5 stated bowing quite low with a huge grin upon his weathered face.

I slowly walked about inspecting the different types of Liberian art when my eyes finally spied those large colorful oil paintings leaning against the inside wall of my bungalow. I was hooked on the unique haunting eyes of the child who was holding a grapefruit in the painting. I not only wanted it but, I needed it desperately! I quietly looked at Bakari's work from afar remembering what someone had told me about bargaining. I was not to pay great attention to something I really wanted. The Charlie's game was for me to ask prices on something I did not want to buy. Then after lengthy bargaining, I would suggest that I will buy something to make the Charlie's stay worthwhile. I was to make it seem I was doing the Charlie a huge favor by taking this item off his hands today. This is when I would say, "Hum, I can only buy one or two things today and I want to help you out so, I will buy this thing here."

Of course, this would be the thing I had wanted all along. I was told that the Charlie would keep going back to the first thing I asked about and lowered the price for me with me declining and stating that thing was still too dear. I also remembered that I needed to gasp in great pain when I would hear the price of the first item even to the point of falling to my knees and begging him give me his good good price! I did exactly this and was amazed at how much Charlie # 5 enjoyed my bargaining act as he danced around mimicking my pain and stating, "Missy, today is Saturday and I need money to feed my ten children and give to my God in church tomorrow. Please, I beg you Missy; help this old Charlie make his Saturday!"

So, the bargaining game continued until I bought the two oil paintings for five dollars each-the paintings that I wanted in the first place. Surprisingly, Charlie # 5 gave me a dash for helping him with his Saturday! It was a small bronze mask of a country devil that I loved immediately! We "Liberian shook" hands and I promised to be his good good customer as long as he gave me his good good prices. Charlie, smiling from ear to ear, nodded in agreement.

Now, here I am in the carpentry shop in search of hooks to hang my painting treasures. The Liberian went looking for the hooks when I heard...

"Bonjour Mademoiselle Mobilia! Je m'apelle Michel." (Hello

Miss Mobilia! I am Mike.)

"Bonjour, Michel….je suis Kathleen." (Hello, Mike…I am Kathleen.)

"Missy, this is the thing you want?" The Liberian voice interrupted.

"Yes, I believe it will work…er…what do you think Michel? I want to hang two paintings in my dining/living room. Will this work?" The French flowed from my lips and he suggested something else and would hang the paintings for me if I wanted.

"Certainement! Merci beaucoup! (Certainly! Thank you very much!) Do you know where I live?

"Mais, oui! J'accompagner immediatement." (Of course! I can come immediately.) He answered collecting whatever he needed to hang my paintings.

Michel or Mike as most people called him laughed when he saw my car, "Jim Smith couldn't get you better transportation?"

I explained, "Jim did, however, I liked 49 D and the independence it gives me. Plus it's fun to drive!" We stood comfortably chatting until there was a lapse in the sheeting rain to make a dash to our vehicles. I learned that he was the manager of Firestone's heavy equipment; bulldozers, tree walkers, road graders, and such and had been with the company for over 20 years.

Leopold was nestled in a cactus plant on the porch and Mike marveled that I had tamed a wild bush cat. Leopold was now about 4 months old and growing steadily. Quickly Mike hung my paintings and we continued to talk while drinking the lukewarm tea Joseph had brewed for us. I told him where my family lived in France. He had an interesting career having worked for a French road-making company in Mali, West Africa during the 50's and 60's. Mike was married and had two children, their son was in 6th grade and daughter living back in France. They had just returned from leave and were at the Guest House for a couple of days while his wife Gabby and their houseboys got the bungalow in running shape. All too soon, he was leaving. I was finally alone and quickly began to correct school papers before my dinner plans with a student's family.

Once ready, I drove 49 D out past the Firestone Hospital to the Agoncillo home for a dinner party. Christopher was in my class and his family had invited me. I followed the road going through the Plantation from one division after another. I was happy to have driven during the daylight and able to have the sun behind my back painting the rubber trees and hills in shades of reds, purples, and at last, coating everything in soft silver luster with the rising moon. I inhaled deeply and became charged with renewed energy filled with the ever constant changing colors and tones of light. Liberia burned deep in my soul!

The Agoncillo children greeted me and showed me around the outside of their bungalow. I saw the places they held secret and dreamed their dreams. Once inside, I was introduced to many other Filipinos, some worked on the Plantation while the rest worked in Monrovia. Dinner was a buffet of delicious foods and afterwards tables were cleared and beautiful small suitcases appeared. Inside the suitcases were unusual colored tiles with characters and numbers on one side. These tiles were slid onto the tables, turned in one direction showing only the solid side. I realized they were going to play a game they called Mahjong. They used strategies with these tiles of dragons, birds, flowers, bamboo, and Chinese writing. I sat at one table with Ming and Pepe Agoncillo trying to understand the many game rules. After about one hour, I still couldn't follow the game. All I heard was Pongs, Kongs, and Mahjong. I tried hard to understand as everyone was extremely excited and it looked like loads of fun! I was invited by Ming's sister to come in two weeks to her home in Monrovia for dinner and Mahjong. I accepted hoping to learn this interesting game. Pepe said that a friend, Noli, would pick me up on Saturday and bring me into Monrovia.

Driving in and out of rain showers, I finally arrived home to find Joseph sitting at the table with Leopold. Right away Joseph told me excitedly, "That cat, he humbug me too much! Joseph no sleep! Take cat now!"

"Joseph, I pay you to watch the bungalow when I am gone and not to sleep. So, don't tell me the cat humbugs you. I, the boss lady now hear me!"

"Ya, Missy, I hear. I no like that cat!" he said stomping off to his room. But later that night while in a deep sleep, I heard a loud sound. Jumping up, I ran to the porch calling for Joseph. There he was with his rifle pointed to the sky releasing another bullet. Yes, that was the sound that woke me up.

"Joseph, what are you doing? Are there rogues about? What are you shooting at?"

"Missy, I see people. They come here to take you. I shoot them! Look! There they are!" He spoke while pointing his rifle into the dark space by the side of the house.

"Go! I come now!" he hollered.

I ran down the stairs towards the people. However, I couldn't see anyone. Or hear anyone fleeing. But, Joseph stood his ground determined to protect my place and me. He continued yelling at the people or rogues and then the gun blasted off again.

Basjaan, Ralph, and Joe came running up the hill with their watchmen. They saw no one. Ralph sent the watchmen back to their bungalows. He said, "There probably weren't any people in the first place. Joseph must feel you're upset with him and might sack him. So, he sees people and shoots a few times to show you how good a watchman he is. My watchman does this every so often to guarantee his job and show how valuable he is."

"No kidding! I did have words with him when I came home. So, perhaps that could be why he did this tonight. I will handle Joseph. Sorry about all this and waking you up," I said climbing the stairs to head back to bed when Ralph suggested that we come down to his place for drinks. "Drinks? Sure, why not!"

We followed. But before I left, I told Joseph what a good, good watchman he was and thanked him for taking care of my bungalow. Joseph grinned from ear to ear and went happily to sit on his chair guarding my home.

We drank, sang, and danced until the sunrise and then gobbled a huge breakfast made by Jeremiah. What was an abrupt ending to a nights rest ended up being a fun-wee-hour-dawn-party that ended at Marshall Beach. Ah, Liberia!

> Dear Mom Dad Stop
> Played game Stop
> Mahjong Stop
> Hugs African kisses Stop
> Kathleen

A week later, Bart Witteveen Sr. and Aldo Holzl were scheduled to give me tennis lessons on the red clay courts near Central Office when the sky opened up and poured.

Bart remarked, "Notice the rains are shorter and not as often, Kathleen? A good sign that dry season is beginning. Rain should be letting up soon so just wait in your car."

I had been taking tennis lessons for the past few weeks and played in light rain or the humid heat and I enjoyed the game. Both men were terrific players and great instructors. Often, I went down to the courts and practiced hitting balls with young Liberian boys. They were very good and so patient with me trying to remember how to hit the ball and hold the racket. These kids also took lessons from Bart and Aldo. They decided to leave and return another time and I stayed hoping the rains would let up so I could hit some balls. While sitting in my car waiting, Mike Martin pulled up in his green pickup and waved.

"Bonjour Katsy! I didn't know you played tennis… Perhaps we could play a game sometime."

"Mike, I'm a beginner and not very good. Would you want to serve some balls so I could get more practice?"

"Bien sur! I also can give you lessons. How about tomorrow early morning?"

"That sounds wonderful but not tomorrow as I plans to travel and explore Buchanan. Ever been there?" I asked.

"Yes of course. Er…you drive yourself?"

"Yes. Last week I drove to Little Bassa on the Atlantic coast.

The area is very different than Monrovia and I've heard Buchanan also has a seaport that I want to visit."

"Of course! Make sure you find the harbor master, Bill, and introduce yourself explaining that you work for Firestone. Also, say you know me. He will give you a tour of the harbor if he has time."

"Magnificent! Will do! Merci beaucoup!" I said au revoir as I drove away.

While at the Motor Pool getting gasoline, Jerry Elam came up to me concerned that I had already driven over 800 miles in September and October and this month I was very close to the limit with a week to go. He wanted to know how I had used up my allotted miles and suggested that I ask Jim Smith to sign me up for additional miles. I thought that was a great idea and drove off with two gas cans filled for my trip tomorrow knowing that I would be adding about 200 more miles with the trip to Buchanan. I hoped Jim was able to grant more miles otherwise, I'd continue to disconnect the odometer when I was close to my allotted mileage and buy my own gasoline.

Joe had our little group over for dinner at his bungalow. His place was shaping up nicely with the FPCo borrowed curtains and some other items and he had added many interesting new African artifacts that he had purchased from the Charlies over the past few weeks. It was fascinating to see how we all had decorated our bungalows. I asked the guys if they wanted to join me on the trip to Buchanan but surprisingly, no one took me up on my offer. Looked like it would be a solo trip. I excused myself early walking home by starlight from billions of stars. It was amazing the number of stars and intensely dark sky we had here compared to the light polluted skies back home. Joseph greeted me with a long face and again gave me a report on Leopold and how my cat had humbugged him as he loudly complained his way to his room for the evening.

By 6:00 a.m. I was driving through Cotton Tree and headed to Buchanan. I made great time arriving at the seaport about 7:30 a.m. and quickly located the Harbor Master's office. Bill was a tall, lean middle-aged Swede with weathered bronze skin and brown hair. He offered me his hand in a vigorous handshake. He was surprised to meet me and more surprised that I had driven from Firestone alone. When I told him that Mike Martin sent his hellos he invited me for a tour of the harbor. He didn't have to ask me twice and before I knew it we were chugging along in the tug passing many different size Fanti canoes and headed through the entrance of the harbor and out to sea to bring in a large tanker ship just outside the entrance of the harbor. What a thrill it was to come alongside the tanker and slowly push it in. Up and down the tug moved with the swells of the waves and slowly the tanker was pushed into the dock. We were invited to have a tour of the Italian tanker which flew a Liberian flag. I learned that more ships and tankers worldwide flew the Liberian or Panamanian flag because of their low taxes. Bill and I were also invited to share lunch with the crew and we feasted on cheese ravioli, spaghetti with meatballs, and a delicious Cabernet Sauvignon! I hadn't realized how much I missed Italian food and my mother's cooking! The crew was proud to show me their ship and explain their jobs and was pleased to learn that I was half Italian. Luckily, most of the crew spoke broken English and with my broken Italian, we got along fine. It was an interesting learning experience especially when the captain gave me a tide chart and a map of the coast marking some seaside villages for me.

  All too soon I said thank you and my goodbyes and headed back to Firestone Plantation but, not before detouring to Little Bassa. Hopefully I would be able to buy some fresh fish. Arriving in Little Bassa I joined in a meal with the villagers eating smoked fish and fish soup. The people were celebrating today's good haul by dancing by a huge open fire on the beach. Drums pounded out a hypnotic beat while warm tropical breezes gently cooled the hot dancing bodies. I joined in trying to do the steps but failed miserably and collapsed on the warm sand to just watch and clap. What wonderful people the Liberians are I thought and smiled at my good fortune of being in Liberia.

  I headed back to the Plantation with the sun sinking into streaks of reds, oranges, and purples with my fish and great memories of this super day.

Dear Mom Dad Stop
Went to port of Buchanan Stop
Met Italian sailors Stop
Ate food miss Mom's cooking Stop
Danced on beach Stop
Hugs African kisses Stop
Kathleen

Italian ship docked in the Buchanan Harbor

Visits from the "tiny beggars" were on all major holidays

Chapter 21

Red Paisley Drapes, The Pass, and Tuna Turkey

Life had fallen into a smooth routine and I was enjoying many dinner parties and meeting people from countries around the world. Everyone was here for the rubber business. We worked and played hard and with no TV and infrequent mail from home, some went quite nuts. Sometimes, one of us would go into a screaming rant and people around them would simply keep their distance but, would always make sure the person couldn't harm themselves or others. We were family and took care of each other as for example…Jim Smith's drapes.

Today, Margaret Hedrick and I were headed to Monrovia to look at some fabric she had seen in the German store. Margaret, a blonde, was a former Pan Am stewardess and married to a Scotsman. While dining at Jim Smith's last week, Margaret thought that some statement drapes would look fantastic framing the enormous window overlooking Hydro Falls.

"I know just what would be perfect," Margaret exclaimed. "I saw what I think would fit the bill. How about you discuss this with Jim since he'll listen to your ideas."

I did just that telling Jim how some dramatic drapes would frame his windows perfectly. Unbelievably, Jim agreed. He really liked the suggestion and money wasn't a problem. Do what I want. Whoa, spending someone else's money; now, this I liked!

So, here Margaret and I were shopping for the fabric at the German Store in Monrovia. I was enthusiastic when I saw what Margaret had selected. The huge 12 inch paisley design in true red on white fabric really was an eye opener and definitely would get everyone's attention when entering Jim's bungalow. We bought the necessary yardage and after more shopping at Water Side, headed to Oscar's Restaurant for dinner. Over the usual delicious meal prepared by Oscar, we discussed not showing Jim the fabric.

"I think I want to go for the total dramatic wow from Jim when he sees the drapes hung framing the window over the Hydro Falls!" Margaret said excitedly.

"Oh…I agree. Do you have a place in mind where we could cut it? It would have to be where no one could see and tell Jim if we want to keep it a total surprise," I added and then quickly said, "I know, my classroom at night! No one is there except the night watchman. I can dash him something so he doesn't talk. Billie Darsey and I both have 6 foot tables that would make a terrific place to lay out, measure, and cut the fabric."

"Deal," said Margaret.

Our meal was finished and so was the day as the setting sun's warm colors were reflecting off the ocean. It was a terrific end to a productive day of shopping.

We headed back to the Plantation, when the driver veered off the road and was headed to the infamous lagoon that Jim had taken me to when I first arrived in Liberia. Margaret and I had partially disrobed and we were dancing in the warm water when she approached me trying to kiss me. I was shocked and didn't quite know how to handle her approach. I had heard stories that some people had relations with the same sex. This wasn't for me and I hadn't seen her pass coming. I thought the lagoon stop was simply to cool off from the heat of the day.

"Gee, Margaret, I'm not interested," I continue explaining why. "I know it's the 70's and the sexual revolution and all, but I'm not interested in even exploring these types of choices."

She kept trying as though she hadn't heard me.

"Stop, please leave me alone," I said jumping backwards. "Margaret, you really don't want to do this. It's the liquor talking and what would your husband say?"

"Husband? We have an open marriage. Anything goes," she slurred dropping face first onto the sand. The liquor had taken effect as she had passed out before her head hit the sand.

Somehow, the driver and I managed to get Margaret onto the back seat of the car and I rode up front listening to her snoring loudly on the way back to the Motor Pool. I phoned her husband to come take her home and called it a night. What a night it was, I thought. As I drove home, I wondered how to handle being around Margaret after her pass? We would be together cutting the fabric at my school, certainly be at the same parties, and along with many other couples, we were helping put on a play called "Sesame Street" for the children. All costumes were made and final practices were winding down, but, I felt I needed a plan just in case.

We scheduled a time to measure and cut Jim's fabric for Margaret to take home and sew. Thank goodness, I didn't have any "passing" problems with Margaret. I believe she has forgotten all about it.

Thanksgiving morning before the sun rose, I had a lesson on the Liberians' unique way of celebrating this holiday and in fact all American and Liberian holidays. I was awakened to banging on pots and pans with sticks and some crazy chanting by small children.

"Ole man beggar, tiny beggar…" over and over they chanted from a safe distance as they didn't know where Leopold was. The ever increasingly chant continued until I went onto my porch. The kids clamored to the bottom of my stairs where Leopold jumped onto the screen door shooing away the noisy kids. However, not for long, as they continued to shout and beat the pans until I came out with some small change. Paying the "beggars" got this group to move on but, others kept coming. Yep, that "ole man beggar" came at all holidays and always very early in the morning.

The bachelors had chipped in and purchased a turkey from the states. A Pan Am crew person had brought it in for us. Ralph's houseboy said he knew how to cook turkey having done it many many times for his previous bosses. I baked pumpkin and key lime pies for the bachelor dinner. Everyone was contributing some other part for our dinner. Our stomachs were already anxious for our special meal.

With everything ready except preparing and cooking the turkey which Jeremiah was in charge of doing and after the early awakening from the tiny beggars, we headed to the beach to enjoy the sun and freedom from the tiny beggars. Lying on the beach soaking up the sun's rays, I inquired, "Have any of you received letters of recommendations from women coming to your bungalows? Because in the past few days, Liberian men have been lining up under my bungalow with letters of references for me to read and select someone to ahh...well...and so, I decided to read some. Well, the first letter I read, I about died! It explained in great detail how he could service me in a sexual manner!"

The guys roared as they always were getting these, but from women and once in awhile from men.

"Hey guys, some of the letters described what he would do to me and many told about their appendage's size! I was especially shocked to read about how big some were! Another young Liberian simply told Joseph to come get him anytime for 'the Missy'. And yes, they were also signed from the women that wrote the letters! I read everyone trying not to laugh while thanking them for their time and said goodbye. Guess, women have their own 'Ten Dollar' person," I laughed.

"You can get your watchman or houseboy to keep them away, as they will flock to the young missy's place," Jim laughed. "Well, that's if you really are rejecting them. Perhaps you'd prefer a Liberian and not have any emotional ties that go with a relationship. You'd simply be a modern woman."

"Gosh, let's change the subject and talk about the Sesame Street play we are acting in on Saturday."

Fortunately the conversation swiftly changed and some of us practiced our parts. I was the Cookie Monster. Stephanie Puckhaber from Pan Am had made my costume. Her husband was in charge of Pan Am at the Robertsfield airport and was able to have needed items brought in by a crew member.

We cut our beach time short so as to get to Ralph's and enjoy our special family Thanksgiving dinner. Our well-oiled suntanned bodies climbed the stairs to Ralph's bungalow almost tasting the turkey and trimmings, when our noses sniffed a rancid odor. Upon entering, we quickly covered our noses and fled from his bungalow. Ralph was calling for Jeremiah.

"Jeremiah, come now. What's that smell?" Ralph demanded.

"Turkey, he cooking, Bossman."

"Yes, I know he's cooking! But the smell is horrible! What did you put in the turkey? You make oyster stuffing like I told you?

"Ya, Boss, I make like you told me…turkey he cook."

"Go get the garbage bin for me to see the oyster tin," Ralph ordered.

Jeremiah did just that and we discovered he had used tuna fish and not oysters as directed for the stuffing. We all found out that Jeremiah couldn't read and simply made a mistake-a grave putrid one at that. There went our exquisite turkey dinner with all the succulent trimmings. We piled back into our cars and headed for the Firestone Golf Club for hamburgers as well as the delicious French fries made by Mr. Livingston. I love how we bachelors were able to turn a stinky disaster into a fun evening of eating, drinking, and playing the dice game called French Ten Thousand.

Ah…sweet Liberia once again had WAWAed us.

Dear Mom Dad Stop
Many different ideas Stop
Still good girl Stop
Tuna attack turkey Stop
Hamburger won out Stop
Hugs African kisses Stop
Kathleen

Firestone's ship at Freeport, Liberia

Chapter 22

Freeport, Christmas Day, and New Year's Day

"My house shipment has arrived!" I excitedly told Ralph, Jim, Ellen, Basjaan, and Joe over dinner at Ralph's bungalow. "Well, it's at Freeport and its being loaded this Saturday for the trip to the Plantation and then my bungalow."

This was the last meal we were to share with Basjaan and Ellen as they were going back to The Netherlands. Their bungalow was all packed and they were staying at the Guest House as was customary for staff entering and departing Liberia. We knew that Mike Martin was moving into their bungalow as he was now divorced and the company rules said that single people were to reside in one bedroom bungalows.

I was thrilled to be getting my shipment that left my parents' home in mid-August. It seemed so long ago. Yes, my own things that I had carefully selected with Mom and Dad's advice, boxes of school materials needed for my job, and of course what Firestone had recommended that I buy and bring to the Plantation.

"Can't wait for my shipment to come," Joe added. "Mine was packed the following week in August and probably will arrive on Firestone's next boat coming from Baltimore."

"Let's go into the Freeport and watch the shipment being loaded onto the Firestone lighter. With the school on winter vacation, we can make it a bachelor outing. Supper at the Ducor Palace afterwards. Maybe get a suite and sit back, enjoy the pool, and views of Monrovia," Jim suggested.

"Deal!" We all answered eagerly.

Saturday arrived and Jim drove to the Freeport. We all were excited to be on this little excursion and had decided to leave the Plantation via 15 Gate and head to the Freeport on the Monrovia-Kakata Road. This road was called the back or old road to Monrovia. Getting to 15 Gate was a long drive heading as if going to the Big Club, Hospital, or Botanical Research department. The ride had us going up and down the red hills, through old and newer rubber divisions, and an occasional latex loading station. Since it was so early in the morning, we saw the tappers moving from tree to tree slicing their knife into the rubber's bark to sweat the latex out and let it slowly seep into the small cup hanging on the tree. This route to Monrovia was definitely interesting with so much less traffic than the Harbel-Robertsfield Airport-Monrovia Road. Because Isobel Lokko told me about some first settlers and places they settled, I convinced the guys to visit two of these settlements on this back road into Monrovia.

"Isobel had told me that some original houses were still being lived in," I said as we drove.

In Careyburg, we found a few original houses which mimicked the styles of the ones from the old south in the United States. All were made of wood with wooden shutters and metal roofs. Most were in disarray, but the beautiful Southern style was still present.

Getting to Crozierville proved to be very difficult as the road was in horrible shape and in need of a good grading! We learned that Crozierville had been founded in 1865 by freed slaves from the Caribbean and not the United States. These settlers traveled about 15 miles inland from Monrovia near the Saint Paul River hoping the higher elevations would have cooler temperatures than those by the Atlantic Ocean and the river's mouth.

We selected a place for our picnic lunch outside of Crozierville. I remarked, "I just can't imagine how difficult it would have been for the settlers to travel by ship back to an area that wasn't where they or their family members had been stolen and sold from. In fact, most settlers hadn't any idea what part of Africa they were from. Their move was to try and make an effort for a better way of living than what they had been forced into. Slavery. I never could understand why one group felt they could own another. No one or group should be able allowed to have power over others' lives, liberties, and fortunes. These new settlers faced more hardships in this new land and somehow managed to eke out a living for themselves and heirs." My fellow travelers agreed.

We were about finished with our picnic lunch when Ralph asked, "Hey, Kathleen and Joe, tell us about dinner at the President's Mansion last night." We had gone for dinner in Monrovia at the Executive Mansion where President Tolbert lived and just as Mr. Brown had promised me, A.B. Tolbert was in Europe on business.

"Boy, you can't believe the opulence of the Presidential Mansion!" Joe remarked. "I never thought this kind of world existed here in Liberia. With approximately 95% of the population below poverty, well, it was hard to be there. Don't get me wrong, I was happy to be Kathleen's guest but, I believe I speak for her too, about this."

"I totally agree with Joe! One can't describe the room we ate in. Beautiful china, gold silverware and goblets, and on and on. It was beautiful but, way over the top considering how the locals live. We did meet many diplomats from most of the embassies in Monrovia. The food was delicious and the wine flowed forever it seemed. How handsome Joe looked in his tux! All the men wore tuxes or Liberian Swearing in suits. My eyes hurt from seeing such beauty from the women's fancy gowns, jewels, and the furniture, just everything. We even saw the elevator rumored that could carry the President's limo up to his private residence!"

"We didn't see it open so don't know if that rumor was true or not. Oh yes, the dancing afterwards was great! I found it interesting to watch the Liberian March and more fun to join in, which we did," Joe added.

"President and Mrs. Tolbert began the Dance March by walking, stepping, walking side by side. People then joined in the side by side steps. The group slowly marched around the ballroom, moving their arms up and down, and paraded in this manner. I enjoyed the Dance March too and was thrilled to see Mr. Brown there. He assured me that A. B. Tolbert was in England on business. What a relief, I had worried for nothing. Mr. Brown had delivered on his promise. President and Mrs. Tolbert were the most gracious hosts walking around to greet and talk to everyone. I had a wonderful, memorable time."

"I ditto that," Joe added. "Something that I shall remember."

Back in the car, we continued on the road to the Freeport. We were all excited to see its operations first hand after hearing so much about it. Firestone had two freighters that made the loop from Baltimore, Maryland to Freeport passing each other in the middle of the Atlantic Ocean. Some Firestone employees had made the ocean journey this way. Something to think about I thought.

We drove into the area by the Freeport and noticed that the traffic continued to grow. We passed through the entrance and followed the guy's information on locating the Firestone freighter which loomed ahead. We were here!

I showed my paper work for the crate my items were stored in but, unfortunately, they had been loaded on the lighter and headed back to the Plantation. Also, no way could we get a tour of the Firestone ship even with Jim trying his best to persuade via dashes.

We left Freeport and Bushrod Island and passed over to Providence Island. This was where the first settlers from the United States disembarked and set up the first settlement. Providence Island was at the mouth of the Mesurado River. This settlement would become the country of Liberia after many trials and struggles.

We continued onto United Nations Drive and passed Water Street to Broad Street. Turning right on Broad Street, we climbed the hill to the Ducor Palace Hotel. I had forgotten what a fantastic sight we had as we entered the round circular drive at the hotel's entrance. The men took the responsibility of unloading the car, dashing the valet, and signing in for our suite while I wandered around staring out the huge windows that showed off the views of Monrovia, Freeport, Atlantic Ocean, and West Point. The floor was a white and brown marble. Aqua was the accent color used throughout. I was amazed at the spiral cement stairway and was starting to climb when Ralph called for me to join the group in the elevator to go to our suite which was luxurious. We quickly changed into our swimsuits and headed to the pool for drinks and the promise of a refreshing dip in the water.

"What a way to enjoy Liberia!" Mike said as he drank his Heineken at the pool's bar. We all agreed. Mike had joined our little group of neighbors on this adventure.

The Ducor Palace's pool was shaped like a large foot with the diving board at the heel. The water reflected the cool aqua blue of the pool's tiles. I was so happy to relax and enjoy my umbrella drink and friendship! Dinner was top notch and we danced and danced. I was spoiled by my four male friends and loved all the attention! All too soon the relaxing weekend was over and we drove back home as Ralph, Mike, and Joe had to get back to work. Jim and I had three weeks off for Christmas break. On Monday I found out that my shipment would be delivered to my bungalow on Wednesday.

Later in the week, Ralph, Mike, and Joe took two days off work for our trip to Edina and Buchanan. Mike's and my friend, Bill, the harbor master, and his wife warmly welcomed us and had rooms for us to stay. We spent the day sightseeing Buchanan and the port. We only found a few old settlers' homes near the Buchanan waterfront. The rest of the afternoon was spent lounging on a white sand beach. Because the bay was protected from the wild ocean waves and rip tide we were able to swim and enjoy the warm water.

We knew that Liberian settlements were founded by freed men from the United States and that their house styles were similar to those in the southern United States Colonies when they returned to the African continent. The American Colonization Society started Edina in 1832 at the mouth of the St. John River. These new residents had hoped to make it a port city, however, a few miles down the shore, Buchanan was founded in 1835 by black Quakers from New York and Pennsylvania sponsored by Thomas Buchanan, cousin of USA's President James Buchanan. Today, the port of Buchanan handled the iron ore from the Nimba Mountains and palm butter and oil from the J. P. Getty Palm Plantation. Edina had never developed as hoped.

After church in Buchanan, we headed back for the Plantation with a stop in Edina. It was an ideal place at the mouth of the St. John River. We wandered up and down the streets and enjoyed many more settlers' homes. This town was more preserved than the others we had visited. Perhaps because it was not directly on the ocean and at its mercy. I found Liberian history so exciting and could see my friends were beginning to get hooked, as there was less complaining about the heat and road conditions and more inquiries about the town.

While wandering about, we made a friend of a young girl about 7 or 8 who volunteered be our tour guide. Hawa walked us around pointing out homes, who lived there, and how she was related to them. At the town's center stood a monument dedicated to President Joseph Cheeseman the 12th president of Liberia. Written on it was "President Cheeseman as he was the 1st president of the Liberian Baptist Missionary Convention appointed April 17, 1886". It was enclosed with a small black iron metal fence and two old cannons were aimed at the river to deter approaching invaders. Hawa was animated as she told us the oral history of Edina. We made a quick tour of the two churches and the Masonic Building before walking through the cemetery.

Hawa's history of Edina was impressive and she beamed when we kept saying how we were enjoying her information (or perhaps gossip?). There was this man's wife and his 2nd wife and here were the children of the 1st wife and so on. She knew it all or made a terrific act of storytelling and keeping us spellbound. She was delightful and gave us all small pieces of quartz that was lying on the ground around the town. Waving goodbye, we left Edina. Traveling down the road a little bit, we turned right and headed to the Fanti village that I so love visiting, to buy some freshly caught fish. Our supper was bought and we headed back to the Plantation for our dinner.

Leisurely days during the week before Christmas were spent unpacking my shipment and arranging and rearranging my items. Ralph and I had found a small artificial tree and we decorated it just before Ralph's children arrived from the States. This way, they had a Christmas tree to sit under and open their gifts on Christmas morning. We all were there for coffee before heading up to church. And lest I forget, yes, the tiny beggars visited at the crack of dawn asking for their "Christmas".

After church services at the Chapel on the Hill by the Golf Club, we all headed up to the Carmichaels' home for Christmas brunch. Jack Carmichael was Firestone's general manager at this time and resided there with his family. Just about the entire Staff were present with children running about playing tag while the adults sipped on Bloody Marys or Mimosas..

It was an elegant affair with men in their swearing in suits or regular suits and women in fancy dresses with hats and gloves. Everyone was in the Christmas mood meeting family members that had made the trip to Liberia for a few weeks as Ralph's children had. People queued up to the long white cloth covered tables for food from fresh fruit to egg dishes and there were also many dishes from other countries. We sat at small card tables under the towering shade trees mingling with our Firestone family.

"Billie, I love the Carmichaels' home! It's like stepping back in time onto the Tara Plantation from the book, *Gone with the Wind*."

Billie agreed and said that it was designed after President Jefferson's home, Monticello.

I remarked, "This will be my last time wearing a girdle and hose! This heat is sapping all my energy."

As the party wound down, many headed to the beach or back home for children to play with their new treasures from Santa's visit.

Christmas 1973 brunch at the
General Manager's home

On New Year's Eve we decided to celebrate the incoming 1974 year at a party hosted by the Pan Am crew at the Robertsfield Hotel. We enjoyed barbecue, specialty dishes prepared by Max the hotel's chef, drinks, and dancing. A pilot explained to me about the most unusual wall decorations and how they were made. A rather large busted, intoxicated stewardess was spun around the walls as someone poured wine onto her nude body and thus the room was "painted" and left as was. We left when someone fired off a gun to ring in the New Year using live ammo. That was it for Ralph, Joe, Mike, Jim, and me.

New Year's Day brought the "tiny beggars" and a recovery day at Caesar Beach.

> Dear Mom Dad Stop
> Merry Christmas from Liberia Stop
> Unpacked my shipment Stop
> Visited some settlements
> Spent holidays at beach Stop
> No Snow! Stop
> Hugs African kisses Stop
> Kathleen

John Francis rolling a rotten mango

Chapter 23

The Come As You Are Caper

Why am I standing outside John Francis' bungalow at 10:30 at night? Ron and Mae Gillian were still in the truck urging me to keep knocking, "Someone will come," Mae shouted. Yeah, right, I thought. Why me? An outside light flickered on and there was a noise and not from the car horn that Ron was now pounding on. I guessed John was home. Well, now I'll be able to get the deed done. His door swung open and there John stood in all his glory…Mom said there'd be days like this. How come I'm the one who keeps getting these days I wondered?

Getting here was a process and now I'm stuck. A week ago I was aghast when I looked at the name on my small piece of paper. It read John Francis! Of all the people I would have to draw his name, I lamented. I was getting into my car when Mae Gillian approached and asked me whose name I had. All she did was laugh and was so happy she and Ron hadn't pulled his name. We had been at a BYOB planning meeting and the theme decided upon was a "Come As You Are Party". We were divided into small groups and given a list of BYOB members to catch, record what they were wearing, and invite them to the party! What a hoot! We had all agreed the time to catch people was 9 on Sunday morning. However, the committee wasn't as lucky as someone had our names and could approach us at any time and place. Thus, I decided to be properly dressed at all times until I was caught.

Over the next few days, I went to where John Francis worked but couldn't locate him. The deadline was drawing near when I decided to catch John at his home. After going there a few times, I finally asked Ron and Mae if they could come with me as this trip was to be late at night when he most definitely would be home.

Ron and Mae picked me up in Ron's green pick-up. No lights were on anywhere and I said, "Rats, let's go and try tomorrow a little earlier in the evening."

"No, way! We're here and you are going to march up to his door and wake him. Time is running out for you to catch him," Ron stated, puffing on his cigarette.

I slowly climbed from the pickup and then walked up and knocked on John's door. Got to get this done I thought. No answer. I knocked two more times and was headed back to the truck when Ron laid on his horn. The horn's noise would wake the dead, I thought.

Both Mae and Ron had exited the truck and were standing with me when John swung open the door and stood there dressed in, well, nothing! Yep, nothing, well, except he did have a wee cigarette dangling from the corner of his mouth and lest I forget, a bull whip tucked under his arm.

"Aye, mates," John quipped stepping back and inviting us into his dark abode.

"Thanks John but, I drew your name for the 'Come As You Are Party' and well, here's your invitation. I am recording what you are wearing or not wearing for the party."

"Yes, if you aren't coming the way we caught you, you will be penalized, remember?" Ron laughed and accepted the John's invitation to go into his bungalow.

Mae said, "Just one beer."

What's wrong with them? Can't they see he's naked and oh yes involved with no other than "Bouncing Irene" who was doing just that. Bouncing! Naked! She was so excited that they had visitors and she continued to jump up and down. Ron and Mae knew Pan Am stewardess Bouncing Irene and I was introduced just in case I didn't know her.

"Yes, I have met Irene before but she was dressed or in a swim suit," I said. So, keeping my eyes looking upward, I said hello and followed the strange group into John's living room. The walls and ceiling were painted black and hanging in the middle was a mirrored disco ball splintering the light over everything as John controlled a strobe light which was on the floor in the corner. He laughed as he made it flash off and on.

We sat and John took our drink orders. I continued to stare at the disco ball and after a few minutes, the strobe light caused a weird visual sensation. Neither John nor Bouncing Irene made any attempt to put something on. Ron and Mae just chatted and drank as if everyone was fully clothed. I was getting dizzy from the music, lights, and was embarrassed by the whole situation. John and Bouncing Irene were disco dancing and were joined by Ron and Mae. Mae tried to get me to join. I begged to stay sitting and realized why Irene was called "bouncing" and wondered if she was the stewardess that decorated the Pan Am's room at the Robertsfield Hotel. Two drinks later, I did join the crazy group but, danced in the corner by myself. All too soon we were driving back to my bungalow. Five am comes around very quickly. "Goodnight guys and thanks once again for helping me out," I said as I climbed my steps.

I was barely in bed when I heard a loud knock on my front door. Thinking it was Mae returning to give me something I had left in the truck, I quickly opened the door to find a tall broad shouldered man in a light blue plaid shirt standing there with a "Come As You Are" invitation in his hand and a huge grin on his face! Frank Field had caught me and here I was in my nightgown! What the…? I was caught and nothing I could do about it. I accepted the invitation. Frank bade me goodnight and headed back down the steps to his car while I went back to bed and tried to sleep.

Early on Saturday morning, the BYOB committee had gathered at Botanical Research where the BYOB party house was located. Men had emptied the huge house of all furniture except long tables and chairs. They quickly brought in more tables and chairs. I was on the decorating committee and we began doing that. Excitement was running high. Everyone had heard about my catching John Francis naked with the bull whip and they were looking forward to how he would come to the party. Crazy penalties were planned and the men had one designed just for John. Bets were being placed as to how John Francis would attend the party; clothed or not. A small group was practicing a skit to reenact the night the Gillians and I went to John's bungalow to invite him. Gosh, these guys are starved for any kind of entertainment. The bungalow was beautifully decorated with huge palm fronds and colored lights everywhere. Candles in wine bottles were on the tables and on window ledges. The group in charge of roasting the goat said everything was going well. The drinks, food, and music were ready for our party. Yes, the mood was set for a great BYOB party.

A long line of vehicles sped down the road kicking up clouds of red dust as they approached the BYOB bungalow. Young Liberian men parked the cars and trucks as members began to party. Everyone was in a party mood eagerly awaiting the arrival of John Francis. He arrived but was not totally nude. John wore a Holiday Inn hand towel tied around his waist however, the bull whip and the cigarette were present. Everyone went nuts! Later after gorging on food and liquor, the committee walked around noting who wasn't dressed as caught and they were asked to line up along the wall. I had made sure I was in compliance by wearing my nightgown. When it was John Francis's turn, he accepted his penalty in great stride. He jumped up and down and danced around imitating a real boxing pro. The crowd cracked up, roaring! John knew how to entertain and didn't disappoint his followers. He graciously accepted his fate and pushed a rotten mango across the floor. Everyone went crazy when the skit about how I caught John and Bouncing Irene was performed!

Oh what a night that was in January 1974!

>Dear Mom Dad Stop
>What a night Stop
>Watched nude man Stop
>Roll rotten mango Stop
>Never a dull moment Stop
>Hugs African kisses Stop
>Kathleen

Timbuktu, Mali 1974

Chapter 24

John "the Duke" Wayne and Timbuktu

Flying high above the Sahara Desert, the Swedish Air Force Colonel called Sven (of course he'd be called this) banked the C-130 plane to the right so I could get a better view of the upcoming landing site. I was perched in the copilot's seat having moved from sitting on the hundred pound bags of flour stacked in the back and I was straining my neck in all directions to soak in the surreal views. My fingers were operating my 35mm camera, framing and snapping the aerial layout. Shivers ran up and down my spine in anticipation of landing at the...

A week ago I had been on a different perch, a stool at the Robertsfield Hotel, along with my friends Jim, Joe, and Ralph, when a drop-dead good-looking silver haired gentleman approached me asking if he could sit next to me and buy me a drink.

"Yes," I stammered trying not to show my attraction to him.

Moving to a nearby table, our drinks came and we chatted with the usual where are you from, what airline do you work for, and so on. Sven was a colonel with the Swedish Air Force and was pleasantly surprised to learn I was a US Air Force brat and had lived in Panama, Ireland, England, France, and with my family traveled all over Europe and Central America.

"We made it to Denmark, but didn't get to Sweden, Norway, or Finland," I told him. "Someday, I hope to visit."

"Places you'd enjoy and by the way, what do you do here for Firestone?" Sven asked.

Answering about my job, our conversation went on with easy questions and answers until out of the blue, Sven asked.

"How about going to Timbuktu with me?"

Well, that comment certainly got my attention and I almost fell off my chair! What a most unusual pick up line! In fact, it was the best pickup line I had ever heard! Timbuktu…yeah right!

Wanting to shout are you nuts, I found myself squelching a snicker. "Sure… when?" And thinking, does he really think I'm that naive?

"We leave at midnight tonight, so be on the far end of the runway about 15 minutes before midnight. Dress in slacks and bring a sweater as it does get chilly."

"Sure thing," I piped up thinking a sweater to go to the desert? Yea, right! And midnight at the darkest end of the runway. He really thinks I'm falling for his line and would show up for some hanky panky. Didn't mom tell me there would be men and days like this?

"Well, see you in a few hours. I must try to get some sleep before my preflight check list."

Gosh, he was going to carry this out to the max I thought. Well, it was an interesting evening talking with Sven until he pulled out that pickup line of the century. "Okay, see you at 11:45 pm on the far end of the runway. And I won't forget that sweater either!" I said in my most over anticipative voice.

He left and I rejoined my friends and thought better of sharing the strange pickup line with them. They wouldn't believe it as I didn't believe that unusual conversation had even taken place. Timbuktu…who would believe the place even exists. Mom would used that place to terrorize us when she needed us to hop to whatever she demanded. I knew it existed but who would ever go there? It's too much of a stretch to share to the guys.

Wednesday after school, I was at the Hotel enjoying its pool and its covered roof. Dry season's sun was so intense and this shelter was a wonderful blessing. I sat next to some bikini clad women and I quickly discovered they were Swedish and nurses with their country's Red Cross! Oh, my goodness, I wanted to scream! Sven was telling the truth about the drought areas in the Sahara Desert and their mercy missions after all. It wasn't a pickup line and he really was flying in food, water, medicine, and medical people to the drought areas. And worse of all, I missed a chance of a lifetime to go to Timbuktu! What the heck! I was shattered and so bummed out over the next couple of days. I went to the Hotel's bar every evening looking for Sven. He was there when I walked into the bar on Friday evening and greeted me warmly.

"Where were you? We waited for 20 minutes, but our flying window would have been compromised if we had waited any longer. What happened to you?"

"Oh my goodness! Sven, I thought you were trying to pick me up for a rendezvous and gee, Timbuktu? That line sounded so phony. I'm sorry that I didn't get there as I so wanted to go to the place my mother always said she'd send me to if I didn't behave," I said, almost crying.

Sven laughed and said, "Well, perhaps all isn't lost. Tomorrow we fly back to Timbuktu. Still interested?"

"Interested? You don't have to ask me twice! When? Still at the far end of the runway? And still the sweater?"

"Yes, and we depart at 8:00 am," Sven said still amused.

We continued talking and laughing about my misunderstanding of his "pickup line". Sven said he would be sharing this story for many years to come.

"How long is the flight? When will we return as I have a Valentine party to attend tomorrow night? People would miss me if I'm a no show."

"Three hours each way and about 3 to 4 hours on the ground. We should be back no later than 7 pm."

Yep, mom, I'm going to the end of the world in a C-130 and returning to Liberia on Valentine's Day weekend. Life is definitely exciting!

Driving back to my bungalow, I decided not to share this adventure with the guys after all. I still didn't have my passport and it doesn't look like Firestone or the American Embassy were motivated enough to locate it. Sven had said I would be flying under the Swedish flag on a United Nations Mercy Mission and did not require any documents. "Don't worry, but also don't spread it around that you are leaving and returning to Liberia as this government could have big problems with it. One never knows in matters such as this."

I got my clothes ready for the party tomorrow just in case the mission ran a little late. I chose my outfit for the trip, white pants and a Liberian tie dye T-shirt, sandals, and of course a light weight jacket. Sleep was evasive as I tossed and turned dreaming of my new adventure and worrying that I might get caught. This thrill was too overpowering for me not to take the risk and so there I was on the far end of the runway by 7:30 am on Saturday, February 15, 1974. I didn't want to miss this special flight again! There was much hubbub going on with securing the huge bags of flour and people bringing other items on and off the C-130. Sven greeted me and introduced me to the flight crew. Everyone was excited I made it this time and laughed at how Sven's pickup line messed up my last attempt. The weather looked good for the entire day and all too soon, the C-130 was taxing on the runway ready for takeoff to the end of the world.

We flew high and watched the many colors of green of the

rainforests and mountains of Liberia and Guinea decrease into grasslands. The first part of the leg was about 45 minutes and there it loomed; the Sahara Desert! The shades of brown and cream colored sand dunes morphed into various shapes and then there was the meandering snake-like river of ancient history; the Niger! It took my breath away. All this texture continued for hours. Every now and then, a small village appeared along the Niger. Sven had told me that the drought area extended through Mali, Niger, and Upper Volta. The area had only ½ inch of rain in the past 7 years. The nomadic desert people were grouping near villages in order to acquire food and water. It truly was a desperate time for the desert people. The United Nations was flying in much needed flour, medicine, water, and medical people. Sven's group made 2 trips daily to different areas. Most of the time they coasted above the sand as items were slid out the dropped C-130's door. Sometimes, they made 4 to 5 drops in one flight at these remote areas. Today was different as Timbuktu had a paved tarmac for our plane's landing and take-off. We were staying here for a few hours.

At 11:45 am, we landed at the "end of the world" to searing heat of 103 F and flies everywhere! We talked through our teeth and kept our noses covered. It was a trying endurance to be sure, but I was here! Sven, along with some other crew men, and I were ushered to the airport's tower to have a quick tour. The glare from the runway and sand was blinding. How do the controllers do their job, I wondered. Our plane looked so very small. The people, clad in white or blue flowing robes, wearing turbans with a piece of fabric draped over their noses and mouths were bustling about like tiny ants below us in this extreme dry heat. How I envied their draped cloths as a method of repelling the flies. What I needed was a scarf and not the sweater that Sven had recommended.

Next, we were taken to a Bedouin camp close to the runway's edge. I didn't take any photos because I just couldn't expose the dire situations these people were in. Only a half inch of rain in 7 years. Gosh, I won't complain about the rain when I get back to Liberia. It's helps to see what others go through in order to appreciate what you have.

I saw few women and no young children on my walk. Interesting, I thought. Most women were probably in the tents taking care of small children shielding them from the extreme heat.

All of a sudden, a tall thin boy boldly approached me inquiring if I spoke French. I answered in French and we exchanged names. "Ali Baby" grabbed my hand and danced while swinging my arm. He was delighted to meet such a famous person such as me.

"Famous? What's this Sven?"

With a sheepish grin on his face he said he had told our hosts I was a princess. Aha, I thought his special way of getting me into Mali with no papers. Clever guy that one was. He did explain that the real Princess Christina was actually a nurse and back at the Robertsfield Hotel.

"Really? I just read in *Time* magazine that she was recently engaged and to marry in June," I said.

Ali Baby and a group of his friends posed with me on a luggage wagon with the name "Timbuktu" on it. Later walking around the camp I saw a camel lying under a low branch hanging tree. He snorted and balked when I mounted him for a really tall ride around a few tents. Getting back to earth was more dangerous than rising up. I wanted to give the Bedouin something for my unique ride. He accepted a silver spoon ring and then the men came from everywhere to trade goods with me. American money, of course, wasn't used and I only had what I was wearing. I traded my last silver ring for a pair of leather sandals when I saw an exquisite sword in an aqua and coral sheath draped around the torso of the Bedouin camel owner. I had already traded my rings, white long pants, earrings, and well the only thing left was my bra. Deal done and it took all my restraint not to snap a photo of the camel's owner wearing my bra hanging over his head and waving to his comrades as he rode off into the desert. John "the Duke" Wayne would be proud.

All too soon, we were saying goodbye and boarding the C-130 to head back to Liberia and me to head out to the Valentine Day party. Thank goodness I still had my light weight jacket as it was tied around my waist to help with modesty even though the tie-dye T-shirt was mini dress length. Nothing would ever top off this trip to the end of the world; right Mom? Over the next 2 months, I flew almost every weekend with the Norwegians and Finns as they also were on the United Nation's mercy missions. I made it to Niamey, Niger, Gao and Nioro, Mali, Gorom Gorom, and Ouagadougou, Republic of Upper Volta and many desert camp drops. Made it back to Timbuktu two more times. My trips almost came to a screeching halt when I was called down to Central Office one day by Jerry Swanson, Firestone's personnel manager.

"Hi Jerry. What can I do for you?" I squirmed trying to look as innocent as possible. I had the faint suspicion that I had been caught and everything was going to come down on me big time.

"Sit. I have some questions to ask you and I want direct answers. No evading them."

"Sure, Jerry, whatever," I said plopping onto the mahogany chair he had pointed at.

Soda bottle thick black glasses framed Jerry's little beady eyes and he began his questioning on how he had noticed my car down at the far end of the runway every weekend. "Your gig is up! I know you're flying off with the Mercy Missions and don't lie. Last Saturday, I watched you board the C-130."

Yep, I had been discovered and I needed a quick way out of this mess. "How about I arrange for you to take a flight to one of the places?" I bartered, quite pleased I was able to come to this solution in record breaking time. And wonders of wonders, it worked. Jerry was as happy as a bug in a rug.

Fini palava.

I smiled.

Dear Mom Dad Stop
World's end exists Stop
Been to Timbuktu Stop
And other drought places Stop
Hugs African kisses Stop
Kathleen

I'm standing next to a Bedouin in
Timbuktu, Mali

Firestone Hospital at Duside.

Chapter 25

Mohawks Charging, Jupiter Rising, and Bathtub Christening

Wearing a pink and white t-shirt, white shorts, and flip flops, I was sitting on a long freezer at Sammy's store sipping on a lukewarm Club Beer. It was hot and humid and I was catching up on the latest news with the guys. The guys were saying the next man and woman who stopped at Sammy's were having a sizzling affair and they were working out the details of their made-up story. Thank goodness I was one of the guys now. Presently, the only news about me was with John Chapman who was giving me weekly updates on his progress of being able to finally meet my expectations we had established months ago on that crazy day with the Nazi problem.

Driving way too fast and skidding to a stop near the large

cottonwood tree came a green Ford truck. Monkey, Sammy's pet chimp chained to the cottonwood, went crazy expecting attention and food but, instead the driver ignored him and strode up to the store.

John Chapman said, "Hey, isn't that your new neighbor Kathleen?"

I never got a chance to answer as a short, wiry, but, muscular man wearing cowboy boots and spurs with the most unusual haircut entered the far door. His head was shaved to his scalp in the front and back leaving a 4 inch tall and 4 inch wide row of hair from ear to ear. Perhaps, he was a long lost Mohawk from the States who decided to wear his hair this way? Without a smile or saying a word, he picked me up, moved me to the counter, got a Club Beer from the freezer, and then put me back on top of the freezer.

Collecting myself after this abrupt manner, I stuck out my hand to shake his and said, "How! Me, Kathleen, your neighbor."

The man just looked, grunted, "How," with his hand raised high and not shaking mine. He threw money on the counter, lazily walked back to his truck, put it into reverse, and made tracks.

"Well, I'll be," murmured Dick Hugg and a couple of the other guys. "Doesn't that beat all?"

"Yeah, and he's Kathleen's neighbor. Hope no 'injuns' go on a rampage," Jim added.

Ralph and Joe piped up stating that they kept a good eye on my place so I had nothing to worry about.

"Well, that can't compare to the horrific time I had with my impacted wisdom tooth two weeks ago," I said placing my tongue in the gaping hole at the back of my mouth. My teeth and gums had been bugging me for weeks when I finally decided to get them taken care of by visiting a dentist in Monrovia named Dr. Jupiter. My Firestone driver stopped in front of Dr. Jupiter's tall narrow two story wooden building that had no distinguishing marks other than a small sign saying I was at the correct place. The driver told me to go up the uneven wooden steps. I did climb them and waited in a small stuffy, hot room until Dr. Jupiter came out to greet me. I was trembling in fear of what Dr. Jupiter would say-not that I had any fear of dentists because I had had a lot experience with them over the years. and they made me nervous.

He wore the usual white coat of a medical person and was quite tall. He beamed from ear to ear as he shook my hand and led me into his office, also not air-conditioned. I was in a lot of pain but he gently, even with his huge fingers, examined my mouth and declared, "Your gums are badly infected and an abscessed partially impacted wisdom tooth is the cause. That tooth needs to be removed and infection cleaned out. Now." Seeing the fear on my face of the dreaded news I suspected was coming, he added to soften the blow, "The infection has gone too far for me to treat and so the tooth must come out. However, I don't have enough Novocain presently on hand to remove it. My advice is to come back in an hour or two after you have drunk enough scotch that you'll feel no pain when I remove it."

Nodding the acceptance of what needed to be, I found a nearby bar, bought a bottle of scotch, sat at a wobbly table covered with a bright purple and green lappa, and proceed to drink. I hate, just hate scotch, but the pain overcame my hatred for the awful taste. Why scotch and not gin or vodka, I wondered as I took one shot after another? Somehow, I managed to scale those even more uneven wooden steps and was back in the dentist's chair. The little Novocain Dr. Jupiter had helped somewhat but, eventually I passed out either from the pain or being drunk. It took a long, long time to remove the tooth and all I remember was Dr. Jupiter, with tears in his eyes, begging my forgiveness for causing me such deep pain as I stumbled down the steps with the Firestone driver's support, who poured me into the car for our return to the Plantation and home.

Over the next three days, I returned to Dr. Jupiter for him to clean the wound and treat me. Nevertheless, I developed a dry socket. The pain was excruciating and I felt so sorry for Dr. Jupiter who was doing his very best to heal the infection. A visit to Dr. Jallah at the Firestone Hospital for stronger antibiotics was what finally did the trick in healing the dry socket and infection. On the fourth day and feeling somewhat better, I drove myself to Dr. Jupiter's office. I was stopped by a policeman at Broad Street and Tubman Boulevard who said I was speeding and he needed to arrest me. I simply opened my mouth, pulled out the bloody wad of gauze, and said, "Okay, my friend, arrest me."

One look at the blood and the policeman wave me on with a wobble of his hand to slow down. I was thinking as I pulled away, how could he have stopped me as he didn't have any car? One time I was happy to have a bloody wound and not face any police palava.

After the tooth nightmare, I'd stop in every so often and visit Dr. Jupiter, "my dentist from outer space" as I used to call him. He would beam when he saw me glad that I got through that ordeal. He always said, I was one of the strongest patients he ever had with a high tolerance for pain and he even understood why now I couldn't drink scotch. He did say that I could have drank gin or vodka as they would have had the same effect, he just so happened to like scotch!

"You know guys," I added to my story, "No scotch for me ever! I am so relieved that the infection has cleared up and I'm on the mend thanks to Ralph, Joe, Jim, and Mike who took great care of me. Mae Gillian's and Eileen Field's chicken soup got me back on my feet and to teaching. Now, hopefully my new neighbor won't give me any palava."

The men were now plotting a skit to depict my meeting with my "Mohawk neighbor". Will they ever weary of their pranks and skits I wondered?

A few days later, Jim, Mike, and I were headed back to Freeport in Mike's truck to get my bathtub, sink, toilet, and tiles that I had ordered for my bathroom redo. My ordered appliances were yellow and the bathroom walls were going to have white subway tiles up 5 feet with a row of black tiles capping the white. We brought two Liberians to help us load and later unload the truck. They were relaxing in the truck's bed

"Got to keep you happy!" was Jim's response whenever I wanted something for my classroom or bungalow and somehow the school's budget covered it. That's why we were on the way to the Freeport to pick up everything for my bungalow's bathroom redo.

The rains had been returning along with the egrets. About three weeks ago, someone in my classroom screamed, jumped up, and ran to the window all the while yelling, "They're back! The egrets are back!"

Everyone dashed to the windows to take in the splendid white long legged graceful birds strutting in a light misty rainfall. It was a sure sign that the rainy season was returning. Every day it rained a little at certain times and each time the durations grew longer.

Rains were holding off at present which was a good thing since we had collected the bathtub, toilet, and sink with the faucets, and the boxes of tiles. All were lying opened in the back of the truck with the two Liberians. Turning to look back to admire my yellow appliances, I saw the Liberians sitting back by the tailgate laughing, bouncing wildly about, enjoying the wind, sun, and the ride.

Soon, we were slowing down to pass through 15 Gate and enter the Plantation when the low hanging clouds opened up and humongous rain drops plopped down. We bounced along for about three miles with the windshield wipers going at breakneck speed, when I turned to look in back to check on things. What should appear but the oddest of sights! I gasped and could hardly speak. I sputtered out that we should stop because the two Liberians were naked and taking a bath in my yellow bathtub throughly enjoying themselves! Mike and Jim just howled with laughter at the spectacle. The men were singing away enjoying my yellow bathtub, rain, and the ride.

"What the heck," I said and joined in the laughter. We were WAWAed once again.

Only wish I had my camera to take a picture, I thought. No one will believe this back home or on the Plantation. Yep, these men had christened my bathtub proper!

When we stopped, Mike yelled at the men to drain the bathtub and get dressed and we headed back to my bungalow to store everything under it. Jim had workmen coming in a week to do my bathroom.

Once my bathroom was completed, one by one, the bachelors each took a long soaking bath with candlelight and wine. I know Firestone was frowning upon what I had started with the bachelors as bathtub after bathtub were ordered. Oh, well…

Bang. Bang. Bang. Someone was wildly banging on my bungalow's door. I was seated at my dining room table correcting school papers and rose to answer the door as the persistent banging continued.

House Joseph followed me grunting something under his breath as he hated being disturbed when he was baking; his usual task on Wednesdays. I had already enjoyed a thick slice of freshly baked bread topped with butter and marmalade and was looking forward to more with my dinner. Most house boys in the bachelor compound baked bread on Wednesdays.

I opened the door to see the "Mohawk neighbor" along with my watchman, Joseph waving his rifle. "Mohawk" stomped in wearing his cowboy boots and spurs. He promptly sat down on my sofa and grunted something.

"That man, he come. I say he go. He no hear Joseph," declared my watchman gesturing his rifle showing how he was defending me.

"Hello. May I help you?" I questioned my neighbor while hoping the gun was loaded and either Joe or Ralph was watching my bungalow just in case.

"Ugh," he grunted over and over. "Ugh."

"I don't understand you. Est-ce que tu parles Francaise?" I pleaded.

He continued to grunt and the noise became louder and louder. I thought perhaps he was related to Banana Mama and wanting to calm this man, I asked if he wanted some fresh bread that Inside Joseph had just taken from the oven.

From hand to mouth and rubbing his belly, I gathered I was correct with my suggestion. I thought he was American however, he spoke no understandable English. Turning to go into the kitchen, I pushed the swinging door, and walked down the short passage between the bungalow's living section and the kitchen to ask Inside Joseph to fix a plate of bread for my guest. Joseph swirled his finger about the side of his head and said, "Missy, that man, he loco!" My man of few words spoke volumes.

"Okay, I hear you, my friend. Just do it. I don't want any palava as Outside Joseph has his rifle and you know he could shoot. Who knows? He might have bullets in it!"

After a few nerve racking minutes, Inside Joseph came out

carrying a tray with a plate of warm slices of buttered bread on it and set it on the coffee table. As he was doing this, Mohawk neighbor grabbed the bread and shoved it into his mouth with much landing on his lap and the floor. Not to worry, as he scooped that up and continued to guzzle to devour the bread, grunting the whole time.

"Wow! I see you are very hungry. Joseph will bring you some loaves of bread when they finish baking."

Wonders of wonders, Mohawk neighbor rose and jingled out. Hopefully, never to return.

Outside Joseph radiated happiness as he returned to once again guard me, my home, and okay, my animals; tamed and wild.

    Dear Mom Dad Stop
    Much palava with wisdom tooth Stop
    Much palava with yellow bathtub Stop
    Much palava with Mohawk neighbor Stop
    Jupiter, rain, and bread took care of palava Stop
    Hugs African kisses Stop
    Kathleen

Selecting fish from the Fanti
Little Bassa, Liberia

Chapter 26

One People, One Fish

Many Saturdays, I drove on the Buchanan road and made the turn onto a smaller road heading north to the Atlantic Ocean. It usually took me approximately an hour after leaving my home and the Plantation to reach Little Bassa. When exiting my car, I would be quickly surrounded by children clamoring to see the white woman. As usual, they wanted to play with my fine blond hair even though it was still quite short. The children giggled and would follow me into the village. They knew I wanted to buy fresh fish-especially lobster. One time I met a happy-go-lucky short man called Two Head. When he was at the village, he would usually make all arrangements of selecting the fish and loading my car.

Every time seeing Two Head, he would say, "Missy, I help you so you can help me some day."

Not questioning what my part would entail, I would agree to his terms. But today something was going on. As a growing crowd of Liberians collected around me.

"Where is Two Head? I come for fish."

"Oh, Missy, Two Head, he come soon. We help the fish in," said David a friend of Two Head.

"Oh? How?"

"Wait small. You go sleep and come back small," David said as I walked through the village. Many houses were cement block with tin roofs while others had thatched roofs with mud walls. Just about every home had an outdoor kitchen and the dirt yards were extremely neat, as usual, in Liberian villages. So, off I headed down the beach to sun bathe. Some children followed me, excited, to have a visitor.

Making an area my own, I nestled down to sun bathe. While enjoying the salty breeze and the sun's heat radiating from the white sand, I was lulled into a dreamlike state, totally relaxed. Resting here on the warm sand was simply heavenly after a week of teaching. Before long, the water crept in to my feet returning me to the present. Ah, tide was rolling in. I quickly joined the villagers as they sighted the two canoes not too far out as the waves pushed them toward shore. Each canoe was paddled in quickly with one end of a huge net forming a closing circle. One canoe came into the shore first with the Fanti fishermen and villagers pulling the canoe out along with one end of the fishing net. Many people, including me, jumped into the surf grabbing the net's end to begin hauling it in along with the fish and anything else they had dragged up from the ocean floor. The chanting also began and the rhythm surprisingly helped make light work of pulling in the heavy net.

Many times I slipped, gulping mouthfuls of salty water, but the exhilarating thrill of working as a team with the villagers to bring in the day's haul of fresh fish couldn't begin to describe my feelings. I just knew I would be back to do this again. I thought, my lobster was well worth this hard labor. I liked the crowd and enjoyed laughing with them.

I continued to help as the other canoe rode the tide in with villagers joining in the process of retrieving the day's catch. Much heaving and pulling, the net finally met the shore with the fish cascading as the women collected them in their large colorful metal basins. I collapsed onto the beach gasping for breath but, thrilled to be part of this experience. I'm sure to everyone else here, this daily hauling in of the fish was simply a chore in their way of life. Haul fish in and then sell in the market.

One happy Fanti fisherman remarked to me, "Missy, you Fanti! You my good friend."

"Wow! I am honored to be Fanti!" I said as Two Head showed up and began begging me to carry him to Harbel.

"Missy, you my good friend. Carry me to Harbel," chimed in Two Head while loping after me continuing to beg.

"No, I can't do that."

"I beg you Missy, I beg you. Carry me to Harbel. You say you help me when I help you with fish."

Oh no, I thought, was this the favor being called in? I was a little nervous about having someone I really didn't know in my car when I was alone.

Now the crowd was chanting, "Carry Two Head to Harbel." And Two Head continued to beg…following me on his knees with the crowd continuing to chant, "Carry Two Head to Harbel". More people joined in and the chanting grew louder as Two Head rolled and twisted on the sand begging and roaring robustly.

Laughing, I agreed to bring him to Harbel. Having selected my fish with plenty of lobsters in the mix, I followed the group back to 49 D only to discover a huge group of men piled into my car every which way with barely room for me in the driver's seat! Arms and legs were hanging out the windows and hanging on the trunk were some young boys.

"Missy, we put fish in boot," they chimed.

"What's this?" I shouted over the din of the crowd who had followed me now chanting, "Harbel, Harbel, Harbel."

I saw no reasonable conclusion to my dilemma...I had agreed to Two Head's conditions over many weeks ago for helping me get my fish, so surrendering, I climbed into 49 D.

"Off we go to Harbel!" I sang out pulling away from the village with a trunk full of fresh fish and my coveted lobster and someone's smelly armpit in my face. Oh well, I thought. This was Liberia and the adventure I wanted. The way back took forever as I didn't want anyone falling off my car. Everyone sang loudly like drunken old sailors. I just smiled and hummed along.

Over the next few months, I made many trips to Little Bassa, helping to pull in the fishing net and buying my fish. I thought back to the time the Fanti fishermen invited me to go out in one of their canoes to drop the nets and haul in the catch. Without a care or second thought, I had jumped into the canoe with the Fanti rowing out over the huge waves and being carried out into the Atlantic. We rode high and plummeted into troughs, as we slowly made it out into the ocean. The high I experienced was incredible! Who would have thought months ago I would be doing this as I was packing to come to Liberia. Never could I have dreamed that I would be in a Fanti canoe dropping fishing nets in the ocean! Life was so good!

It was a humid day when I next decided to go to Little Bassa. I hadn't seen Two Head since that adventure with him and the car load of his friends. Here he was again begging as if nothing had occurred a few weeks ago.

"Eh, I see my good good friend," he said. "Missy, you carry me to Harbel?"

"No, Two Head, I will not take you or anyone else to Harbel."

"Missy, I beg you, I beg you, my good good friend. I go Harbel with you. Only one people go."

Well, this dialogue went on for perhaps 10 minutes, with a growing chanting crowd following the two of us. They chanted, "One people, one people, go Harbel."

"No", I said loudly, "No, no, no people!"

I selected my fish after I helped haul in the net teeming with the day's fresh catch. Everyone was in an extremely happy state, pulling, chanting, and begging for me to carry Two Head to Harbel. And yes, Two Head continued to grovel at my feet, even kissing my toes. Exasperated, I gave in to Two Head and the people.

"Only one people go to Harbel. One people!" I said laughing.

"Ya, Missy, one people. One people go to Harbel."

As I approached my 49 D, I couldn't believe it! The people followed with many fish in their pans and only Two Head was empty handed. He opened the car's back door and one by one each person threw in their fish...I stood with my mouth open unable to speak. Words escaped me. What was going on? It was then that I recognized exactly what was going on in my car. The lobsters were trying to claw their way over the piles of fish and this sight I found to be hilarious. Who would believe that once again Two Head and the villagers had outsmarted me? I threw up my hands and agreed to take Two Head and the car full of smelly fish and clacking lobsters to the market in Harbel.

I drove away with the crowd clapping and chanting, "One people, one people go to Harbel".

Yes, indeed, they were correct. It was after all only one person going to Harbel with me. And it was Two Head.

Now I found myself concerned about going back to Little Bassa to buy fish. What do the villagers have in store for me next I wondered? However the lure of lobster overcame my fear and off I went one overcast Saturday.

Rain pelted down as I tooled down the Buchanan Road. I was in my new car, a 73 Volkswagen bug. How I acquired this car was indeed something that was still amazing to me. About a month ago, I had been over for dinner at the Petersons' bungalow. So, Linda and I had eaten supper having given up on Chuck. When it was almost time for me to leave, Chuck came up the stairs and was noticeably intoxicated as he had won at playing golf that afternoon. I stayed for a while and then said my goodnight and went down the stairs to go home. The rains were coming down pretty hard as I went underneath their bungalow. Through the immense raindrops, I noticed that my car was not where I had parked it. I blinked and blinked again.

I asked the watchmen, "Where's my car?"

The old man looked and looked again surprised to see my car was missing and clapping his hands announced, "The car, he go."

He kept clapping his hands and shaking his head every time I again asked him where's my car?

And again he repeated, "I don't know where that car go, Missy. The car, he go."

I climbed the steps back up to the Petersons' front door and crying explained what had happened. "Someone has taken my car!" I was scared that Firestone would think I was irresponsible with their property. Linda instantly took charge of the situation, calming me down and made a phone call to PPD. In a short time, the PPD were interviewing the old watchman and me. I was still very upset having to report that my car stolen. Then it dawned on me, "How was I getting to work the next day?" I queried.

Linda said, "Don't worry. I'll pick you up and take you to school and PPD will find your car. They know who to look for and where."

Linda drove me home and again promised to take me to school in the morning.

True to her word, Linda brought me to school where I explained to Jim Smith what had happened to my car. He also had great faith in PPD locating my car.

"In the meanwhile, I'll act as your personal chauffeur until either your car is found or I get another one for you from the motor pool," Jim said encouragingly.

So for two days Jim did just that. Then he came to my classroom with an envelope from Chuck Peterson. Quickly opening it, I read that he wanted to see me after school and to go down to his office with his driver. A set of keys were also in the envelope. There, parked in front of my classroom was the VW with a Liberian that I recognized as Chuck Peterson's driver.

I did tell Jim that Chuck Peterson wanted to see me after school and sent his driver to bring me to Central Office. Disappointment flashed on Jim's face, but he did agree.

When the last student left, the driver asked me if I could drive this car with a stick.

"Stick? You mean, you want me to drive to Central Office in this car?"

"Ya, Missy, Bossman say for you to drive car."

"Sure, I can drive a stick car," I said getting in behind the wheel, turning the engine over, and then realizing that I didn't know how to get into reverse. "Help me put it in reverse. I have only driven a stick that was on the steering wheel and not the floor," I begged the driver.

He did a great job explaining the "H" and all too soon I was buzzing along and shifting smoothly on the way to Central Office. A secretary ushered me into Chuck's office and he soon entered.

"Glad to see you Kathleen, how was it driving the VW?"

"No problem. Has PPD located my car?"

"Well, yes they have but before I tell you any more, I must swear you to secrecy. Can I solicit a vow of silence from you? I will release you from this vow upon my death. Can I rely on your word?" Chuck implored and not in a joking manner.

"I…I… am having a difficult time wondering why you would ask something so serious of me and especially not being able to speak of it until you die. Gosh this is serious."

"Uh, this is sort of embarrassing for me and I do need your oath."

"Yes, I give you my word," I said now thinking where was this oath thing going?

With great hesitation and almost stuttering, Chuck told me that my 49 D was located and couldn't be repaired. He continued to explain that the night it went missing, well, it was accidentally pushed over the ravine at his bungalow and pushed over by Chuck himself! He had a sheepish grin on his face mixed with embarrassment.

"Wow! I see why the oath. I am glad that the mystery was solved and no one was injured in the process. What am I to do for a car?"

"Okay, that's covered and since Firestone doesn't have another vehicle at this time, I bought you the VW from Franz De Roos. This was his wife's car who doesn't need it anymore. Franz has agreed not to speak of the matter, too. The car is yours to use and sell when you leave the company, but it is yours on the condition you tell no one how this came to be. Motor Pool will continue to service this car and your gasoline allowance has been increased. Jerry Elam has been notified and has agreed to service the car."

"No problem. My lips are sealed. Thanks for getting the car. I really like it and know it will be so much fun to cruise around in," I promised Chuck. I smiled remembering this episode as I shifted down to a low gear turning onto the Little Bassa road. All too soon I was at the village with a crowd gathering around my car.

"Ah, Missy… the car… he good-o!"

People were clapping and cheering for me getting a new car. If they only knew the circumstances I thought smiling. Two Head was pushing his way to the front of the crowd and of course begged to be taken to Harbel.

"No way will I take you to Harbel. No. No. No."

"Missy, I beg you carry me to Harbel. Only one people and one fish," he chanted and sure enough the villagers joined in. I was working my way to the beach where the Fanti fishermen were just about ready to come onto the shore. Every able body joined hauling in the fishing net. The catch was plentiful and I made my selection including lots of lobsters.

The crowd's chanting and clapping was becoming hard to ignore and I relented and gave in to Two Head.

"Okay, Two Head, I will carry you and only you. You can bring one fish to Harbel market."

"I thank you Missy. My God thanks you, Missy," he said kissing my feet, crawling on his knees and howling. The crowd went wild. Oh my, I thought, what have I created?

"One people, one fish, one people, one fish," they chanted as they followed me to my car. I loaded my fish into the front trunk. Two Head jumped into the passenger seat as I started up the car.

"Where's your fish?" I asked over the loud chanting of the people when I happened to glance in my review mirror to see something simply unbelievable. I blinked and blinked again not truly comprehending what was coming at my car.

"It couldn't be…I can't believe it." I stammered.

Two Head smiled from ear to ear and proudly exclaimed, "Ya, Missy, it one people, one fish."

There it was. Eight Fanti carrying on enormous fish and struggling to lift it over my car. It was the largest fish I had ever seen.

"Stingray," Two Head told me smiling.

"I can't see and breathing is difficult…" I said to Two Head gasping for air.

"No problem, Missy, wait small. The people take good good care of Two Head and you."

Sure enough as he was speaking, holes were being carved out of the fish on both sides and where the front and rear windows were. The wind was able to pass through but, I was still gagging. The smell was thick and I just wondered how I was to make it back to Harbel without getting sick. Two Head continued to be thrilled with his plan to WAWA me and the crowd followed us down the road chanting, "One people, one fish! One people, one fish!"

Ah, Liberia, sweet Liberia.

> Dear Mom Dad Stop
> One new car Stop
> One people one fish Stop
> Sweet Liberia Stop
> Hugs African kisses Stop
> Kathleen

My VW that I named "cat" in front of my bungalow

Monkey bridge near
Bolahun, Liberia

Chapter 27

Monkey Bridges, Lepers, Mrs. Nixon, Oh My!

"Zor Zor? I can't believe this is a real place!" Joe said as we drove through this town. "Almost like being in Timbuktu. I remember my mother saying I'm sending you there if you don't listen better."

"Hey, my mom said the same thing! Joe, you do know there really is a place called Timbuktu located in the Sahara Desert and not all that far from here. That would be a great place to visit someday," I said secretly smiling.

"Not for me. This trip is enough. I probably won't be able to walk for weeks with all this bouncing about on these horrible roads!" Joe complained as he down shifted the gears on my VW.

We had been driving for 4 hours having left the Plantation at 4 am headed to a town near the Guinea and Sierra Leone borders called

Bolahun. We had heard there was a leprosarium mission run by Holy Cross Fathers and we would have a place to stay. Joe and I tried to get Ralph, Jim, or Mike to come with us, but no way would they venture that far away. Kakata was their limit along with maybe Buchanan and I was lucky to get them to do that. Joe turned out to be more adventurous than I had thought because he always drove over to our neighborhood bungalows and never walked.

"Our trip is going well, but I am still afraid of snakes and bugs. And animals. Remember what Leopold did to me a few weeks ago?"

"Yes, and Leopold is still traumatized over the whole thing," I said. "I can still hear both of your blood curling yells when Leopold was trying to escape from the back seat of your car. I do believe your scratches are healing nicely since the stitches were removed. Sorry to say, but thanks to Leopold's attack, the Liberians walk far away from our bachelor's compound. They say, if that cat get white man, what he do to Liberian?" I laughed.

So, we all have accepted Joe's real and imaginary fears I silently thought.

"Yeah, your cat is a mean one and I don't understand how he worships you. It's amazing how he nurses on your fingers and sleeps on your lap. You have that cat and most men under your magic spell. I see how Jim Smith treats you. Man, that guy's in love with you and hangs on every word you speak. He's like a love struck teenager."

"I know and it's a big problem. I've told Jim I won't date anyone I work with. It seems to be working for now at least. He's quite attentive and always trying to give me small presents. I just don't understand why he refuses to take 'no dating' for an answer."

"He's a guy and crazy for you. Just enjoy it."

The morning was still cool. We had been in dry season for about five months with almost no rain but later on the heat would become intense. Both of us wore bandanas over our noses to shield us from the red dust, however the fine grains of dust still invaded our noses and eyes making it difficult to see and breathe but the thrill of exploring a different place prevailed.

From Willie, I had learned how to pack for upcountry travel by carrying water, snack food, gasoline, and yes, toilet paper. When we came to the end of the Plantation's road at 26 Gate the going got rougher, but nothing like the roads we were driving on now. Huge ruts that you could lose your car in. Sometimes, I got out to see how deep the water hole was before we skirted the hole's rim just in case Joe slipped a wheel into the hole. We plowed onward. Adventure lured us like a drug. We craved it. The quest was to see something new and different. The iron-rich dust that draped the green leaves on nearby bushes and trees kept us moving. We went up and down hills and passed by some people walking; carrying goods on their heads. Most of the villages we drove through were small and didn't look promising for a pit stop until we reached Gbarnga. It was a large town and already vendors were setting up their stores in the marketplace.

Joe and I walked around purchasing oranges and bananas to snack on and once again were headed out to Bolahun. Switching drivers, I drove to Voinjama which was bustling with market activity. We stopped an old man to ask how far away Bolahun was.

"It not far," the man said, "Please Bossman, you carry this poor poor man there?"

"I say no room in da car," Joe answered in pretty good Liberian English. He was learning it faster than me.

"No problem, I go there," he said pointing to the car's hood.

"No way, man. It too dangerous to carry you there. Next time we come, we bring truck for you to ride in. Okay?"

"Yeah Boss, I thank you proper," he said walking off to find another way to Bolahun.

By now it was beastly hot and humid with us back on the dusty road praying for rain.

"Funny how it hasn't taken long to want rain again when during the rainy season it's we all complained about it," I remarked.

"Yes, I agree," Joe said. "But the only way to travel upcountry was between seasons. Well, that's what I've been told."

We passed more cars loaded with people with their goods tied to the hoods and trunks. Some vehicles were vans again packed with people traveling. The drivers drove fast and were all over the road. There weren't any signs or speed limits to follow. Just go, was the general rule, until you stop or something stopped you. Once in a while, we would pass a few vehicles that had been in a horrific accident. They were just left on the road and we maneuvered around them saying silent prayers for the families. Slowly over time, the wrecks were stripped of any good parts that could be recycled.

"Hey, it's my turn to drive," Joe said and I pulled over near a three car wreck.

The rest of the trip went on with us taking turns driving and resting. We saw rolling hills become mountains of the Nimba Mountain Range. It was a glorious day and we were anxious for adventure. Joe and I shared family stories, places we'd lived, and what we wanted out of life.

Joe asked, "What's this I heard about you and a scorpion?"

"Oh, yeah, a few weeks ago, I was walking around the Golf Course when I saw a scorpion coming towards me. I simply took my walking stick and managed to get the scorpion onto it and back to my car. I placed it in the trunk and drove like crazy to the Chem Lab. Al Nonemaker took it and got it into some resin to make a paper weight for me. What a conversation maker this will be once I am back in the States."

"Wow! I had heard from Dick Hugg that you caught it with your bare hands and put it into your purse to take to the Chem Lab."

"Well, he's sort of right as I did put it into my purse and then into the trunk. I was afraid it could somehow get from the trunk to the inside of my car and attack me!" I added laughing. "That little insect did put up a struggle getting it into my purse." And then the conversation turned to golf.

"Joe, how do you like playing golf on the Firestone's golf course?"

"I like it swell, but it's a difficult course to play. I have found some interesting information about the course. It all began in 1938 when

Charlie Woelfel, at that time a young planter in the Estates Department, applied and received management approval to build a few holes for the golfers at Harbel. The present first four holes and 9th hole were the outcome. The following year with more space available, four additional holes were built, thus completing the present nine-hole layout."

"That's incredible knowing it was done by hand as they didn't have any heavy duty equipment back then that Firestone has now," I remarked.

Joe continued, "Correct, all work to smooth the course was done by hand. They dragged a fifteen-foot section of a 12 inch I-beam over the fairways to level them. It was decided to use oiled sand instead of grass for the putting greens allowing golfers to play in all weather."

"I was told that the first hole opens on a 'dogleg' and it's a most difficult one to play also. I heard Charlie Woelfel was dissatisfied with the course as he thought it played too easily and so he added 17 new and deeper sand traps and repositioned the teeing areas. Lots of golfers complained about these changes and told Charlie what they thought. Many golf course records have been made, broken, and rebroken over the years. Hugh Darsey set the course record for nine holes which is 30. It has been equaled but not beat. Only seven golfers have had a hole-in-one with the last one being made with a No. 4 iron on the 7th hole by Franz de Roos in 1965."

"Wow, you golfers know the most interesting trivial."

"Yeah, we do," Joe agreed. "But listen to this, some famous people have played golf there including Sam Snead, Lowell Thomas, and Liberian Senator Shad Tubman, and of course the Firestone clan. I hope to break Darsey's record by playing a 29 someday! It's a dream of mine."

"A wonderful aspiration," I responded. "Awhile back, I tried to play and hired a couple of Liberian caddies to teach me. I passed out from swinging the club too much. Over 30 on No. 1 hole and that's when I actually hit the ball! I told the guys not to count the air strikes. I'm sure the boys are still laughing about my attempt at learning golf. I do putt very well, however, golf isn't my sport."

"A sport I enjoy and wish I was playing now instead of swallowing all this dirt!" Joe laughed as we were finally reaching our destination. Bolahun was nestled between rolling hills and was a very small village. Joe and I parked by a small white washed building... maybe a medical clinic...leprosarium? While Joe waited outside, I went inside.

I called out, "Hello, hello. Anyone here to help me? Hello?"

I heard voices and then a scream-a long deeply disturbing scream. I entered a small room on the right of the four room clinic and saw to my dismay two older women were pulling apart the legs of a girl who was sitting on the dirt floor. Oh my goodness, the girl was about to give birth! One old woman had an old rusty knife between her teeth for cutting the umbilical cord or I hope that was to be its use. I called out for anyone else to come and help. No one came. Joe answered. I yelled stay out! The eyes of the young girl who I believe to be about 14 said it all to me. I dropped to the dirt floor and talking softly, cooed her into a kind of trance-like calmness. I began the rhythmic breathing and she followed. I was drawing upon that birthing class film and follow up discussions I had when at St. Benedict's Academy. Who knew that one day those techniques would kick in to assist this young girl? The old women had dug a small hole and the girl was sitting on top and gravity was finally taking effect. The baby's head appeared and with one long hard push, the baby popped out into my hands. The shoulders unfolded and its scream proved it to be alive. I was shocked to see the baby's skin was very pale, almost white. Could the baby's father be? Perhaps? The baby girl, with a great set of lungs, announced her arrival as all of us beamed, laughed, and cried. I reached into my bag and brought out a small pair of scissors I use for my embroidery work. I saw nothing for sterilizing the scissors and so I shouted for Joe as he smoked and carried a small Zippo. Joe came dashing into the room to what was probably a place he didn't want to be.

"Zippo? For what reason?" Taking one long look, he threw the lighter to me and fled.

Cord cut, baby at its mother's breast, old women cleaning up, and

I finally stood up. Still no one was coming around. I watch in amazement the baby girl's skin gradually darkened in the room's natural light. The baby's father was black after all I thought when saying my goodbyes to the little group.

"I'm impressed that you knew what to do back at the clinic," Joe said putting away his Zippo. "How'd you know what to do?"

"I saw a film in high school and I paid attention as most of my classmates closed their eyes or passed out. I found the whole procedure fascinating," I revealed.

Joe and I continued to search the village. We found women preparing their evening meals and some children who were chasing one another and they began to follow us.

"Where's the Mission?" I kept asking.

People just smiled and spoke in a language other than English but, we did follow their finger pointing direction and we saw a long bearded white man wearing a faded blue tie-dye t-shirt!

Joe yelled, "Stop!" The man slowly turned around staring in disbelief as he approached us with a growing smile.

"Who are you? What are you doing in Bolahun?"

We filled him in and exchanged names. Joshua told us that the Mission was closed, priests were also gone, and the leprosarium was about 15 minutes away in the bush operated by Father Stevens the remaining Episcopal priest. Joshua was with the Peace Corps and in Bolahun teaching for almost two years. He offered us his hut as it was getting late to walk to the leprosarium. We happily accepted because sleeping in the car wasn't an attractive option. We joined a group of Joshua's friends for dinner which was fufu and chicken served over rice.

Joshua explained to Joe what fufu was, "It is cassava root that's been pounded, mixed with water or palm oil, rolled into small balls, and allowed to rise. It is then placed in the bowl with ground spices, boiled okra, smoked fish or chicken, goat, or other meat. Then a spicy soup is poured over your bowl for you to enjoy. One swallows fufu. Do not chew it."

No need to encourage us anymore as we devoured our meal.

Musicians began playing drums and people danced to the beat. A party! Liberians were always celebrating any little thing and so Joe and I joined in with the gyrations. We were today's "little thing"!

All too soon the sun was setting which helped cool down the hot humid air and bodies. Bug-a-bugs, with wing spans of 2 1/2 inches tip to tip, were swarming and young children caught them, plucked their wings off and popped them into their mouths. One little girl who spoke some English, brought Joe and I some wingless wiggling termite bodies to consume. Joe declined and I wished I hadn't said, "I like mine cooked." Shortly, she came back with a dish of cooked bug-a-bugs! Everyone cheered me on to eat and I did! "Not bad," I said crunching away. And I really meant it. Not that I was going to add them to my diet any time soon.

Joshua showed us to our rooms and the outside bathroom with shower, well, kind of a shower. It was an enclosure where you poured a little water on you, soap up, and then rinse quickly. All this was from a large tin tub like my watchman and house boy had under my bungalow. "G.I. shower," Joshua explained.

We each had our own tiny rooms because Joshua had taken over the convent when the nuns left. I notice my window didn't have any screens but, there was a net over the mat on the floor. The mat was my bed. I was almost asleep when Joe asked if he could stay in my room. He did have that fear of creepy crawly things and well, I said yes. He slept sitting up at the end of my mat with one eye open and his Zippo in his hand…just in case a python crawled in through the screenless window. I on the other hand had no difficulty sleeping knowing I had a Zippo-toting savior protecting me!

After an uneventful night with no attacks from snakes or other creepy crawling things and a breakfast of left over rice and strong coffee, Joe and I went to the market in the center of Bolahun. The Bush girls were there because later today they were to be initiated into the tribe. The school was a secret society where girls learn many different things to become good wives and mothers as Joshua explained to us. Kind of like home economics class back home I thought.

We left the village and headed on the well-worn path to the leprosarium toting our bags just in case we would stay overnight there. Next thing we knew, some young boys took our bags and led the way to the leprosarium and new adventures.

Word of our arrival had reached the leprosarium and the people came out welcoming us. Father Stevens approached us with an outstretched hand, smiling, "Welcome to our home!" He was a tall man with salt and pepper hair wearing a flowing black robe.

After many introductions, Father showed us around the clinic and we watched in fascination the warm wax technique used on the lepers' hands and feet which were then massaged to help loosen the muscles and ligaments to keep them from freezing up. We learned that the disease attacks the digits first and because the person can't feel anything, they end up cutting themselves, and infection sets in. Most of all, the lepers wanted us to touch and accept them for who they were. We moved over to the vocational therapy area and saw the lepers carving different woods. They created incredible wooden masks, statues of people and animals. Both Joe and I bought some to add to our collection of Liberian artifacts at home.

Father said, "I'm happy to see you show no fear and accept my patients. Most people have such a poor image of the lepers and think they are the untouchables. We work very hard to educate village people to the contrary. The lepers know how to take care of their disease and are able to return to their families, villages, and continue to work."

After a quick snack, Father asked, "While here, would you like to visit a monkey bridge? There is one fairly close over a small river but it's a hard trek through some rough bush."

Neither of us had to be asked twice as we both answered with a resounding, "Yes!" And after changing into long pants and long sleeved shirts, we were off. My bell bottom jeans flopped around as I walked which made walking even harder. Father was correct, this was an arduous trek. Soon we were both dripping with sweat and the flies drove us crazy. Every so often, I snapped a photo and sipped some water from my army canteen. We both were excited and didn't pay attention to the saw grass blades that cut through our shirts. Fortunately, the jean material was much more durable. We could hear the small rapids as we approached the river. The monkey bridge didn't disappoint. It loomed ahead and with great caution, I climbed up the ladder, onto the bridge, and began to put one foot in front of the other. Clenching the waist high rope for support, I crossed the expanse. In the middle, I gave my best Tarzan shout with relief that I had made it after the long hard walk to get here.

I observed that the bridge was suspended by braided vines both vertical and horizontal. Many of these vines were slung over strong branches so high above that we couldn't see where they ended. Our leper guide explained how the bridge was made when I asked who and how was it done.

"The monkey people, who live in trees, come at night and make bridge good."

"Monkey people? For true?" I asked with great skepticism.

"Yeah, Missy, the people fly and make bridge good. No people can see. Only monkey people see. The bridge it fine-o."

Both Joe and I nodded in agreement but one never knows. After all we believe in a fat guy wearing red and delivering toys to all boys and girls and then yes, there's the chimney thing too. So anything was possible.

Once our photos were taken, we crossed back over the monkey bridge and returned to the leprosarium. However, on the way back, walking up a hill with sweat blocking my vision and amid the noises of the jungle, I didn't quite understand what the men were yelling to me. All I knew was they were pushing me to the ground and removing my pants before I passed out from extreme pain.

Joe and Father Stevens told me what had happened. Someone had told me to move away and avoid stepping over the "log" as it really wasn't a log but driver ants moving to another location. Unfortunately, I stepped on the "log".

"When driver ants move their queen, they form a log-like structure and they all move together. The queen is never exposed to sunlight," Father told us. "You were badly stung and the boys had their good wits about them to help you. Oh, by the way, your crazy pants were left back on the trail. They quickly took you to a witchdoctor located near here to treat your swollen leg. You were fortunate the boys were there to help. Everyone got you back to the leprosarium and I gave you something to help with pain. I'd advise you to see the doctors at Firestone."

"I will," I whispered as Joe and I shared the round mud hut with its dirt floor. Father Stevens laughed when I told him about being protected by Joe holding his Zippo.

I felt much better in the morning and we attended mass. Father Stevens said the mass in three languages, Vai, Bandi, and English.

Thanking Father Stevens I said, "What a trip we have had. Joe and I wanted some adventure…well, we certainly got that and then some! I am so delighted to have met you and your patients. I admire their strengths in not allowing their disease and deformities to hinder their life and belief system. They live with grace and I'm proud to call you all my friends."

Joe agreed as we waved goodbye to Father and our new found friends. "We'll be back and bring those supplies you asked for on our next visit," Joe said as we walked back to my car to continue our trip with a visit to Koindu in Sierra Leone.

There wasn't any border crossing gate or people to ask for papers; we just went over some river and once in Koindu parked and walked around. Koindu was much larger than Bolahun and people were bustling about gathering their needed items for the week. Joe and I wandered around and took photos from our hips which we had become quite adapt at doing and ran no risk of any palava as this place didn't look as friendly as back in Liberia. For one, we saw two policemen carrying rifles. If you saw any Liberian police, they never carried weapons. At one point, a policeman came up to me questioning me in French. He demanded, "Give me camera. No photos allowed. Why you in Sierra Leone?"

"Sierra Leone? No, I'm in Liberia," I answered back in French.

He grabbed me and said I was under arrest for taking photos.

"Photos? No, my camera is here by my side. I didn't take any photos."

This arguing went back and forth with a small group gathering around staring at our theatrics.

Finally, the policeman accused me of not respecting the laws of Sierra Leone. I accused him of not showing respect for my husband, my country, and me. This stopped him cold as he just stared... probably wondering just who I was?

So, I said forcefully. "I say. Do you know who I am? Who my husband is?" Of course he didn't and so I told him.

"My husband is the President of the United States, Richard Nixon and we are visiting your beautiful neighboring country of Liberia. That man over there is my body guard. He will report back to my husband, President Nixon, and big palava will come down on you! I am Mrs. Nixon. Take your hands off me now!"

For a long moment, the policeman considered what I had said. Perhaps he thought about his career along with the possibility of the wrath of the American president and country. He may have regarded the looks on the crowd's faces and he slowly formed a plan on how to save face. Before long, his demeanor began to gradually change and a huge smile broke on his face. "I say to all that hear this. This woman is my good, good friend and we must welcome her to our country!"

With enormous fanfare, I was shown all around and Joe was told what to photograph and of course my new friend was in many of the photos with his arms around me, Mrs. Nixon. My new friend promised me that I wouldn't have any more palava if I wrote letters to him. I wrote my newly-found friend my address at 1600 Pennsylvania Avenue Washington, D.C. in the United States of America.

"Stop and be our guest," I offered. Of course, he was impressed. As we left Koindu and began our return trip back to the Plantation, I asked.

"Hey, Joe, do you think I should give a head's up to the President and Mrs. Nixon and the White House of a possible letter and or visitor?"

"No way; do you really think he is going to write you?"

"Yes, I do as he is my good, good friend," I laughed.

We made good time going home. "Always getting to the place takes longer than the trip home," Joe said. I nodded in agreement.

Soon I was nestled back in my own bed after receiving a loud meowed greeting from Leopold. He was happy I was home however, Joseph had his usual list of never ending complaints about my cat. Life was good.

> Dear Mom Dad Stop
> Upcountry trip great Stop
> Visited leprosarium Stop
> Monkey bridge Stop
> Warn White House Stop
> Nixon Stop
> Visitor may come Stop
> He my good good friend Stop
> Hugs African kisses Stop
> Kathleen

Monkey bridge
Bolahun, Liberia

Robertsport, Liberia 1974

Chapter 28

Vaitown, Cat Palava, and Robertsport

For weeks, Mike and I had been planning a trip to a diamond mine located somewhere near Vaitown, sometimes called Bomi, and the St. Paul River. We also were going to Robertsport, a town on the Atlantic Ocean about ten miles from the Sierra Leone border. Mike wasn't exactly sure where the diamond mines were located but had been to the Liberian Mining Company (LMC), near Vaitown and had heard about them. Mike had helped LMC with parts for machines in need of repair many times in the past as he was in charge of the department for heavy duty equipment for Firestone. Caterpillar machines were his specialty and Mike said that companies helped each other out in times of need. Rumor had it that this area could be dangerous because of diamonds being discovered and mined. Ralph, Joe, and Jim nixed going on the trip, not through fear but, because we had to take the truck due to rough road conditions, so only three of us could go. I had the time and Mike who had been there before to do some work on a broken machine felt the region was safe. The sun hadn't risen when we got to 15 Gate and the rains were holding off.

"Still can't understand why no one else would join us in our search for a diamond mine," Mike said as we got on the back road to Monrovia.

I said, "Yeah, I agree. I'm so excited to try to find a mine but, especially a diamond one."

Disturbing chickens and a few goats, Mike turned abruptly to avoid a hole the truck could have been lost in forever. We then turned onto the rutted road that led to Careysburg.

"Thought the road would be in better shape," Mike said. I just bounced all over the seat trying to hold onto the truck's top with my arm out the window and getting coated with red dust. Yes, of course, I wore my bandana over my nose and mouth. Every now and then we drove in and out of rain.

"I am glad to be going to Vaitown and Robertsport. I did find out that the latter was named for the first president of Liberia, Joseph Jenkins Roberts."

"Oui," Mike added, "Robertsfield Airport was also named for him."

"Mike, did I tell you I stumbled upon a diamond mine once when driving around by myself? I wandered into some hidden area close to some small river. I knew it was something big. There were armed naked guards who were taken aback seeing a white woman traveling alone. I convinced them to let me see what they were doing and reluctantly they agreed. I do know my dash spoke volumes. I did however, have to remove my clothes, shoes, leave my camera in my car but, was allowed to keep wearing my bra and underpants. I suspected it could be a diamond or gold operation they were taking me too, or at least I had hoped so," I said.

"Wow!" Mike remarked.

"Yeah, a guard carrying a rifle led while another one followed us.

They told me I needed to ask permission to move my arms even to scratch my head! At the river's edge, there were many armed men stationed all around carefully watching the diggers and men panning for diamonds. Yes, diamonds! All unarmed and armed men were naked so, I was happy I didn't have to follow suit. Everyone had to ask to itch or move in any direction that might be considered suspicious."

"Might be the same situation if we do find a diamond mine today. Workers are treated this way as they could slip a diamond into a skin pocket on their body like in their mouth, leg, between toes," Mike said. "When they leave the site, they are carefully body searched.

"Wow! Didn't know that and thank goodness I wasn't body searched! Well, back to my story. I was sitting on the river's bank, I motioned to let me pan for diamonds, the head guard nodded in agreement, and I slipped into the murky gray water not even fearing getting any germs or any attaching critters like leeches. I just wanted the experience. One guard, putting down his rifle, jumped in, showed me how to pan, and what to look for."

"Some magic makes the diamond go here," he said pointing to the middle of the tin pan.

"Mike, I knew that diamonds are the heaviest of minerals and specific gravity makes them settle in the center of rings of different stones weight. The diggers picked at the river's edge and others shoved the muck onto the banks. Men pushed muck into their tin pans and slowly sluiced them in the water. This was fascinating to do and nope, no diamond, but I did find a black hematite stone and got to keep it. The operation I found was small. There weren't any machines for digging or scooping the river's bottom and edge. All work was done by hand."

"You really took a big chance," Mike said, "You'll do well on this trip if we find a diamond mine." Slowly, we drove though the towns of Franktown, Bensonville, Clay Ashland, and turned off a somewhat traveled road.

"This road looks like a good possibility of being near a river or stream and maybe a diamond mine," Mike announced as we bounced all over the road which started off pretty good but grew increasingly worse.

"Perhaps, we should turn around and try another road branch."

Turn we did, traveling up and down what looked to be promising roads but weren't. On one of these side roads, we got stuck proper as the Liberians would say. Try as we could, the truck wouldn't budge and all four wheels just spun. I even went into the bush to pee as usually when doing this, someone would stop and start up a conversation not paying any attention to whether I understood them or they the business I was doing.

The truck was stuck "proper"!

"Mike, no one stopped to chat," I said upon returning to the stuck truck. "I don't think anyone lives out here. In fact, come to think of it, we haven't seen any people in over two hours! That's so unusual. Don't you think?"

"Oui! I got a thicker branch to use as a lever. You drive the truck in reverse and I will bounce on the branch. Hopefully this will jar the truck loose."

So, following the plan, I drove backwards and Mike bounced and bounced. Wonders of wonders as his plan worked!

Then carefully negotiating the deeply rutted road, we managed to get back on the main road when we heard someone shouting. "Monsieur Martin! Monsieur Martin!" and out of the deep bush, came a small Liberian still calling Mike's name and, "Arrêtez, s'il vous plait." (Stop, please)

"Well, I'll be! We haven't seen anyone for hours, I even peed in the bush and no one came by, and out of the bush comes someone who knows you!" I exclaimed.

Mike stopped and the Liberian spoke quickly in French that his "cat was broke" and begged Monsieur Martin to fix it. Mike glanced my way and his eyes said it all. Cat meant perhaps a diamond mine and maybe, just maybe, I could even get one. I nodded my consent and the Liberian hopped in front to direct us to the "broke cat" and swore us to secrecy. We agreed that we knew nothing and furthermore would remember nothing. After many miles, more rough roads, and turns and more turns, we came upon a small river and naked armed guards. Stuck in the middle of the river was a huge backhoe/digger Caterpillar and it wasn't operating.

At last, we had found a diamond operation! I only hope that we would live to return to the Plantation. Mums the word and my eyes saw well, nothing. Mike scampered up onto the cat and was examining it while I sat on a hill of freshly dug muddy stuff from the river trying not to appear to be searching for anything that glimmered.

Getting up to stretch my legs, the guards became agitated, excitedly chatting, and scrambled to push me back to our truck. Everyone was behaving oddly and soon I understood why. A Liberian woman came stomping out of the bush screaming at Mike since she had noticed him first. Mike quickly jumped off the machine, forded the water, and headed to her. I decided to catch up to both of them. She continued to holler in some Liberian language to the workers and turned to us and in English asked, "What are you doing uninvited at my diamond mine?"

Mike explained how we were going to Vaitown when a man that knew him, flagged him down, and asked him to come check out a broken Caterpillar machine.

"We were brought here under a vow of silence so I could examine the broken caterpillar," he said skipping the information about our searching for diamond mines.

"We are from Firestone and were asked to help you with this palava. My name is Mike Martin and this is my friend, Kathleen, a teacher at the Firestone Staff School."

I stammered as I put out my hand, "Madam, I am privileged to meet you and aren't you Miss Angie Brooks?"

The in-charge Liberian woman dressed in a purple print lappa skirt wearing a white blouse and another colorful lappa wrapped on her head, stared and then threw her head back and laughed as she said, "I am Miss Angie Brooks and will always be Miss Angie Brooks! How do you recognize me?"

I explained about my community's local high schools and how they ran a model United Nations every year.

I said, "My school represented Liberia and me, you."

Miss Brooks nodded and a smile spread over her face when I added that knew she was the President of the United Nations General Assembly in 1969. She shook both our hands.

"Miss Brooks, I feel fortunate to meet you and thank you for your dedication to representing women and children worldwide. I also agree with you that women's voices need to be heard and respected."

Miss Brooks was appeased and then addressed Mike about repairing her machine. He promised to return with the needed parts and would fix the Caterpillar for her with Firestone's compliments. Of course, Miss Brooks was happy with this and allowed us to continue watching the men work and Mike to check out some other Caterpillar machines nearby. She also promised me a raw diamond upon Mike's return to repair her machine. To this day, I still await my diamond. I guess, it's the Liberian way. She rapidly hurried away back into the bush. My only regret was I hadn't taken any photos as our cameras were banished to the truck. Later, I thought, not even an autograph.

"Mike, who would ever believe we met Miss Angie Brooks, a President of the UN General Assembly, at her diamond mine? Gosh, a photo would have helped with this memory…" I remarked as my voice trailed off.

Our newly found Liberian friend took us back to the main road and we were once again headed to Vaitown making a stop in Clay to eat. Soon, we were in Vaitown and seeing a table of gasoline filled jars, we decided to gas up the truck. The gas in Mike's truck was there for emergencies. Buying gas whenever you can was a traveler's motto going anywhere in Liberia. We headed to LMC and discovered the huge operation they had going on! A German, Frederick, gave us a tour and told us that this mine only had a few years left to get the iron ore out however, he recommended that we travel via train up to Bong Mine near the Guinean border as it was a much larger open pit mine that was also very impressive to see.

"Well, it looks like another trip to plan," I said. "Please, Frederick, explain why the water collecting in the bottom of the pit is such a deep sapphire blue and the edges are a softer aqua blue?"

Frederick explained, "The surrounding rocks contains much copper which gives the water the unique shades. Many local people have named this Blue Lake."

"Definitely well named," said Mike as we climbed into Frederick's truck to head back up the steep pit's rim and for us to get back on the road to Robertsport.

"Robertsport is a beautiful town," said Frederick and Lake Piso is another incredible blue lake but was formed naturally and is a salt water lake. Oh, yes, stay at the new Hotel Victoria on the Robertsport's beach. Very nice accommodations. Enjoy all the area has to offer and come back to visit us any time."

Retracing many miles to get on the road to Robertsport, we arrived there at last, very late. No lights of any kind were on however, we drove around and down the hill towards the beach and found Hotel Victoria. We unloaded our bags and checked in. A cook was awakened and he prepared something for us to eat and we headed to our rooms. Exploring Robertsport was scheduled the next day..

I hardly got to sleep when Mike was knocking on my door and saying, "You must see the beach and ocean. C'est belle! I see a lighthouse down the way to explore and also a ship wreck on the beach's edge. Remember, I want to see where Benson Base was located that was built by the United States and used during WWII. Norman Hayes speaks about Pan Am, Firestone, and the United States establishing military bases here near Lake Piso or Fisherman's Lake as it was first known and the other was of course the development of Robertsfield."

"I had heard Norman talk about this also. He had said that our United States Army cleared the bush and put down special planks for a runway like they did at Robertsfield. Allied seaplanes landed, unloaded, and shuttled passengers and cargo to Monrovia and then onto Robertsfield. Benson Base was a connection to Brazil and the United States however, Robertsfield became the major base supporting the Allies' war effort," I added.

We spent the day exploring the area, enjoying a swim, helping the local fishermen haul in their nets teeming with the day's catch, and loaded up the truck for the long trip back to the Plantation.

"We must return to Robertsport with the guys for a weekend at the Hotel Victoria," I said as we got back on the road home.

>Dear Mom Dad Stop
>Trip to Vaitown and Robertsport Stop
>Diamond and iron ore mines Stop
>Cat and truck palava Stop
>All is well now Stop
>Hug African kisses Stop
>Kathleen

Peter Cottle

Chapter 29

Peter Cottle and Liberian Adventures

Climbing the steps of the Central Office building, I was headed to see Jack Carmichael. Hoping I hadn't done anything wrong, I went early to visit with George Kohout to see if he knew why I was being summoned. George was out and so I chatted with Ottilie Thompson, his secretary. Ottilie might be able to give me a clue as to what Jack wanted. George always said she was the best secretary he ever had so, maybe? Her mischievous eyes told me she knew but, she denied knowing, "What Mr. Carmichael wants, he doesn't share that information with me and I can't help you. May I get you a Coca Cola?"

Just at that time, Jack's secretary said, "Mr. Carmichael will see you."

Jack met me at the door and offered me a seat. He was smiling.

So far so good, I thought, I'm not in any trouble. I sat in the chair. Jack was a very tall man and with a big smile. He removed his thick black glasses, cleaned them, and replaced them on his nose as he spoke, "Kathleen, thanks for coming down as I have something quite important to go over with you. Word has it that you like to travel around Liberia and I have a proposition for you."

Oh no, I panicked, he knows about my flights to Mali and the drought areas in the Sahara without any passport. Or maybe he's upset about how I masqueraded as his wife, Ann, when traveling around the country. I thought, this is bad, really bad, even with that wide smile Jack was displaying, it could be just to fool me. That Jerry Swanson blabbed on me even after I got him onto flights to the Sahara with the Red Cross…that…

Jack continued, "I have discussed this with Jim Smith and he's all in for you to help Firestone out. Next week a guy, Peter Cottle, who was born on the Plantation, is coming for a visit. Peter will be in and out of Liberia as he will be taking photos for National Geographic in the drought areas of the Sahara," he said with an awkward chuckle.

"Er?" I said but thinking, not again! They want me to date this Peter guy, another A.B. Tolbert palava. I sat quietly waiting and tried not to jump to conclusions, one thing I have learned to do.

Jack continued, "I can't lend him a car and driver to go around the Plantation and Liberia so here's where you come in. Would you be willing to be his driver and take him wherever he wants? Jim said he'd cover your class when needed and you won't be missing that much school as you have an Easter break. All that is required is your agreement. Do you need time to think about this or not?"

Hum, not what I was expecting at all I thought, and said, "I agree to be this guy's chauffeur."

Peter Cottle arrived on the next Pan Am Sunday flight. Many Firestone people were waiting and warmly welcomed him. Turns out, he was the first expat baby to be born at the then newly built Firestone Hospital. The Cottles and Peter, who was 12 when they left Liberia, were known by many Staff. This was Peter's first trip back in eighteen years.

He was about the same height as me and had dark brown hair. I could tell he was excited about returning to Liberia and to see his "family" again. David Sharwellie greeted his long-time childhood playmate and helped him to collect his luggage and get through customs. Peter had one large suitcase and three larger silver suitcases, a small silver one, and his camera's heavy-duty tripod. Hum, what's in those silver suitcases I wondered?

Everyone headed to the Guest House where he would be staying when in Liberia. The stewards had an incredible spread of food and drinks for a wonderful welcome-back-home-brunch. Wow, I thought, Peter was some kind of celebrity as the red carpet was rolled out for him. And, I'll be driving him around no less. This will be lots of fun!

Peter shared photos of his parents who had passed away a few years before. He also shared a photo of his wife and where they lived in Santa Barbara, California. I learned that he was a photography instructor at Brooks Institute in Santa Barbara and freelanced for a variety of magazines. Peter was doing a shoot for National Geographic and wanted to take photographs around Liberia for a photographic show back at the Santa Barbara Institute and perhaps publish a book. Did I say this was going to be fun? Well, I could feel the excitement rising!

A week later, Peter and I were on the dusty road, bandanas in place, passing through 26 Gate headed to Bolahun and the leprosarium there. Over the past week, I had taken Peter all around the Plantation and Firestone's factory. Already, I was learning so much from him about how to plan and compose photos. I found that I had a knack for putting people, especially children, at ease and getting the photographic shot. I loved using his equipment, having discovered what was in those silver suitcases. The small one contained slide film which Peter kept in the refrigerator at the Guest House. He likes to keep his film "on ice" or tried to as many places we were going to wouldn't have any ice.

Peter took photos using a Swedish Hasselblad camera. Its many interchangeable backs and lens were used to get the right shot. His equipment was expensive and out of my price range so, my Nikon camera would continue to be my camera.

We stopped whenever Peter saw what looked to be a promising photo opportunity. Seeing Liberia through his eyes was so exciting. I was enjoying this wonderful opportunity that Firestone had given to me. We made it to Bolahun and the leprosarium where Father Stevens greeted us. The next day a guide took Peter and me to the monkey bridge and I was careful not to run into any driver ants remembering my last encounter with them. It was a perfect day to take pictures with the sunlight filtering through the trees.

I explained to Peter that I was nixing driving into Guinea as I didn't want to run the risk of meeting that policeman. Father Stevens and Peter enjoyed my accounting of that day with "body guard Joe" and being Mrs. Nixon.

That evening, the villagers put on a dance show for the "silver box man" as Peter had become known as. We laughed and enjoyed the show. I even joined in and let loose dancing wildly.

We managed the long tiring return trip to the Plantation without any incident. The next day, we drove to Division 33 and hiked to the waterfalls and then drove over to the water hole at Division 36 ending the day at a BYOB party at Dick and Polly Huggs' bungalow. The theme was Hawaiian and included a roasted pig that had been basted and turned all day. Peter remarked how he had watched a similar theme party held at his neighbors bungalow 20 or so years before. The music blared from the stereo and most were dancing and enjoying the luau. Our small group called it an early night as we were going to Marshall Beach with Ralph on his boat and he liked to leave early from the SNAFU dock.

"The fish are early risers and so must we," Ralph would always tell me.

Ralph was the most gracious host and the day was fantastic! Ralph, Joe, and Peter caught grouper and they were put on "ice" in the cooler. Good eating for another time together. Ralph's cook had prepared fried chicken and other munchies for us to enjoy. We returned to the Plantation tired, sunburned, but relaxed and happy. Ralph picked us up and we met Jim at the Hotel for dinner. Peter marveled at how Ralph played his number game with the waiters.

On Monday, Peter left to travel in Mali and nearby areas and I went back to teaching, much to the delight of my students. I sure did miss them and easily slipped into my routine for a few days before the school's Easter break began. I used this time to make arrangements for our trip to LAMCO in the Nimba Mountain Range. LAMCO was an iron ore mining operation established in 1963 by a Liberian-American-Swedish Mining Company. I had been hearing about their open-pit mining for some time and wanted to see it for myself especially after seeing the pit mine at LMC. I decided to put my car on the LAMCO train and ride it from Buchanan up to the iron ore mine. Then we would drive back to the Plantation, showing Peter the Mission and leprosarium in Ganta. I thought that seeing the Liberian countryside via train would be a wonderful thing.

Peter returned from Mali and shared his adventures with everyone. And, no, I didn't tell him that I had also been there as I didn't believe it was necessary. Me, still without my passport, I was afraid that Liberian government would deport me for exiting and entering Liberia without my passport. I did check in with the American Embassy every few weeks to see if it had shown up on someone's desk under a pile of forgotten papers. I was going to go to Europe in July no matter what. The Embassy said they would give me a document to present at any borders I would cross and it would get me back into the United States. They were working on getting me a replacement passport that would be at my home in Erie when I arrived there in August but, they were still hoping that it would show up here in Liberia before I left. What a huge palava this has been since I arrived that Sunday almost eight months ago. There were so many people trying to locate my passport.

Peter, Joe, and I drove to Buchanan and met up with Bill, harbor master and we spent the night at his bungalow. Rising early, we drove over to the LAMCO area and my car was driven onto a rail car. We all went into the front car and had incredible views of the scenery along the track. At one point, I was lulled into a peaceful sleep as the train rolled on the tracks. We passed 9 stations on the single-track line and each station had passing tracks. Our ride was 5 hours long and we arrived in

LAMCO around 2 pm. Watching my car come off the train, I felt suddenly exhausted even though I had dozed on the train. Someone told us it was because we were in the mountains at about 5,000 feet above sea level. It would take some time to adjust to the altitude. Soon we were on route to LAMCO's guest house where we cleaned up and met at the poolside bar and pool to await our dinner.

"Gosh, this pool is super!" Joe remarked as he stepped out of the Olympic-size pool. "The pool alone would be an incentive for people to come and work here since there really isn't much else to do."

"True, however, I would miss shopping and eating in Monrovia."

"Yeah, and don't forget the Ducor Palace and embassies parties," Joe added.

Continuing to enjoy LAMCO's hospitality, we rose early the next morning, ate, and had a tour of their mining operations. All the while enjoying the amazing views of the Nimba Mountains. LAMCO was interesting with a great pool and incredible views. However, even with their own school, this place wasn't for me.

In the afternoon, my car was placed back on the train and we rode the train down to the station closest to the town of Sanniquellie. Driving once again, we were headed to the Mission and leprosarium in Ganta which was a mile from the Ivory Coast border and still in the mountains. We met up with the missionaries who ran everything and had a tour of the leprosarium and we were invited to spend the night at the Mission. This was wonderful, as we had planned to camp out in or by my car. We departed early in the morning with Joe doing most of the driving and arrived very late back at the Plantation.

After a couple of days recovering, Peter, Joe, and I flew on Air Liberia to Harper and Firestone's Cavalla Plantation in Maryland County. We were the guest of Charlie Lorenz, the managing director. Peter knew Charlie from before as he was a friend of his parents. They spent time reminiscing about the "good old days" and I spent time in the library set up for the staff. Joe really enjoyed being at Cavalla and indicated he would like to work here. I would also if there had been a school.

"Our Plantation has less staff and so, no school," Charlie told us while giving us a tour of the Plantation and then of Harper.

"Harper was named for Robert Goodloe Harper who was an American politician and a member of the American Colonization Society. It was settled in 1834 by freed blacks and former slaves from the state of Maryland in the United States," Charlie told us. "This area always had trouble with the Grebo and Kru tribes and finally, after many skirmishes, the independent State of Maryland asked for help from Monrovia in 1857. They then joined Liberia becoming known as Maryland County with Harper as its capital. By the way, former President Tubman was born and raised here in Harper."

"I just love learning about the history of Liberia," I said thanking Charlie for our tour and stay at the Guest House which was attached to his bungalow.

The day ended with us going to the beach where I tried to climb out on the rocks to the farthest point of Liberia. I didn't make it as far as I had wanted because the rocks were just too slippery. Early in the morning, three weary travelers flew back on Air Liberia to Robertsfield and the Harbel Plantation.

Peter had only a few days left before returning to Santa Barbara, California and we drove to places on the Plantation for his last photo shots.

"I don't know if I'll ever get back here," Peter said. "When I'm home, I am going to check and see if any private companies need a jet flown here. And, yes, I do have my pilot's license."

Peter did return over the next two years to Liberia flying jets for companies in nearby areas. Of course, he flew back commercially to California. He managed to take more photos for his show and future photo book of Liberia and her people.

A going-away dinner party for Peter was given by Dory and John Muir and Mr. and Mrs. Carmichael had a brunch at their home. Many people were at the airport when Peter left. Sadly, I said goodbye to him and went home with Ralph, Mike, Jim, and Joe. I was both happy to get back into my routine, but sad to not continue my exploration of Liberia. I had so many incredible adventures and memories of my time traveling with Peter.

> Dear Mom Dad Stop
> Opportunity to be tour guide Stop
> Took him around Liberia Stop
> Miss exploring Stop
> Happy to be back in my routine Stop
> Hugs African kisses Stop
> Kathleen

LAMCO in Nimba County, Liberia

My third grade class 1974-75

Chapter 30

Chinese Dragon Attack and the Christmas Visitor

I was back in Liberia after my month leave in Europe and the United States. My second year at the Staff School had begun smoothly. Once again, I established my routine. Both my Inside and Outside Josephs were still employed by me. Yes, Outside Joseph was still humbugged over Leopold and immediately complained when I returned. Both Josephs had taken care of my animals while I was on leave. By now, I had Leopold, two domesticated cats, and Fred, the Rhodesian Ridgeback. Fred had joined my little family just before I left for my leave. His family had returned to The Netherlands and were unable to bring him. I happily adopted him and extended his "juju" along with all my cats. They weren't going into anyone's soup, that's for sure.

I was sitting on my porch sipping some wine and enjoying the light rain. A smile came to my face as I remembered that day in mid-July when I boarded the Swiss Air flight for my driving tour of Switzerland, France, and Italy for two weeks. A group of us had decided to drive around visiting small villages, sampling the local wines, buying and shipping the ones we enjoyed back to Liberia. We were now waiting for the arrival of these boxes. This wine buying trip almost didn't happen. I was buckled into my first-class seat on the way to Zürich/Geneva, Switzerland when Mr. Brown stepped onto the plane. He addressed me as he handed over my passport.

"Hello Miss Mobilia, I have located your passport under a pile of papers and also notified the US Embassy of my find. Please accept my apologies for its loss and any stress this has caused you over the past year."

"Oh, my! Thank you, Mr. Brown!" I said taking my precious passport. "You have saved Firestone, the Embassy, and me a lot of time. I don't have to apply for a new one when back in the States and can travel without worry on my European trip."

"Well, about your trip and flight on Swiss Air," Mr. Brown spoke hesitantly. "I will be joining you because I am accompanying A. B. Tolbert who has already been seated in the rear of this flight."

"What?" I unbuckled, stood, and turned. I couldn't see him. I spoke hurriedly, "I am getting off and taking another flight," I said as I started to gather my belongings.

"Please, Miss Mobilia, don't do this. I have some guards to assist me in keeping Mr. Tolbert at the rear. You need not be concerned. I have made all arrangements with Firestone and paid for these first-class seats and section for you and your group. You all are my guests. Please reconsider and stay. By the way, the middle section of the plane won't have any passengers as that too has been arranged."

I looked at my small group of friends whose eyes pleaded for me to take this flight and the wine tasting trip with them. I weighed everything and decided to stay. After all, Mr. Brown had helped me over the past year with the A.B. Tolbert palava.

Remembering that flight now and smiling, we had a great time and loved how John Chapman stood and sang the French National Anthem when the pilot announced we were in French air space. Food and champagne flowed and not once during the entire flight did I see A. B. Tolbert.

Outside Joseph called for me, "Ma, come now."

Ever since I returned from my leave, Joseph has taken to calling me Ma. I object and beg him to not do this. He would laugh and say, "Okay, Ma, I no call you Ma."

"Joseph, what you want?"

"Ma, you carry this old man upcountry to the village? My wife had baby."

Well, my first thought was how could you be having babies at your old age? But, I said, "Okay, I will take you on Friday after school." I decided to go to the Firestone Store to pick up some baby clothes and stuffed toys. Also, a bottle of Bourbon for the new father. He usually drank cane juice or palm wine so, this would be a treat.

We left for Joseph's village after I had lunch and put Leopold in charge. Inside Joseph frowned as he felt he had more rank than the wild cat.

Our ride was bumpy and uneventful. Arriving and parking my car I looked over the wide river of lush green forest. This is a pristine paradise I thought before we walked down the hill to the river and Joseph's village. We needed to ford this river in order to get there. As often was the case, Loco-man (named this as he moved very fast like a train) greeted us and insisted on picking me up and putting me in the canoe. Once across, he then carried me up the hill to the village. I had given up some time ago as protesting didn't work with Loco-man. Joseph carried the presents grinning from ear to ear. He was so proud to be meeting his new baby which turned out to be a son. Everyone came out to wave and clap for the new father and the drums pounded their hellos. The villagers also knew how I enjoyed the drums and dancing.

We entered Joseph's hut and met the baby boy. Well, you couldn't call him little as he was a big boy with a huge cry. He only wanted his mother's breast. Joseph went outside to meet with his family and friends. I joined them once the baby was asleep.

Joseph approached me and asked, "Ma, my baby want your name."

"What?" Thinking the baby is a week or so old and can't speak. "What do you mean, Joseph?"

"Baby want to be called Mobilia Free Man!" He proudly grinned.

Well, I thought a baby with my last name…this is quite interesting and added, "Joseph, I'd be honored to share my name with your son!"

Later after we ate, I held Mobilia Free Man and gave him my name. The dancer matched the drummers' beat and everyone celebrated this new life and name.

The next day back at home, I shared my news with the greatly impressed guys.

"Does this mean that you will be putting Mobilia through college? Start the saving fund now," Ralph laughed.

I'm holding Mobilia Free Man

Life was back to normal.

I continued traveling upcountry whenever possible and of course, partying. BYOB parties were held every other month and usually with a theme and because of this, we usually were busy planning for the party. Our next BYOB party was going to be on Saturday, November 23 and it was themed a costume party-not a Halloween costume-but, any costume. The BYOB committee had suggested that small groups get together to come up with a group costume. My phone had rung early yesterday and it was Jacques Koops. He had a costume idea and wanted to run it by me and the guys. Jacques's wife, Hil (the Staff School's former secretary) was back in Holland with their daughter Marjanne who was attending high school there.

I met Jacques up at the Golf Club for coffee about an hour later. He thought our costume should be kept secret and included an unusual group of people. In fact, Jacques had worked the whole thing out and even had made drawings of the costume! Wow! I was impressed and especially liked the idea which was a long, long, fierce Chinese Dragon that would include a moving tail, head, and maybe even fiery breath!

I suggested Ralph Welsch, Jim Smith, John Chapman, Kevin Estall, Sammy Adonis, and Mike Martin to be in our group. He added Charles Cooper, Brad Hathaway, Andy Butler, John Francis, and Jack Van Dam. With Jacques and me, we were a total of 13 in this group costume. I loved this idea with people from different departments, some married and some not. I would be the only woman and would sew the costume.

With less than 2 months to design, sew, and create the moving head and tail, we planned how to contact the above people. Our first meeting was at the school at 11 pm where we decided who would be in charge of what part of the design and small groups were created. We agreed keep our identities secret, even from wives, and this included during and after the BYOB party. We were to be the best kept secret group ever! These small groups would select their own meeting places and times.

I was in the group with Brad, Charles, and Sammy. We were in charge of the fabric part; buying the fabric and sewing the costume. Because Sammy owned the store just off the Plantation, he was able to buy bolts of muslin fabric with no one becoming curious as to the large amounts being purchased. Brad, Sammy, Charlie, and I went to Monrovia to buy Rit-Dye. We had planned on a dark gray body with deep purple accents to make our dragon as scary as possible.

"Are you kidding? The only colors we can get are aqua and orange?" Brad said. "I wanted our dragon to be in fierce colors of gray and purple. Somehow, aqua and orange don't say I'm a fierce dragon."

Sammy also agreed, however, these were the only bulk colors of Rit-Dye we were able to find. The muslin and dyes were at Sammy's store the night our group met for the dyeing part of our project.

We all carried our large wash tins to Sammy's and we began the tedious job of dyeing the muslin. Once the fabric was dyed and hung, we rested drinking Club Beer and talking about our big secret dragon.

"Any word from the other groups and their progress?" Brad asked.

Sammy filled us in on what he knew. "They are still trying to work out the fire breathing part but, the tail is swinging up and down, left and right. Wow, Jacques did have a great idea."

I suggested, "Because our dragon is aqua and orange and not a fierce color like we had thought...perhaps we should make it dance and prance around crazily. I am going to run this by everyone at our next large group meeting. What do you think?"

The guys liked the idea and we tried coming up with dance steps which weren't easy to do after many bottles of Club Beer. What a fun time we had in this part of our planning stage.

Brad suggested, "Perhaps, we should do the dancing when we are

Part of our dragon drying in the sun

clear-headed."

The whole group met late the next night at the school. Sammy brought the dyed, dried, and folded pieces of muslin. I explained to everyone the plans of covering our arms, legs, and heads by sewing pillow-like parts out of the orange colored muslin. The body was going to be aqua. I figured out that the dragon was going to be about 52 feet long! Each group gave an updated report on what they were working on.

My group met after church and we measured, cut, and sewed the pieces. Charlie and Brad labeled and bundled each person's costume. We finished late, tired, but happy our part was completed. Last night I had given both the head and tail groups their fabric since they were going to glue and staple it onto the chicken wire designs that they had created for the head and tail. Our dragon was coming together and still we were under the shroud of secrecy. Our houseboys had been sworn and duly bribed.

The next day, the whole group met in my classroom for the reveal of the head and tail. The guys had actually made them move and swing! Unbelievable! Each night for the rest of the week we met and practiced our dance steps wearing the costume and prancing around as the fun aqua and orange dragon! This was incredible! The BYOB party was this coming Saturday evening at the Big Club and we were ready to dance and entertain.

"Costume party is tonight!" Ralph said to us at breakfast at his bungalow. We four bachelors were going together to the Big Club as people expected us to be together. What we were responsible for was loaded in Ralph's trunk and we were psyched.

Later on at the Big Club and chowing on my huge burger, curious people kept asking, "Where's your costume?" My answer was I had decided to not dress in costume and to enjoy the efforts of others.

We had shared with the head of the BYOB committee our plan and to announce a guest who flew in from the Land of Make-Believe to entertain the BYOB party group. I can still hear the cheers, whistles, and applause when we entered, dancing, prancing, hopping, and bobbing to the music, *The Monster Mash* and other monster theme songs. The dragon's tail swished and shook and the head with the extended arms grabbed people's arms causing them to scream and run around. The dance act was incredible and finally, the dragon disappeared into the dark of night. We quickly undressed and stored everything and rejoined to party remarking, "What a terrific costume! Who were they? I loved the dragon's dance moves."

Most thought the dragon was some group from the US Embassy or even some Pan Am crew. To this day, the dragon people have remained anonymous until I wrote about it in my book. Guess the gig's up-now.

American Thanksgiving came and this year I hosted it and was in charge of the turkey. No tuna turkey this year. I made a traditional spicy stuffing and everyone brought their favorite sides to dinner. A day at the beach enjoying sun and water, followed by a family-style Thanksgiving dinner. Life was great and I was sharing it with good friends.

I received an unexpected telegram a couple of days after Thanksgiving from my former boyfriend, Tim. I hadn't heard from him since I last saw him on my leave in August. He cabled that I was to meet his flight arriving a few days before Christmas. Yep, he was coming to Liberia for a visit !

"What do you mean he's coming for Christmas?" Jim asked. "I thought you had said the relationship was over between you two."

"I thought so too," I said. "Don't know what to expect since I haven't had any correspondence with him in months and only saw him that one time when I was home and that didn't go very well."

A small group of us met Tim's Sabena flight that Wednesday evening. Tim was excited and extremely tired (as were most visitors coming from the States) and after a few drinks at the Hotel's bar, we headed to the bachelor compound. Ralph had offered for Tim to stay at his bungalow.

Since my Christmas break had already begun, I was able to take Tim around Liberia. Joe or Jim joined us to help with the driving. We managed a trip to Kakata and the zoo, Ganta and the leprosarium, the beaches that we frequented, and yes, Monrovia. I wasn't surprised that

Tim never contacted my parents before he came to Liberia. This act spoke volumes to me. I knew he was self-centered and this proved it to me and was why I put a nix to our relationship. I didn't understand why he had come for a visit.

At last, Tim's two-week visit was over and my friends were with me to see him off. Tim had had some palava trying to take two elephant tables through customs until I dashed the customs agent and then he, at last, was able to board his flight back to the States via Belgium. Wobbling up the stairs, he truly was a funny sight. Then, Tim turned, waved, and disappeared into the plane's interior. Hopefully gone from my life forever, I thought.

Speaking to the group that evening over dinner at the Hotel, "I had a good time entertaining Tim, but, don't understand why he visited. He didn't even let my parents know he was coming to visit me. Strange, huh?"

Jim sat and smiled. I know he was thinking, now's my chance. No Tim on the scene or in her heart. Room for me? No way would I consider dating Jim. I considered him a good friend, someone I could rely upon in need, but not to get romantic over. I always made sure not to be alone with him or to give him any ideas that our relationship would be anything else.

The Harmattan winds came in mid-January and we were draped in a blanket of fine Saharan sand. My bandana was back in use until the winds changed and blew from the ocean.

After a day at the beach and dinner in the Hotel's restaurant, we were enjoying drinks in the bar when I said, "Later this week, my cousin Ruth and her boyfriend, Chuck, will be visiting for a few days. Her job has her working in different African countries over the next year and Chuck is in the Peace Corps and teaches in Sierra Leone. I'm excited for their visit."

"Chuck is more than welcomed to stay at my bungalow," Ralph offered.

"Thanks Ralph. He will appreciate sleeping in a bed versus on the floor at my place." I said.

"They will be here for our progressive dinner on Saturday." Jim added. "I'll let everyone know to expect two more guests."

The week went by quickly and Ruth flew in. Chuck joined her arriving via buses and taxis from Sierra Leone. I showed them around the Plantation and nearby areas of interest as we were getting everything ready for our progressive dinner. Our dinner had an Italian theme. Polly Hugg, Mae Gillian, and I had made trays of lasagna because we were in charge of the main course. Each course was at someone's bungalow. We began with an assortment of cocktails and hors d'oeuvres at Mike's. Next, we drove to the Boleratz's for Italian wedding soup and wine, then over to the Huggs' for lasagna and more wine. The Coopers hosted dessert and we ended up at the Lawton's for aperitifs and yes, we were stuffed!

Ralph suggested as he opened and moved his belt buckle another hole, "I love this idea of progressing around to eat and drink, but let's not plan another progressive dinner for a few months or until I lose 10 pounds!"

Laughing, we agreed.

Chuck returned to Sierra Leone, Ruth flew somewhere in Africa for work, and I went back to teaching. I enjoyed partying and the holidays but, loved getting back to my routine.

> Dear Mom Dad Stop
> Merry Christmas Stop
> Tim visited for Christmas Stop
> Happy 1975 Stop
> Cousin Ruth visited Stop
> Hugs African kisses Stop
> Kathleen

At the end of 1974, we celebrated the wedding of Werner Schaub (Swiss Air manager) and Christine who were married outside the hotel by the pool and Farmington River. This was a much quieter celebration for us all and a wonderful way to bring in a new year.

Happy 1975!

Rev. Dixon married
Christine and Werner Schaub
on December 30, 1974

Air Liberia

Chapter 31

New News, New Teacher, and New Dogs

We were dining at the Hotel after a long day of sun and beach. Two announcements from our friends floored us. The first one came from Joe. "I am leaving next week for a new job at Firestone's Cavalla Plantation. They offered me an incredible opportunity for upward movement in the company and I have accepted this position."

"Well, knock me over," I said. "I knew something was up when I saw you going back and forth to Cavalla over the past few weeks. That Charlie Lorenz never said a word the entire time I was there!"

"Nothing was finalized until today, Kathleen. So, I didn't want to jump the gun especially if the deal fell through."

"I'll come down to visit as often as I can," I said.

"I believe we all will give it a go," Ralph added.

The next whopper came when Jim said with a strange look on his face as he looked around the table, "I am moving from the school into a new department that Firestone is establishing. I will set it up and get it running. Firestone has been investigating this for a long time. They want to use the cut-down rubber wood to make furniture and flooring. It's a wonderful challenge for me to undertake and I have accepted this job move. I will no longer be the headmaster at the Staff School."

We were stunned. What's going on? What's with Jim's strange look? If this doesn't beat all.

Breaking our shocked silence, Mike asked, "Anyone have more news? I, for one, am staying in my job."

Everyone nodded in agreement with Mike.

Over the next few weeks, we saw Joe move to Cavalla, Jim became more and more involved at his new job and was less and less at school. Billie Darsey was stepping in Jim's place as headmistress. All teachers at school were helping both colleagues with their transitions. Because Billie was becoming our headmistress, another teacher was hired to replace her in her fourth-grade job. A couple of days later at a quickly called faculty meeting, Billie announced, "Patricia Ryan, from St. Louis, will be arriving on this Sunday's Pan Am flight. Hopefully, many of you will be there to welcome her to Liberia and our school. I understand she's coming very quickly not having the same opportunities as most of you had with shopping and packing for your move. She'll need as much support as possible and I know I can rely upon you."

Patty arrived as planned and most of the teachers were there to welcome her. She was a tall, trim woman with raven black hair, blue eyes, and as Irish as Irish can be. Patty looked exhausted, hungry, but eager to see where she'd be living and teaching. I took her to the Guest House to freshen up and then to her bungalow-Joe's. Yep, Joe's. Once her bungalow was repainted, she could move in as Joe had it in great move-in condition. Patty was as thrilled as I was that she had another single woman living nearby.

Even though, I missed Joe terribly, my friendship with Patty grew. She fell into the rhythm of life on the Plantation. Before Joe left for Cavalla, he had given me his German Shepard, Willie, since the dog was more at my home than at his. So, my little pet family continued to grow.

Willie was extremely protective of me and got along great with Fred, the other cats, and even Leopold much to the chagrin of both Josephs. More work for them, I guess. Often when returning home, I would find everyone asleep.

One late night upon returning home, Outside Joseph was asleep on his chair with a blanket on his shoulders, hat on his head, and his arm cradling the machete. Leopold slept on the machete and Fred and Willie were under the table. None of them woke up. I gently touched Joseph. No movement. None from either of the other guards. What gives? I thought as I took the hat off Joseph's head. No movement. Next, I took his blanket. Again, no movement. Well, lifting his arm and moving Leopold, I took the machete. No movement from anyone; Joseph, Leopold, Fred, or Willie.

I carried the hat, blanket, and machete upstairs placing it inside on my living room floor and went to bed.

In the dim morning light, I arose to yelling, barking, and meowing. Next, I realized that Joseph was banging on my screen door with his chorusing back-up group. Joseph fell into my arms with the cat and dogs clamoring in support as he gasped, "Oh, Ma, the people come. The people beat old man Joseph. The people bad-o. People no get you. The people bad, bad, bad. I thank God you good."

I looked at this crazy sight before me not believing my ears and eyes. "Joseph, what people?"

"People, they come, they beat me up, they bad-o."

"Yeah, I know, you told me this. What about the animals? What happened to them?"

"The cat tied up. Dogs tied up. The people beat poor poor old man Joseph. No gun to shoot."

Yep, here we go again about the gun. I had taken it away some time ago as he kept shooting it off in the middle of the night while I slept. The machete was to replace the gun. No noise from it.

"How many people were there?"

"Plenty people. Plenty people. They beat poor poor old man Joseph. They take old man Joseph hat, blanket, and ah, Ma, they take machete," he said hanging his head with a tear running down his cheek.

Boy, was he ever good with this Oscar winning performance. Needs to explain where the missing machete went and thus the fabricated story. "Plenty people? How many?"

"People, people, people," he quickly answered. This meant probably almost fifteen to thirty with my understanding of the multiple of the word people.

"Ma, this old man save you from the people. This old man save cat from the people. This old man save dogs from the people. This old man, he good-o man."

"Well, Joseph, I want to believe you about the people. However, I am the people! You sleep. I try to wake you. You sleep. Cat sleep. Dogs sleep. I take your hat. I take your blanket. I take your machete. You no move. You no wake up." Beating on my chest, I stated, "I, the people!" Bending down, I reached inside and brought up the hat, blanket, and machete showing these items to Joseph.

I kid you not, Joseph blinked and blinked in astonishment and declared as he fell to his knees, kissing my feet, exclaiming, "Ma, you see the people too! You save this poor poor old man. I thank you! I thank you!"

Well, what was I to do but, blink and laugh at how this old man tricked me once again.

Ah, Liberia, sweet Liberia.

A few weeks later when I came home from school, my Rhodesian Ridgeback, Fred, was missing. Neither of the Josephs could locate him anywhere nor was there any news from the camps. It turned out that his juju had lapsed and well, Fred must have ended up in someone's soup. I quake whenever I thought about what had happened to Fred. I made sure the other jujus were up to date with an extra 6 months tossed in. Besides Willie and Leopold, I now had seven cats, well, two cats and five kittens. The kittens were adorable, frisky, and promised to families on the

Plantation.

Over the weeks, Patty and I went often into Monrovia however, she didn't have any interest in traveling upcountry. Boy, did I miss my traveling buddy Joe. He liked living and working in Cavalla and I managed to fly down every few weeks. When at Cavalla, we got to travel around the area, even going into the Ivory Coast.

The last time I was there, Charlie Lorenz's German Shepard had puppies and he promised me one. The puppy I chose was a roly-poly one that I named Bidon as it means round drum. When Bidon was old enough, Joe flew to Harbel for a few days and Bidon came with him.

"Boy, it was a good flight this time as Air Liberia placed seats for me to sit on. You know, I'm just not a crate sitting person. Remember that time when we flew down with the cow and three goats?" Joe laughed as he handed me my little puppy who licked and licked. And of course, peed and peed. Puppies, gotta love them. Joe had adopted Bidon's two brothers and he said they did the same thing.

"Don't forget the chickens who were squawking and carrying on. That flight was a nightmare," I added. "One never knows who your seatmates will be on Air Liberia. Or if you will even get a seat. Wonder if there were any regulations about animals riding in cabins when they weren't crated or even tied down?"

"Don't know, but I will be flying back and forth once a month. Just one of my many perks for the promotion," Joe said grinning. "Perhaps, I'll bring up my puppies to visit with their brother."

A few weeks later our friends, Peggy and Rich Boleratz, went on leave to Europe and then to the States. Patty volunteered to dog sit, Pumpkin, who was a miniature dachshund. Pumpkin was adorable, but yappy.

Every morning, when he was let out to do his business, Pumpkin came flying over to my yard to yap at Willie. Day by day this routine went on with Patty dashing over to grab the little dog. Willie would sit at the end of my driveway without a sound.

Today was different as Willie stayed by the steps with me as I drank my coffee. Pumpkin scampered over and dashed across the road and into my driveway. Before I could grab Willie, he jetted after, picked the little dog up, and with one shake of his head, set the little dog down. Both Patty and I reached Pumpkin at the same time only to see drops of blood coming from a small puncture wound. Patty and I both screamed and she picked him up. We both went back to her bungalow to examine him out of view of Willie. Of course, Outside Joseph wasn't anywhere to be seen to chain Willie.

"I don't think he's breathing," Patty said.

"Get a hand mirror and we'll check to see if there is a fog on the mirror. Then we'll know the dog is still alive," I directed.

No such luck. I did mouth to mouth resuscitation and again no luck. We wrapped the dog up and still wearing our PJ's, sped out to the hospital just in case they could electrically shock him back to life.

Patty kept crying, "The Boleratz trusted me with their pet and look what happened."

"They'll probably sue me because my dog, Willie, did the deed. What are we to do?"

Pumpkin didn't get zapped and Patty had to send a cablegram to Rich and Peggy telling them about their dear pet's passing. All our worries were in vain as the Boleratz were understanding and sympathetic towards us for having to deal with this tragedy. They returned from leave with two miniature dachshunds. Patty never dog sat again. Or me, for that matter. And yes, Willie now ranked right up there with Leopold. The Liberians would say, "That Missy, have killer cat. Killer dog." Not something I wanted to be known for, that's for certain.

I watched the clock as I was timing the Sun-In application I had painted on my hair. I had used this product when I was in the States and brought some boxes back with me to use when needed. Tonight, I was going to an American Embassy party with John Francis and wanted to freshen up my hair streaks. My phone rang and I chatted and totally forgot about the hair color application.

Jumping in the shower, my hair felt strange almost straw-like as I shampooed it. What's up, I thought. The water looked okay maybe a little redder than usual. Finishing my shower, I wrapped my head and body in towels. Facing the mirror and removing my hair towel, I jumped and screamed in horror! My hair was wild and with strange colors but mostly, it was bright orange. I blinked and blinked and of course, cried. Quickly dressing and wrapping a bandana (one I use to travel upcountry as a dust guard) and raced down to the Firestone Store. I hoped I could get some hair color to dye this disaster. Screeching to a halt and racing up the store's steps, I begged the man to let me in. The dash helped.

"You know there's still 5 more minutes till closing time," I said.

He just smiled holding his dollar. Liberia, sweet Liberia, I thought as I dashed to the aisle of personal products.

Oh, no, I gasped almost ready to scream aloud. Only two boxes of hair color and they are in German. I can't read German, but being desperate, I bought them anyhow. Driving back home, I thought. German. Who reads German? Ingrid Holzl was back in Germany on leave. Who else? A Dutch person? Perhaps…Corrie Witteveen came to mind next. Possibly she could read German and help me out.

I drove directly to the Witteveen's and was met by Corrie's daughter, Leonie, jump roping under their bungalow.

"Leonie, mommy home?" I asked getting out of my car.

"Oh, Miss Mobilia, yes. Go on up."

"Please, Corrie, may I talk to you in private?" I asked looking at Leonie and hoping her mom would ask her to leave. I didn't want Leonie to know what happened to my hair.

"Done." Corrie said something to Leonie in Dutch and she left waving goodbye as she closed the front door.

"Corrie, I have a huge palava and hope you are able to help me out," I said as I removed my bandanna.

She looked at the boxes, touched my hair, and said, "I can help you but not with those boxes of hair dye. Both boxes are the color black. They won't work changing the orange of your hair. Your hair needs to be neutralized."

"Black?" Oh, no," I wailed. I have an American Embassy party tonight. I can't go with this orange hair. Please cut it short for me."

"Cutting some hair off will help a little, but this damage must be neutralized and I have some product to do this. You must not talk about what I am going to do to anyone on the Plantation. I take care of someone's hair who isn't a true blonde. These products are hers. I know she'd understand why I need to help you out."

"Sure, anything, Corrie, please make this nightmare color go away," I pleaded.

Two hours later, I left the Witteveens carrying my bandana and relieved I wasn't bald or orange-haired. Over the next few months, Corrie applied the neutralizer and the damage grew out. Thank goodness. No one was any wiser about what was going on with my hair. No more Sun-In for me, I swore.

Today I was traveling from Buchanan back home after a day visiting and shopping. The sun was descending and I was hoping to be home before it set in about 2 hours. Driving through a bunch of chickens, goats, and loose dogs, I felt a jolt on my back left tire. Oh, my goodness, I thought as I stopped and quickly got out of my car. I hoped I didn't kill an animal remembering the horrible stories of the palava of doing this. Children of the dead animal and grandchildren of the dead animal, etc. Sure enough, there it was behind my back tire. A chicken. Dead. I heard people yelling and running from a nearby village. I knew the owner of the chicken was being summoned and that I was in deep trouble.

I fell down by my car's tire and let out a banshee wail, "My car's foot. My poor poor car's foot." I continued wailing and then took to pulling my hair and rolling a couple of times on the ground. People had gathered and screamed at me that I killed that poor chicken.

"Oh, the pain. My car's foot hurt plenty." So, reaching around and grabbing the dead chicken, I raised it above my head and shouted, "Who own this stupid dead chicken? I will sue them. Da stupid chicken has hurt my car's foot. See," I said pointing to the chicken's blood on my car. "I said my car's bleeding. I want the people who own da chicken."

Again, I shouted and waved the chicken, "Chicken. Chicken. Chicken. Who owns da chicken? I sue the people. Where's the people who own da chicken? Where's the chief?"

"Aw, Missy, da chicken, not from village. No one knows da chicken. He bad-o chicken to hurt car."

After much back and forth with absolutely no one owning or even knowing the chicken; I threw it into my trunk and drove off glad to be done with the palava and hopefully be able to remain in Liberia.

Arriving home, I yelled, "Hey, Joseph, I have a chicken for soup." He was pleased and I never explained the blood on my car or how I came to have the chicken. Also, I didn't go down that road for a long time.

Billie gathered us in her office early on Monday morning, a week before the end of our school year. She was crying and slowly told us about a tragic accident that had occurred and that Mrs. Agoncillo hadn't survived. We were shocked and speechless. Some had heard about the accident but didn't know Mrs. Agoncillo had passed.

"Dr. Agoncillo is sending his children into school as he wants them here and not at home. He has arrangements to make and feels that the best thing for his children will be with us."

We all agreed to do whatever was needed to help the family as four Agoncillo children attended our school. This was my saddest time of being on the Plantation. Our family was hurting and gathered together to help when needed. School ended and the Agoncillo family flew to the Philippines to bury Mrs. Agoncillo in their family cemetery.

Before I left for my leave, I made sure my animal jujus were in order and fully paid. Plenty of food for them and money for the Josephs covering their salary, bags of rice, and for any unforeseen needs. I spent a month traveling around Europe and visited family in England and Ireland. After a few weeks back home, I returned to Liberia for my third contract.

Dear Mom Dad Stop
New teacher, new dog Stop
Orange hair gone Stop
I the people, lost battle Stop
Sadness hits us Stop
We gather and gain strength Stop
Family Stop
Hugs African kisses Stop
Kathleen

My new puppy, Bidon

The Van Dam's Wedding on August 30, 1975

Chapter 32

To Be Wedded or Not and Gone Leopold Gone

I was back in Liberia after my month leave in Europe and the United States and my third year at the Staff School had once again started smoothly with another small class. The Agoncillo children had returned with their dad and were in school. Everyone was happy that Dr. Agoncillo and his children had returned to the Plantation. He was our beloved doctor and had cared for us and many times our pets. I was also pleased that my friend, Patty, had returned for another year of teaching.

My life was good with both my Josephs, Inside and Outside. As always, when I traveled, both Josephs took care of my animals and my bungalow.

After dinner at Ralph's and enjoying aperitifs, there came a loud knocking at his door interrupting our bachelor group. Ralph staggered as he opened the door.

Outside Joseph stood there with Willie and Bidon at his heels and he ordered, "Ma, you come now. School tomorrow."

"What? I will come home when I want to come home," I barked back. The nerve of him ordering me around. "Joseph, you go back and put your eye on my bungalow. I pay you to watch my home. You go now."

"No, Ma, you come," And Joseph stood his ground.

Patty said, "Gosh, it's late and I must be going, too. Thank you, Ralph, for another lovely evening." With that Patty ushered me out and back up the hill to my bungalow followed by a smiling Joseph and two happy dogs who also wanted to go to sleep.

"Patty, Joseph is correct, it's late and I need my sleep to work tomorrow but, I just hate how he finds me and bosses me to come home. All so he can go to bed."

"At least your watchman cares and looks out for you. Mine just sits and watches. There is no communication at all with him. You're lucky," Patty said to me as I climbed my stairs. "See you in a couple of hours."

A week later on Saturday, August 30, 1975, I was sitting on the white shag rug at Jim's bungalow, wondering how this came to be. I looked around the room at the most unusual group of people gathered for a wedding. Just about everyone was drunk or near to it like I was. It was steamy and humid following the recent downpour. We were here to witness the wedding or, maybe not, of Jack Van Dam. Jack, who to this point, had been a confirmed bachelor. He was drunk and seated on a white chair in Jim's beautiful living room with the huge windows overlooking Hydro Falls. Yes, the red and white paisley drapes I had helped with, looked fantastic and set a modern ambiance. Perfect for a wedding if it was going to occur. We had been waiting for two hours for Reverend Dixon to come and perform the service. And he was late and so the drinking had begun and continued as we waited. How did we get to this point I pondered.

Early yesterday morning while getting ready for school, I

answered my phone on the third ring to hear Mae Gillian ordering me to sit down as she had some earth-shattering news. I sat and couldn't speak at first and then found my voice. "I thought he was gay and now you're telling me he's getting married? To who?"

"Jim Smith told me she's a mail order bride from The Netherlands and she speaks no English. She arrived on KLM last night. She's quite young and scared to be among strangers and also seeing Jack so drunk when she met him last night. All this has added to her stress."

"I see. Imagine how you'd be in the same situation. What can we do?"

"I think we need to step in to help her and Jack with this wedding; if it's to take place," Mae added. "So, here's a plan."

Well, after that phone call from Mae, John Francis called followed by a series of calls from Jack's friends. They were just as surprised as Mae and I were. Jack's wedding, if it occurred, was going to be a huge event!

Jack had decided to have a small wedding inviting only a few of his closest friends. "I must have it this way so I don't back out."

Jim inquired, "Do you really want to marry her? Why not wait a while? What's the rush?"

Jack insisted that it was now or never and so the wedding was on and Jim offered his bungalow for the wedding ceremony and reception.

Yesterday, before going over to Jim's to help, I met with the bride-to-be, Ingrid, at the Gillians. Mae and I realized that she didn't understand she was getting married at this time. She had thought she was meeting with Jack however, Jack wooed her and here she was a bride-to-be. She refused to wear any of Mae's wedding-like dresses and wanted to wear what she had brought. It was a pretty soft printed patterned short dress and not what one expected for a wedding dress. Mae thought that maybe in The Netherlands this was what brides wore.

We went over to Jim's and spent hours helping him and his stewards get his bungalow ready for the wedding ceremony and reception. Paul De Longchamp, Ralph, and Brad joined us arranging flowers they had brought from their gardens and adding their finishing touches to the beautiful room. Food was being prepared and linens ironed. Tables were set in place for the lavish dinner reception to follow the wedding. Boxes of wine and champagne were cooling and there was a hustle about. The transformation was completed around eight o'clock. I went home exhausted but got my clothes ready for the wedding.

After a few short hours of sleep, I went over to Mae's bungalow to help fix Ingrid's long hair into loose curls with some flowers added in the back. She did look beautiful. Ingrid finished dressing and shortly, Mae and Ron drove her to Jim's. I hurried home to dress and about 30 minutes later, Brad Hathaway and John Francis, who looked smashing in his tux, picked me up to go to Jim's. Yep, the cigarette hung in the corner of his mouth which I believe was permanently glued there.

We arrived behind the Gillians and Ingrid. Surprisingly, Jack was already at Jim's and of course with a drink in his hand. Soon the wedding guests had gathered and were waiting. The excitement was running high and we tried to ease our anxiety by drinking. We drank and waited. Waited and drank. Music was playing loudly and everyone was dancing and did I mention drinking? Lots of drinking. All waiting for Reverend Dixon to come and marry Jack and Ingrid. The food had been devoured long ago, however, the liquor continued to flow. We were wondering if the Reverend forgot and just when we decided to send out someone to find him, he arrived and it was evident that he had partaken in drinks at his other wedding.

Reverend Dixon had us gather around him facing the bride and groom. Jack couldn't stand up and remained seated as they exchanged vows, in Dutch. Only Pim Kraaij understood as he was Dutch. I sensed that something was wrong from the look on Ingrid's face. Everyone gathered around the bride and groom and some photos were taken before things really got crazy. Next thing I knew, Jim led me to dance the tango; slow and extremely sexy. Remember, Jim was an Arthur Murray dance instructor and a marvelous partner. Once the dance was over, Jim got down on one knee and proposed to me! I was shocked, to say the least.

"Jim, this isn't the time or place. Get up and let's dance." I knew he had feelings for me but, didn't know they were this deep. I kept saying it was the liquor making him act this way. Then he grabbed me and was forcing himself on me. Kissing and blabbing all kinds of crazy things.

"You said you wouldn't date someone you worked with. I moved to another department and you still won't give me a chance!" He became uncontrollable and next thing I knew, he pushed me away, yanked his stereo from the wall unit, and hurled it through the large window overlooking the Hydro Falls. At first, the group was shocked and then the free-for-all began. They started throwing furniture and other items out of the broken window.

I felt someone grab my arm and whisper in my ear, "You must get out of here now!"

I looked into Aldo Holzl's eyes.

"Now!" He pleaded.

I followed. Once in his truck, Aldo said, "You can't go back to your bungalow. It's the first place Jim will look providing he gets sober. You can't go to my place either. How about the Hotel? Lots of people are around and you should be safe. I'll stay with you just in case."

Later the next day, Mae called me as Jack said Ingrid didn't believe they were married as he sat while their vows were exchanged. "Are we wedded or not?" Jack and Ingrid asked.

Mae assured the bride and groom that they were married, standing or sitting down as wedding vows were wedding vows in Liberia, the United States, or The Netherlands. Mae announced, "You are married!"

"I have an inkling that Ingrid is going to ask that question many more times," I laughed. We discussed Jim's bizarre behavior yesterday and how horrified I was.

Mae agreed and said they left right after me as the guys were losing it. She did add that most spent the night passed out and probably didn't know how the window was broken or why the furniture was down on the rocks of the falls. "You know how these guys are. They'll remember nothing!" Mae added.

In the following months, I was careful not to be alone with Jim. I continued to see him with the guys and we did things together in a group, but never would I be alone with him.

At dinner one night after a day of beach, sand, and sun, Ralph told us about the crazy message he had received from Akron. For months he had been asking Akron for more computer help and they kept nixing his request.

"I don't know who is responsible for this cruel joke, but I'll get them," he said and continued, "Akron said they were sending two computer guys for my department. Get this, their names are Larry Clarry and Dick Ricks! Do they think I'm stupid or what? Larry Clarry and Dick Ricks. Couldn't they come up with better names for their joke?"

Of course, we all laughed and went on with life.

And yes, low and behold, the two computer men arrived with their families as scheduled with no one to meet their Pan Am flight. Hum, a repeat of my arrival I thought. Of course, Ralph apologized and both families did settled into life on the Plantation.

"What's going on, Kathleen?" Ralph asked me in the early morning phone call. "Last night, I heard you calling for Leopold."

"Yeah, I haven't seen him for two days now. This is so unusual for him not to come home. I am used to him dragging all kinds of dead animals back here, but he's never been gone for more than a day."

"Have your Josephs checked in the camp?"

"Of course and his juju is paid for the next year. I'm worried that he's met his match and another bush cat or animal killed him," I cried.

Leopold was gone for more than three months when one day while in my kitchen, I heard a faint but familiar cry. Could it be? I ran down the back stairs and into the rubber calling his name over and over. And there he was, a bloody mess, lying under a low bush. At first, I didn't recognize him until he cried again. I swept him into my arms and smothered him in kisses. On the way back up the stairs into my bungalow, I realized how light he was and how badly injured.

"That cat, he sick," Inside Joseph remarked.

"Come with me, Joseph, as I must take him to the hospital for treatment."

I was surprised that Joseph sat in the back seat holding Leopold whom I had wrapped in his favorite blanket.

It was the longest ride to the Firestone Hospital and I was relieved Dr. Agoncillo was on call. He examined Leopold, cast his broken leg, and stitched his many deep cuts.

"You have a very lucky cat, Kathleen. He lost most of his body weight and blood," Dr. Agoncillo stated. "Give him this medicine and keep him confined and quiet for the next few weeks. He needs time to heal. It's incredible he made it back to you with these severe injuries."

"I know and thank you for taking good care of him."

Over the next few weeks, Leopold slept, ate from my hand, and gradually regained his normal weight of 35 pounds. We had a special unique bond and I was elated he had returned to me. The Liberians were in awe of his recovery and were afraid more than ever of Leopold. I secretly believed that the Josephs were building up his fierce reputation in the camp. Leopold was now a super cat having risen from the dead.

>Dear Mom Dad Stop
>Went to crazy wedding Stop
>Cat lost and found Stop
>All is well Stop
>Hugs African kisses Stop
>Kathleen

BYOB Easter Party 1976

Chapter 33

Surprise Wedding, the Playboy Bunny, and Going Home

Just after Christmas, Patty told me that she and Dr. Pepe Agoncillo were dating. They wanted to continue to do so quietly and needed my help. Before making this relationship public, they needed to know if any relationship between them would work and so, we planned their meeting places to date. Just to confuse people, sometimes, I went out with Pepe and we met Patty. Other times, Patty went out with him alone and then sometimes, the three of us went out together. We even included Ralph and Mike just to keep any gossip away.

This scenario continued for two months when on March 2, they quietly became engaged and shared their happy news with me.

At first, I was surprised and thought, "April Fool's isn't until next month. I hope you're not fooling with me?"

"No, no, it's not a joke and yes, we are getting married," Patty answered.

Of course, I was over-the-moon about this union. I loved them both and was happy that they had found each other.

Pepe made the announcement up at the Golf Club the next day to an astonished group. He stated, "Patty and I are getting married and because we are joining two lives and cultures together, we will marry on American-Filipino Day, April 9th. Everyone is invited to witness our vows at the Harbel Chapel and come to our reception afterward here at the Golf Club." Thunderous applause erupted and champagne was served with many joyful toasts being said.

However, back in the men's locker room, bets were being placed for the wedding deal to fall through. The guys had even made a chart where you could sign up for a date and time you thought the announcement would be made of the break-up. Patty and Pepe laughed it off while I realized I was losing another bungalow neighbor. That's the third in less than two years.

The Firestone family gathered around the couple and supported their decision to marry and celebrated their union. The staff was pumped for this wedding.

Patty and I were in a tizzy shopping for a wedding dress which was more difficult than we at first thought. Patty did manage to find the only wedding dress in Monrovia and laughingly said, "It looks like it came off a K-Mart clothes rack!" However, she did look fabulous in it and with the veil, Stephanie Puckhaber had made for her bridal present, Patty was the most beautiful bride. Pepe's mother had hand-embroidered on a pale blue satin ribbon their names and wedding date and Patty basted it on the inside bottom of her dress. Something new and blue was covered…old? Patty never shared this with me.

After church on April 4th, I gave Patty a bridal shower at the Gulf Club. The cooks had made tiny sandwiches and beautiful hors d' oeuvres and we had a champagne punch. Just about every woman was present and Patty received many incredible wedding gifts proving the women believed in love and were not betting on this union breaking up. Even after the wedding had taken place, the guys' bets continued.

All of the Agoncillo children were in the wedding party. Tina's, Joyce's, and Noela's bridesmaid dresses were made and both Christopher and Louie had new suits. I had the job as the wedding photographer. Others had taken charge of arranging for the reception food and seeing that the room was decorated. Many women made bouquets, table centerpieces, cookies, and so on. It did seem we were all joined in this union because Patty and Pepe made sure to include as many people as possible. We were their family away from home.

The morning of the wedding began with rain showers which eased up and the church was overflowing with well-wishers. The entire school had shown up dressed in pretty Sunday clothes. The day finished in the wee hours of the morning with the bride and groom slipping away for their secret honeymoon. I wasn't even given that information.

The next event held at the Golf Club was on Saturday, April 10th. Back in March and being on the BYOB party committee, it was decided our theme would be an Easter one since Easter Sunday was the next day. Invitations were made and we asked the attendees to dress in Easter costumes from decorated eggs to bunnies or chicks. A smaller committee met and made a 9-foot decorated Easter egg using chicken wire for the base and covering it in paper mache. The enormous egg was painted and paper straw was placed around the egg. What a centerpiece we had we all thought!

Stephanie Puckhaber, who was also on the BYOB committee, thought I could go as a Playboy Bunny and offered to make my costume. I hesitantly agreed and went over to her house many times for my fittings.

"Gee, Stephanie, I can't believe you found black and white satin fabric."

"Darling, you can find anything at Waterside in Monrovia if you search. And search, I did. Now your tail is proving to be more difficult. I can't find anything to make it and so, I have asked a stewardess friend to bring me some cotton batting on her next trip. And yes, I will have your tail made in time for the BYOB party."

"Fantastic! My parents would die if they saw me in this costume. I am still unsure I want to wear this. I feel almost naked standing here in it and you're the only one looking. What will it be like with so many people looking at me?"

"Get over your fears because you look fabulous and so sexy! The guys will go nuts and you'll do a great job!"

"Hopefully, I'll be able to pull it off," I said still uncertain about the skimpy costume.

"You will, and don't forget the Easter basket you'll be holding. That should help."

"Has Bill gotten the jelly beans and Easter Peeps yet?"

"He's been told they'll be on the Wednesday flight and more than a month before the party. We will need to refrigerate and hide the candy from my kids," Stephanie laughed.

"What a wonderful idea to pass out jelly beans and Easter Peeps and for Bill to have them flown in from New York."

Ralph, who was also on the committee, said he was shaving the little remaining hair left on his head and wanted someone to paint it as an Easter egg. I loved the idea and said that I would do the painting. It turned out that my cousin, Ruth and Greg were here for the BYOB party. Greg designed and painted Ralph's head and everyone got a big laugh from this. Ralph was a great sport!

I welcomed BYOB guests with the jelly beans and Easter Peeps and yes, I wore the Playboy Bunny outfit and blushed at the wolf whistles. John Chapman made an announcement he was now up to 25 minutes upon seeing me as a Playboy Bunny.

"Come, let's go into the locker room," John said hopefully.

"Four hours was our deal, remember," I said laughing.

"You are one hot lady and if you quit teaching, I'm sure Hugh Hefner would hire you in a flash," Jim remarked as he snapped photo after photo. I knew these photos would soon be hanging in the men's locker room.

Ralph won the egg contest having the largest egg decorated at the party. The committee had hidden small chocolate-covered Easter eggs all over the room and our egg hunt was a huge success. What a party we had! However, with the past few weeks charged with so much excitement, everyone was ready for some peace and quiet.

The following Sunday after Easter, we couldn't wait to see it as we had heard about the camera and making movies for a couple of days and today at Caesar Beach it was making its debut. According to the rumors, you could film something and then play it back immediately! This seemed incredible to us all.

"How could it all be done with no developing? I see how both you and Mike take movies and they must be processed. A few weeks go by before you get the movie back to show. I just don't understand how this camera works," Ralph said.

"I can't believe it either! I enjoy using my Dad's 8mm camera and making little movies of my students, however, sending it away takes time. This would be cool if we could see what we did immediately!"

"Just think…" Mike added as we drove down the road to Caesar Beach.

Sure enough, a huge group was gathered around a palava hut and laughing hysterically. They were watching something on a TV? Yes, it was a TV.

"Hey! How can you do this without electricity?" I asked.

Dick Hugg said, "It operates on batteries and we've got plenty of them! We also brought a generator to use when the batteries die."

John Chapman was rolling on the sand, holding his side, and snorting, "This is awesome!"

For the rest of the day and for many weeks following, the camera and TV were the latest hit. However, there was a problem as they had to use the same film over and over as there was only one. Ordered everything else but they forgot to get extra film. We all had a go at filming, directing, and acting. Skits were performed and watched only to have another one made. We never lacked for ideas as many were becoming writers and directors even wearing hats, capes, and holding huge cigars. Eat your heart out Alfred Hitchcock.

Two weeks later, my phone rang around 4:30 am. It was Billie telling me that school was canceled because a wounded python on loose.

"Don't go outside until I call you back that it has been captured and killed."

Rubbing sleep out of my eyes and now more alert, I asked, "Python? What's going on?"

Billie went on to say, that Sammy Adonis had let his dog outside as usual to guard his store and property. Then Sammy heard all kinds of commotion coming from his chickens and dog who was barking fiercely. Sammy knew he was after something or someone because Prince continued to bark. So, he grabbed his flashlight and a sawed-off shotgun and went outside to investigate."

"Is Sammy okay?"

"Yes. Sammy followed the sound of his dog and then he couldn't hear him barking anymore. Venturing further; he turned the corner on the side of his store when he came upon a huge coiled snake that looked ready to attack him! Sammy placed his gun directly on the section that was level with his chest and fired into it. He reloaded his gun and again fired into the snake. The snake finally uncoiled and slithered into the bush. That's when Sammy saw that his dog had been inside the snake. No shot gun marks were on his dog and Prince was dead."

"Oh, my," I stuttered, "I really liked Prince."

"The Plantation is on shut down and the Army has formed a hunting party in search of the wounded snake and perhaps its mate. You know how pythons like to travel in pairs. Please call the bachelors in your compound and asked them to spread the word out to people in their departments. PPD is moving into the camps to inform the locals. Stay inside!"

"I will!" I hung up and called everyone thinking of our snow calling lists back at home when school was called off due to road conditions and massive snowfall. Who would believe that school and the Plantation had come to a halt with a loose wounded python? Later in the day, the Army had located the python and killed it. Tying it onto a pole, it took six men to carry it back to Sammy's Store!

Sammy Adonis's dog was killed by this 17 1/2 foot python

The next day was back to normal, however, just about everyone went down to see the 17 ½ foot long dead python lying next to Prince, Sammy's dog. The python's mate was never found. Villagers near Sammy's Store paraded around the python and exuberantly cheered when Sammy said they could have it for snake soup! We often wondered why the snake went after Sammy's dog and not the loose goats, sheep, and chickens.

In May, Ralph announced that he wasn't renewing his contract and would be returning to Firestone in Akron. I was bummed out. Basjaan, Joe, Patty, and now Ralph. Life here just would not be the same without Ralph.

I could feel that things were changing in Liberia, too. Every time I went into Monrovia the past few months, I could feel the mood fluctuating. People were around that didn't fit in with the Liberians. Many came in from Guinea and were starting trouble. Also, the concession agreements with Firestone and the Liberian government weren't moving along quickly enough. I felt it was time to decide on my future and with a heavy heart, I handed in my resignation to return home to Erie.

I got positions with good families for both my Josephs and believe it or not, Outside Joseph took Leopold! He had grown to like Leopold after all. I also bought him a small rubber farm near his village as part of his retirement. And yes, it was probably a bribe to take the rest of my animal family which he did.

    With only three weeks to pack, I decided to go back home by traveling eastward and visiting other countries. With the help of Swiss Air agent Werner Schaub, I scheduled a three-month tour via plane, boat, bus, car, and even rickshaw.

    The school year ended and my personal items were packed and on the way back to Erie. I was ready to leave Liberia and take my trip around the world. Many people were at the airport for my send off.

    "Whoa, only one suitcase? Pepe asked seeing only one.

    "Well, I have three and they are packed inside the largest suitcase. I decided to travel light and with laundering daily, I should be good. Also, I won't be seeing the same people on my trip so, who cares what I wear?" I laughed. "And, I will have empty suitcases to fill with goodies from my adventures."

    Ralph asked, "What did you pack?"

    "One dress, one t-shirt, 2 bras and underpants, and a pair of sneakers. Plus what I'm wearing. Like I said, light as I will be traveling in all very warm countries."

    "Here you must take my jacket. Just in case you need it," Pepe said.

    As it turned out, that jacket served me well as many places got cool at night which I wasn't used to living here in Liberia.

    Everyone knew my itinerary and had given me travel tips especially for my safari. I had always wanted to do a safari and so that was added onto the my trip. I would travel for 10 days through Kenya and Tanzania and then continued to India with stops in Ethiopia, Egypt, and Yemen. I met Werner and Christine Schaub who had relocated to Bangkok, Thailand and explored the countryside which wasn't that much different than upcountry in Liberia. I visited many friends that I had made at Firestone along the way.

    The three days I spent in Hong Kong, I only cat-napped as there was so much shopping and places to experience. I had to be in Manila, Philippines to visit with Patty and Pepe before they returned to Liberia. I loved the Philippines and visited as much of the country as possible over

6 weeks. I flew to Singapore and Malaysia visiting with the Robb's. Andrea had been in my class at the Staff School and the family returned to Liberia at the end of their leave in Malaysia. Departing from Singapore, I continued eastward to Guam and Hawaii and explored the islands for a week.

Finally, after traveling for three months, I arrived in California and visited with Peter and Amber Cottle. I made it back home to be able to brag of traveling the world and doing it solo. Not many can say that I thought as I greeted my family and friends who were happy I had decided to return to Erie and not dash off someplace else.

I had lived my dream of working and living in Africa. Three years ago I went there a young teacher looking for adventure. Life in Liberia and on the Plantation didn't disappoint me at all. Most of the time, the struggles and changes were for the best. I grew up there and Liberia will always hold a part of my heart.

All hail Liberia, hail. Ah, sweet, sweet Liberia.

> Dear Mom Dad Stop
> Patty got married Stop
> Maybe new career as a bunny Stop
> Time to come home Stop
> Returning the long way Stop
> By traveling the world Stop
> Solo for 3 months Stop
> Hugs African kisses Stop
> Kathleen

The view from my kitchen window
Goodnight, sweet Liberia...

Photo Credits

Front Cover	A Friend's Jewelry Collection
Back Cover Author Photo	Kathleen Mobilia Collection
Inside Back Flap Author Photo	Kathleen Mobilia Collection
Introduction	Kathleen Mobilia Collection
Map of Liberia	@ Nations On line Project
Map of Firestone Plantations Co.	Nickie Kohout 11/3/1959
	Kathleen Mobilia Collection
	Kathleen Mobilia Collection
	Kathleen Mobilia Collection
Chapter 1	Kathleen Mobilia Collection
Chapter 2	Kathleen Mobilia Collection
Chapter 3	Kathleen Mobilia Collection
Chapter 4	Kathleen Mobilia Collection
	Barrie Johnson Collection
Chapter 5	Nickie Kohout FPCo Map
Chapter 6	Kathleen Mobilia Collection
Chapter 7	Kathleen Mobilia Collection
Chapter 8	Kathleen Mobilia Collection
Chapter 9	Kathleen Mobilia Collection
Chapter 10	Kathleen Mobilia Collection

Photo Credits

Chapter 11	Kathleen Mobilia Collection
Chapter 12	Kathleen Mobilia Collection
Chapter 13	Goodreads.com
Chapter 14	Kathleen Mobilia Collection
	Kathleen Mobilia Collection
Chapter 15	Kathleen Mobilia Collection
Chapter 16	Frank Ardaiolo Collection
Chapter 17	Kathleen Mobilia Collection
Chapter 18	Kathleen Mobilia Collection
Chapter 19	Kathleen Mobilia Collection
	Kathleen Mobilia Collection
	Kathleen Mobilia Collection
Chapter 20	Kathleen Mobilia Collection
	Kathleen Mobilia Collection
Chapter 21	Kathleen Mobilia Collection
Chapter 22	Kathleen Mobilia Collection
	Barrie Johnson Collection
Chapter 23	Kathleen Mobilia Collection
Chapter 24	Kathleen Mobilia Collection
	Kathleen Mobilia Collection

Photo Credits

Chapter 25	Kathleen Mobilia Collection
Chapter 26	Kathleen Mobilia Collection
	Kathleen Mobilia Collection
Chapter 27	Kathleen Mobilia Collection
	Kathleen Mobilia Collection
Chapter 28	Kathleen Mobilia Collection
	Kathleen Mobilia Collection
Chapter 29	Kathleen Mobilia Collection
	Kathleen Mobilia Collection
Chapter 30	Kathleen Mobilia Collection
	Kathleen Mobilia Collection
	Kathleen Mobilia Collection
	Werner Schaub Collection
Chapter 31	Kathleen Mobilia Collection
	Kathleen Mobilia Collection
Chapter 32	Kathleen Mobilia Collection
Chapter 33	Kathleen Mobilia Collection
	Kathleen Mobilia Collection
	Kathleen Mobilia Collection

About the Author

Kathleen Mobilia retired after teaching elementary students for 37 years. She taught in Clarion and Erie, PA, Harbel, Liberia, West Africa, and Symi, Greece.

Mobilia's father had a career in the United States Air Force and her family lived in many countries fostering her passion to travel, meet, and interact with new people.

She has published 2 books
Liberia Remembered
That One Last Second; Lance Corporal Peter Caulfield's Story.

Miss Mobilia resides in Erie, PA.

Contact at **HugsAfricanKisses@gmail.com**

CPSIA information can be obtained
at www.ICGtesting.com
Printed in the USA
LVHW010241241220
674973LV00002B/222